I09023O1

IMAGES
*of America*

# HASTINGS

## THE QUEEN CITY OF THE PLAINS

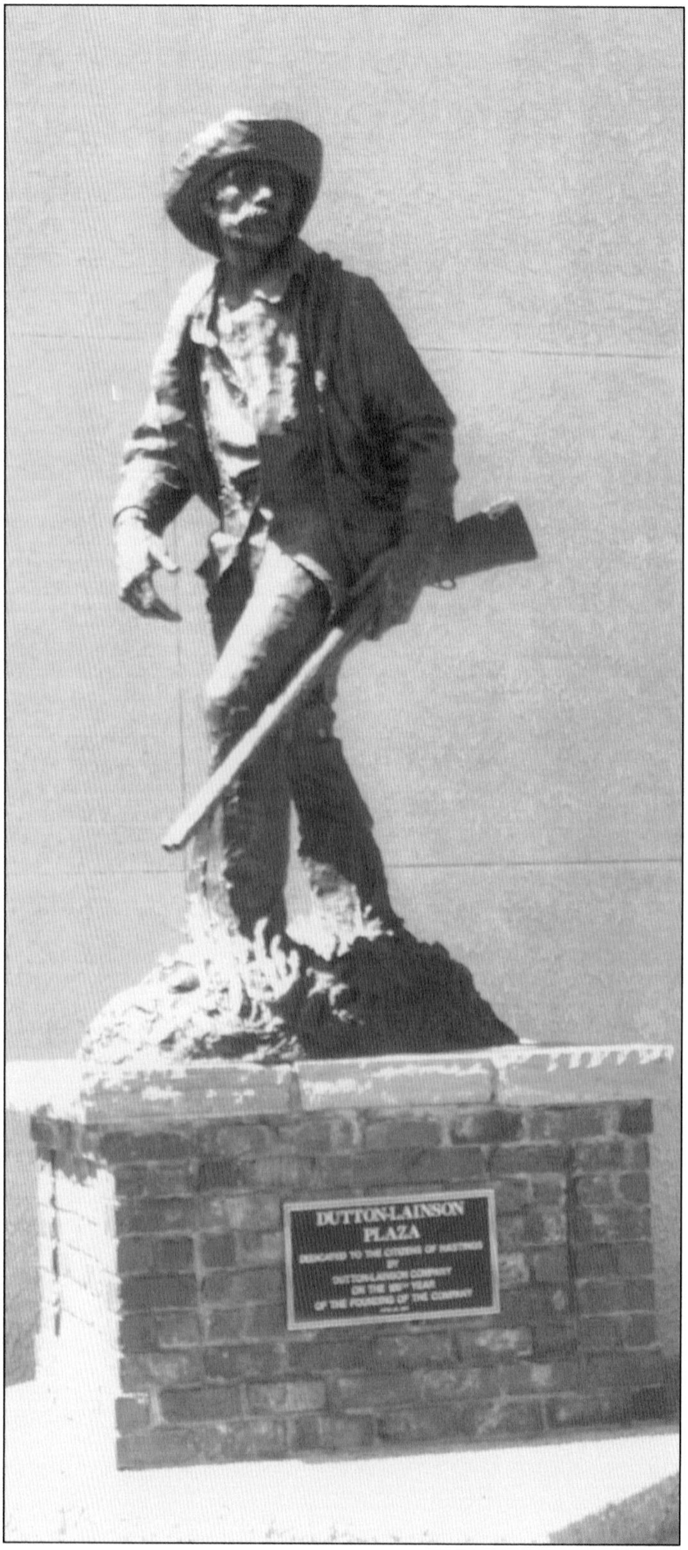


The Dutton-Lainson Plaza was initially conceived in 1987, after a downtown improvement study was completed. Herb Mignery, a former employee of the Cornhusker Press Division of the Dutton-Lainson Company, was commissioned to create a monument-size piece of sculpture, which would serve as the plaza's centerpiece. Mignery's creation, *Prairie Odyssey*, a 14-foot, 1,000-pound bronze sculpture was unveiled in April 1992. Initially, 50, 24-inch versions were made and sold to individual collectors, which provided funding for the plaza project. Located west of the Dutton-Lainson Victory Building, the plaza serves as a place where shoppers can rest in the midst of the business district. In the *Prairie Odyssey*, the sculptor explained that he tried to capture that spirit of self-effacing humility and quiet commitment of the common settlers who were truly the Old West's everyday heroes. "Hopefully, for future viewers this piece will rekindle that spirit of sacrifice, self-discipline, and personal responsibility, qualities that are desperately needed in today's society," Mignery said.

IMAGES
*of America*

# HASTINGS

## THE QUEEN CITY OF THE PLAINS

Monty McCord

ARCADIA
PUBLISHING

Copyright © 2001 by Monty McCord
ISBN 978-0-7385-1900-5

Published by Arcadia Publishing
Charleston, South Carolina

Printed in the United States of America

Library of Congress Catalog Card Number: 2001091395

For all general information contact Arcadia Publishing at:
Telephone 843-853-2070
Fax 843-853-0044
E-mail sales@arcadiapublishing.com
For customer service and orders:
Toll-Free 1-888-313-2665

Visit us on the Internet at www.arcadiapublishing.com

# Contents

# ACKNOWLEDGMENTS

I would like to take this opportunity to express my appreciation for the assistance given to me while writing *Hastings, Nebraska: The Queen City of the Plains*. Most of the fine vintage photographs presented in this work came from the extensive archives of the Adams County Historical Society (ACHS). The ACHS was formed in 1965, with its quarterly publication, *Historical News*, appearing three years later. The *News*, written by volunteers and funded by contributions of local individuals and businesses, is now issued bimonthly to members. During its 36 years, an impressive archives collection was established, and is housed in the Society's office at the Hastings Museum of Natural and Cultural History.

I sincerely appreciate the approval of my fellow ACHS Board members so that I could fully utilize the archives. The officers are as follows: President Steve Buss, Vice-President John Quirk, Treasurer David Carpenter, and Secretary Dick Witt. The directors are as follows: Thomas Creigh, Lloyd Dragoo, Mary Golgert, Phil Jordan, Dale Joynt, Will Locke, Verna Roeder, Renee Laegreid, and Catherine Renschler (executive director).

Thanks also to the staff of the Hastings Public Library who fulfilled my numerous requests, and especially Bev Whitsel who guided me to this project in the first place. My appreciation is also extended to the Hon. Tom Osborne, U.S. House of Representatives; Peg Wallace, Executive Director of the Cottonwood Prairie Festival; the *Hastings Tribune*; Mike Wallace, Executive Director of Kool-Aid Days; Gayle McClure, Dutton-Lainson Co.; Don Reynolds; LaMont Kehoe; Herb Mignery CA; Claire Sharrick, Hastings Police Dept.; and Pat and Mary Jo Randolph, OK Cafe.

# INTRODUCTION

During an exploration in 1819, Major Stephen Long wrote a report in which he described the region, "destined by the barrenness of its soil, the inhospitable character of its climate, and by other physical disadvantages, to be the abode of perpetual desolation." It was declared part of the Great American Desert.

A very differing opinion was given by Tamsen Donner, a member of the ill-fated Donner Party. While traveling through this part of the frontier West, she wrote a letter dated June 16, 1846, "The prairie between the Blue and Platte Rivers is beautiful beyond description. Never have I seen so varied a country, so suitable for cultivation." It was (and is) a beautiful area, but a dangerous one. Early pioneers had plenty of hardships. They built homes from the sod they walked on, because few trees meant little lumber. The weather consisted of terribly cold winters, hot summers, and occasional twisters. Although many Native Americans lived in the territory, it was the Sioux, Cheyenne, and Arapahoe tribes that went on the warpath in south central Nebraska during 1864–65. It was estimated that 40 people were killed during raids in the area.

The pioneers continued to travel west on the Oregon Trail through Adams County, and some settled here. Railroads expanded through the West and were responsible for establishing many towns, including Hastings. The location of the city was determined by the junction of two railroads, the Burlington and Missouri River and the St. Joseph and Denver City. Hastings, founded in 1872, was named after St. Joseph and Denver Railroad construction engineer, Major Thomas D. Hastings.

The first home in the new town was Walter Micklin's "soddy," located near Third Street and Burlington Avenue. When Samuel Alexander came to Hastings in 1872, he built a general store, which housed the first post office. Hastings College was founded in 1882, after 93 civic-minded men donated $11,050 for purchase of land and construction of buildings. Heartwell Park was originally established as a private park by James B. Heartwell in 1886. The park, now listed on the National Register of Historic Places, was purchased by the city in 1899.

Few realize that Hastings is the birthplace of Kool-Aid. The Perkins Products Co., located in a building on First Street, is where Edwin C. Perkins invented the famous soft drink mix. Each summer, "Kool-Aid Days" are held to celebrate the birthplace, the product and its maker. One of the most identifiable landmarks in the city is the Fisher Rainbow Fountain, located in front of the utilities building. Built for an electrical exposition at the 1932 county fair, it continues to delight all who watch its night-time streams of water, lit by a variety of colored flood lights. It was named for reigning mayor, Jacob Fisher.

The largest impact on Hastings was during World War II, when the U.S. Naval Ammunition Depot was built. The influx of construction and naval personnel required the building of the 840 unit Spencer Park housing project.

The end of the 20th century was a time for expansion with a purpose. Nebraska's first IMAX theatre was built at the Hastings Museum. A softball complex was built, and major additions were made to Hastings College and Mary Lanning Memorial Hospital. I hope this glimpse of Hastings provides the reader with a sense of the city's progress over nearly 130 years, its difficulties, its successes, and its promising future.

# *One*

# A Prairie Town 1872–1899

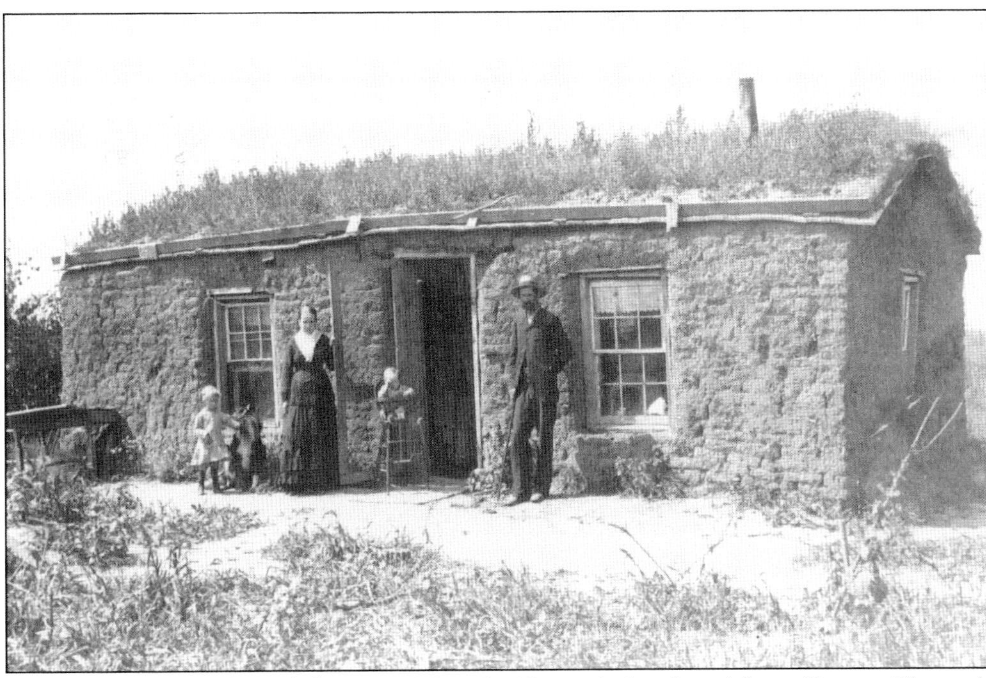

The U.S. Census indicated that in 1870, only 19 people lived in Adams County. The early settlers built their homes from the only plentiful material available at the time, the sod they walked on. Walter Micklin built the first house (a soddy) in Hastings, near the corner of Third and Burlington Avenue. Shown is a sod house owned by James Dean in 1885.

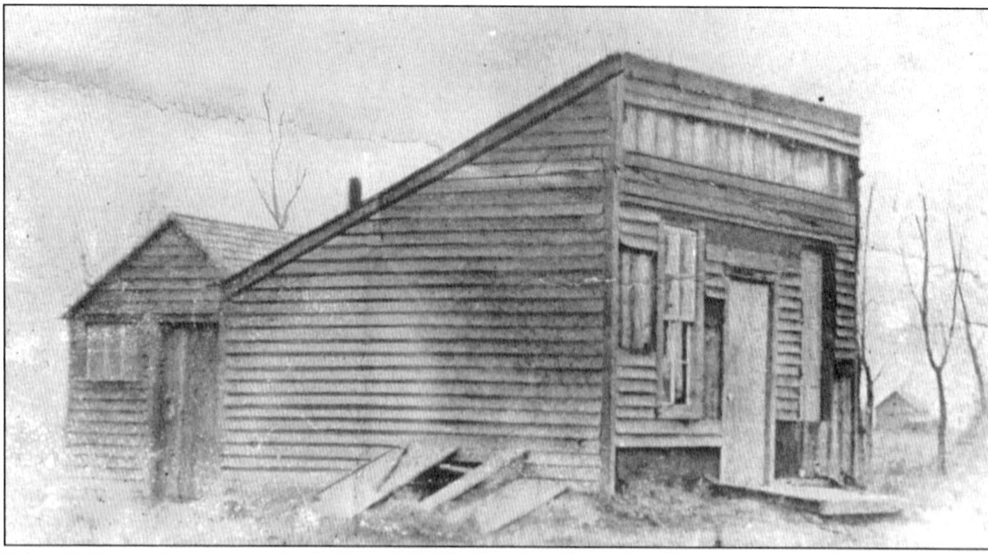

John Gillespie Moore, an Englishman, built the first frame building in 1871, a year before the town's founding. It was located on Saunders Avenue between Second and Third Streets. The lumber used was hauled by wagon from Grand Island, some 30 miles away.

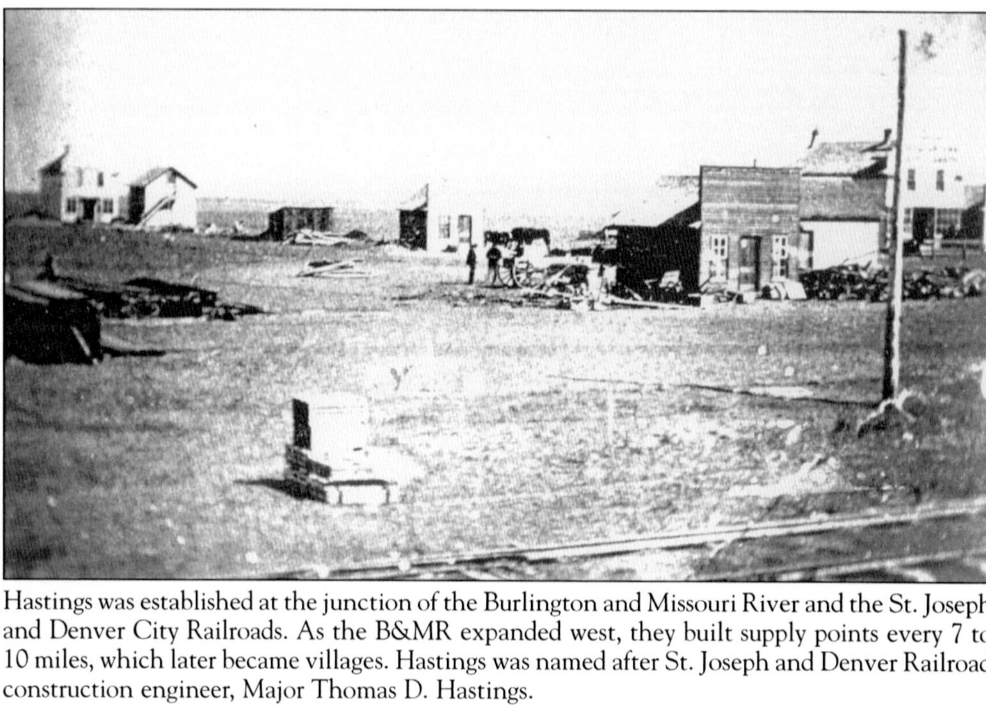

Hastings was established at the junction of the Burlington and Missouri River and the St. Joseph and Denver City Railroads. As the B&MR expanded west, they built supply points every 7 to 10 miles, which later became villages. Hastings was named after St. Joseph and Denver Railroad construction engineer, Major Thomas D. Hastings.

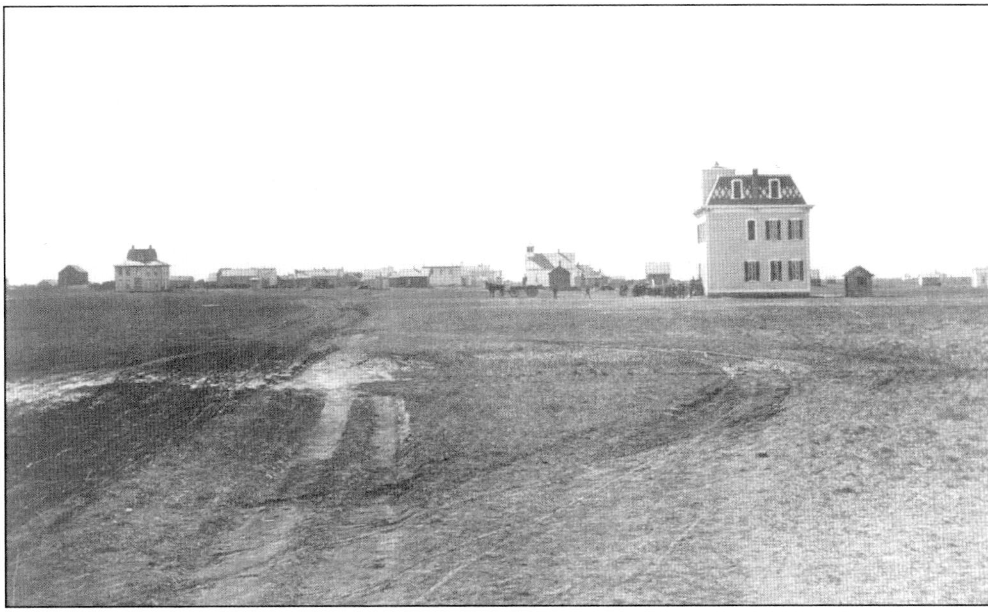

As the prairie town grew, the need for a schoolhouse was evident. In 1874, a fine three-story school was built, which was visible from a long distance away. It could accommodate nearly 300 students. Crops that year were doing well until the end of July, when a massive invasion of grasshoppers destroyed every green leaf within 48 hours.

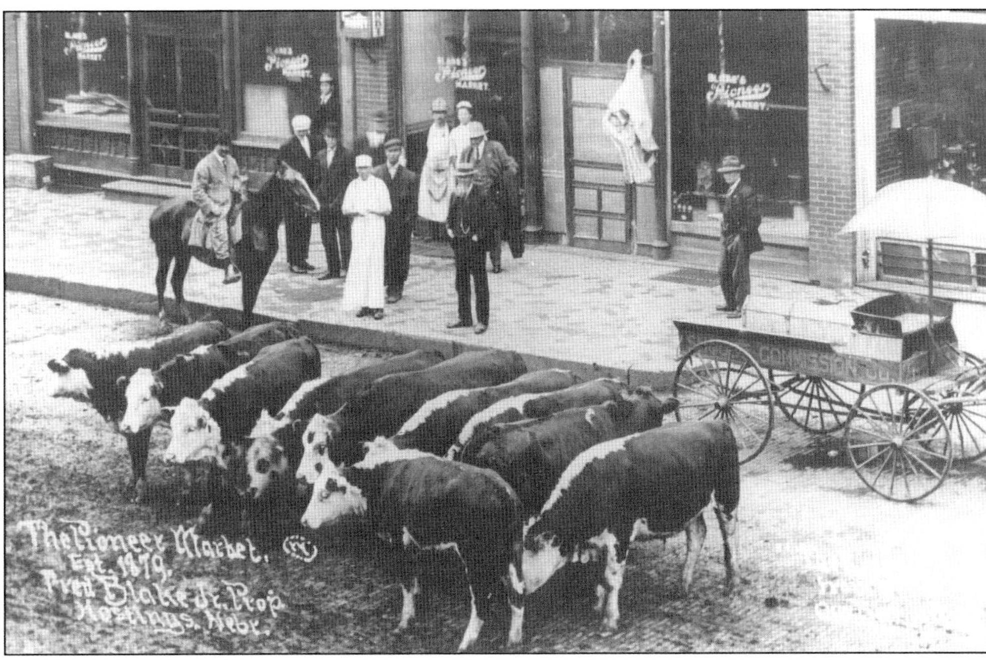


Blake's Pioneer Meat Market was established in 1874, located at 707 West First Street. Fred Blake Jr. is shown wearing an apron standing near the window, and George P. Klein is mounted on the horse. Bringing cattle to the local market was common by 1879. Only a year earlier, county seat status had changed from Juniata (5 miles west) to Hastings after hotly contested elections.

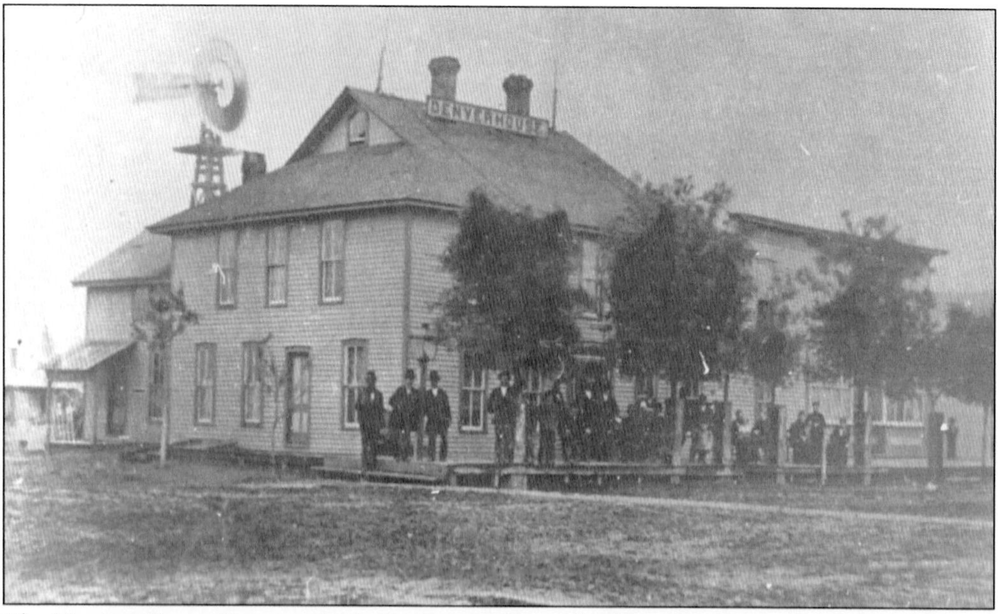


The Hastings Town Company built the Denver House hotel on the northeast corner of Second and Denver in 1878. It was managed by J.M. "Denver" Smith. In 1884, the building was moved, and the Bostwick Hotel was built on the site. The new Denver Hotel burned in 1905.

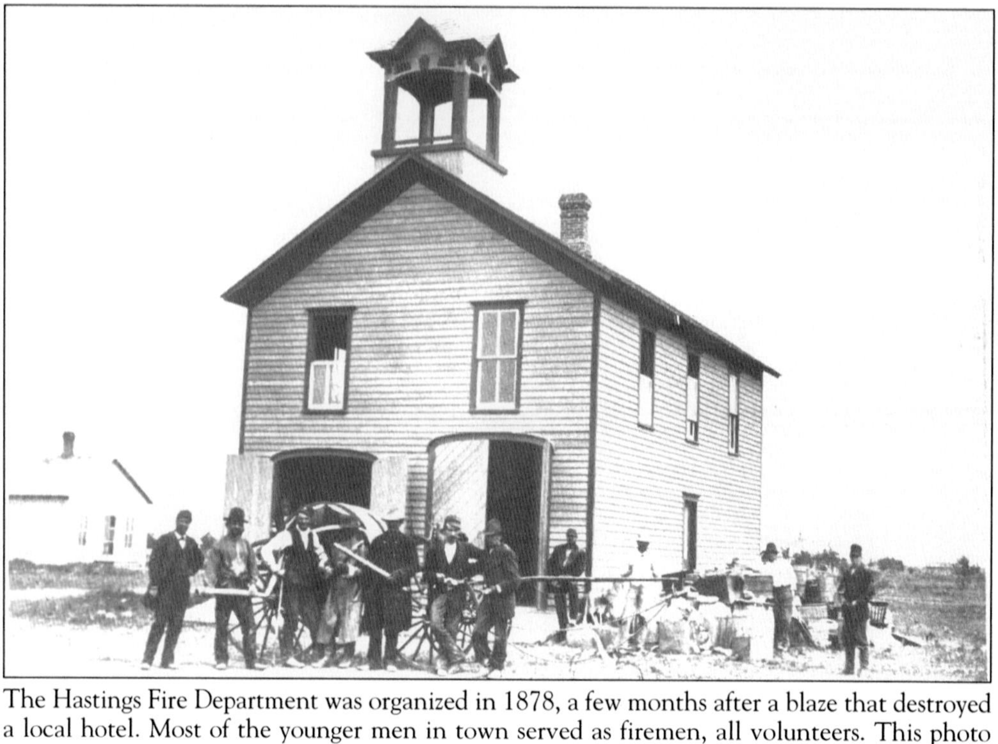

The Hastings Fire Department was organized in 1878, a few months after a blaze that destroyed a local hotel. Most of the younger men in town served as firemen, all volunteers. This photo shows the first engine house (and first city hall, upstairs) which cost $1,000 to construct. It was located on the southwest corner of Third and Hastings, which would become courthouse square. A small jail was located just east of the engine house.

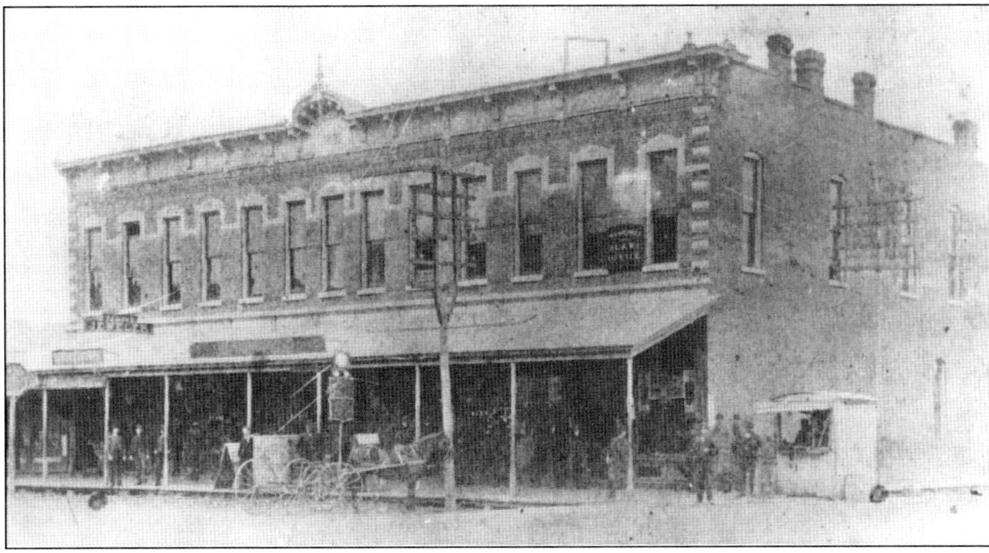

The Chilcote Building, 100–106 North Hastings Avenue, was built in 1881, at a cost of $16,000. Along with stores and offices, the building housed the post office after the prior location burned. Early Hastings post offices had considerable problems with fires, as the Chilcote Building burned in 1887. Ironically, it burned the night before water was available from the new waterworks.

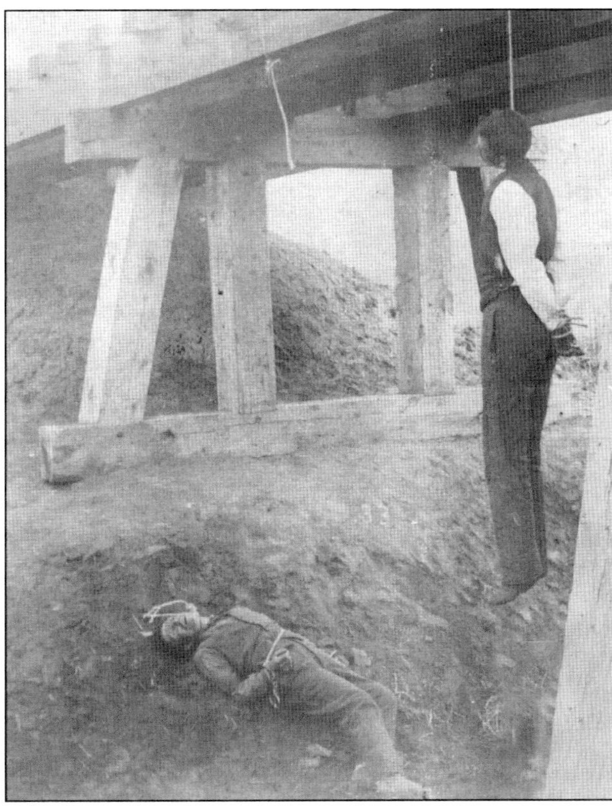

During the late evening of March 26, 1883, store owner Cassius M. Millet headed home. Three masked men attempted to rob Millet, but he ran and was shot and killed for his effort. Tensions ran high after the three were arrested. Before the trial was over, a vigilante group known as the "Committee of the Thirty-Three" forced the prisoners from officers and took them to a railroad bridge north of town. One was saved, but the other two were hung.

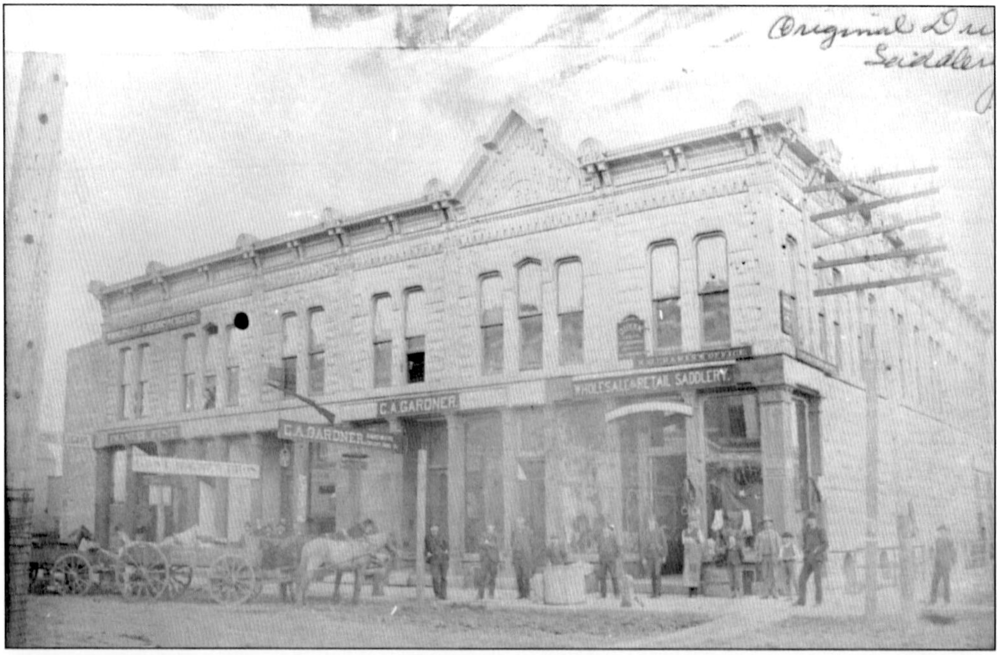


The Farrell Block, still located at Second Street and Denver Avenue, was built in 1880. The main floor housed stores including the J.H. Haney Saddlery, while the second floor was partially occupied by county offices. It was here that vigilantes forcefully took the Millet murder suspects from officers and lynched them. It continues to house businesses with apartments upstairs.

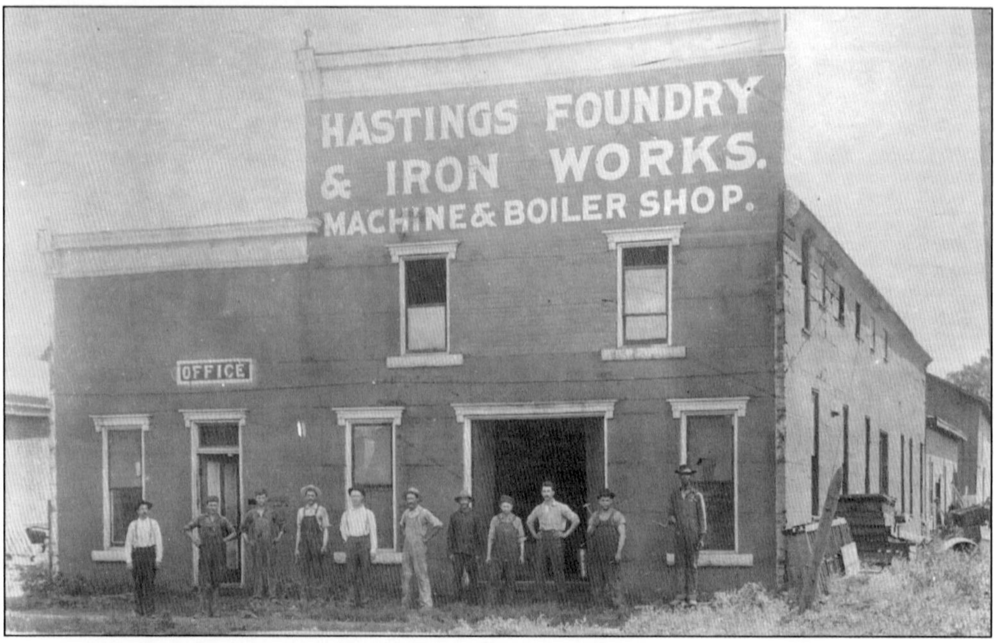


Mayor Clarence J. Miles promoted Hastings by reviving the Commercial Club (later the Chamber of Commerce). New industries were attracted to town, including the Emerick Brothers of Blue Hill, who manufactured their new trip hammer. In 1907, they were bought out by A.H. Ferrens and C.B. Hutton, and became the Hastings Foundry and Iron Works.

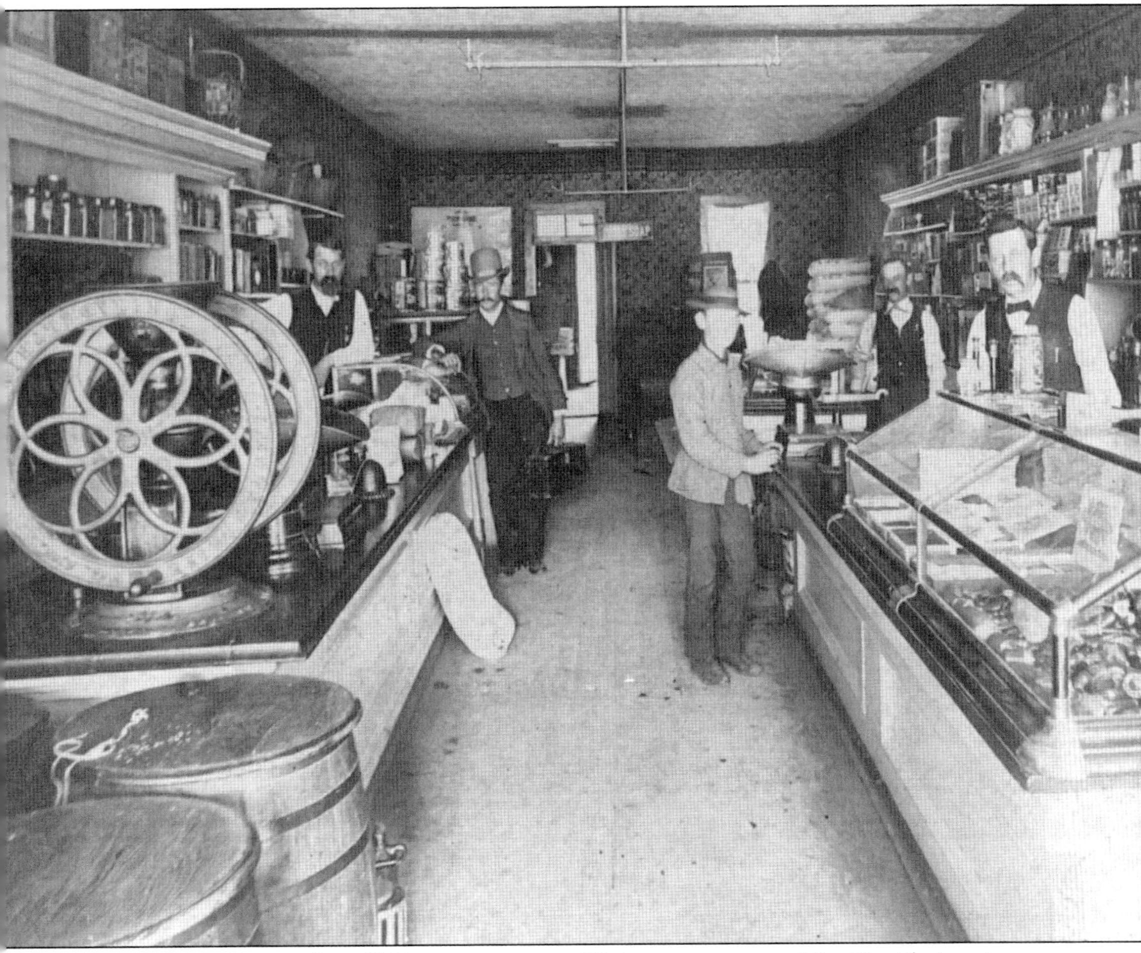

This is a classic scene of an 1880s grocery store. This one was owned by Danish immigrant A.W. Binderup, who moved to Hastings in 1879. He soon established a business selling coffee, tea, and spices, which was destroyed by fire in 1881. He immediately rebuilt the business and retired six years later.

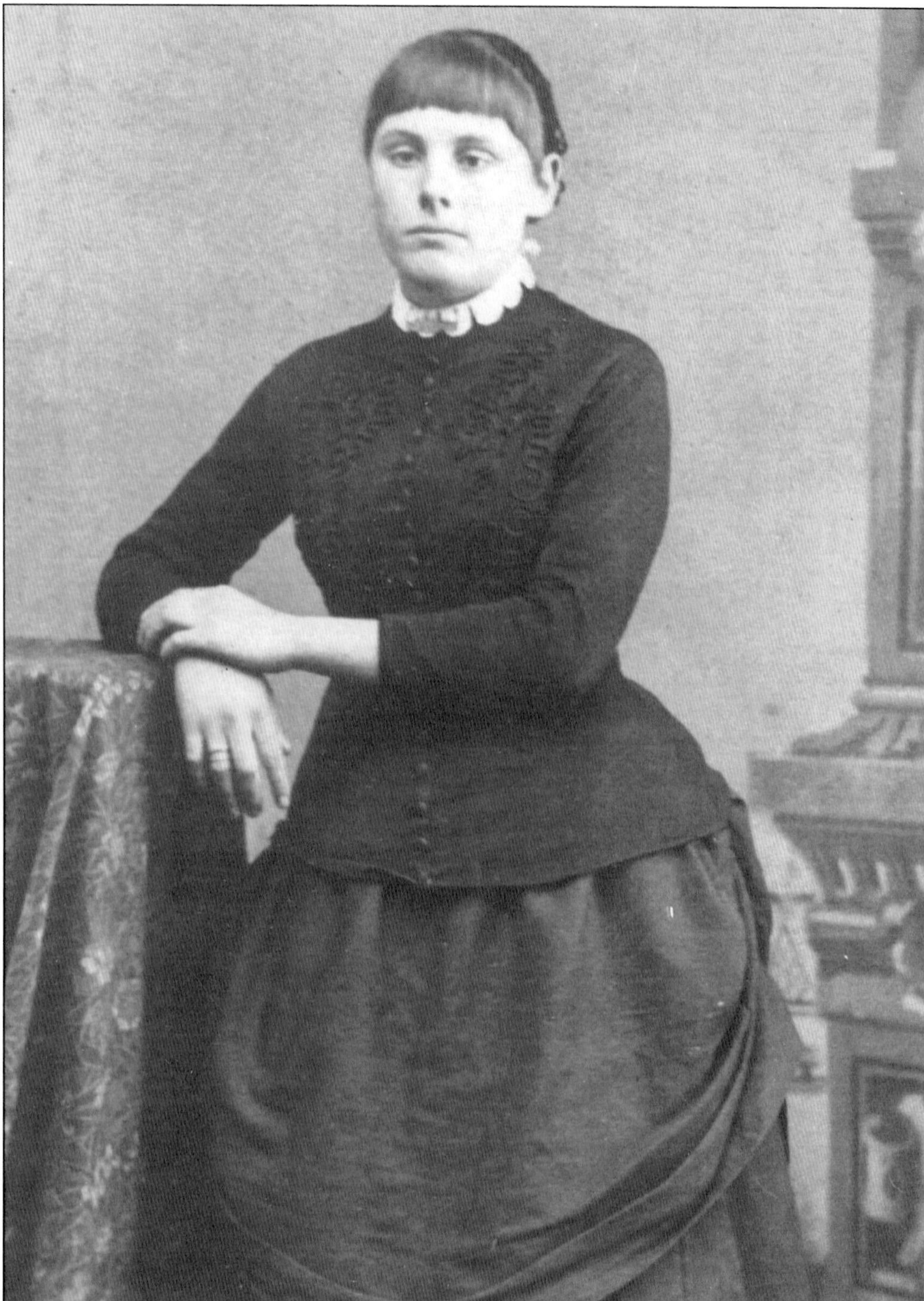

In 1908, Amy Robinson started one of the first hospitals in town. Born in Pulaski County, Kentucky, in 1870, her family moved to Adams County in 1882. Robinson entered the Lincoln, Nebraska, Medical School in 1897, after teaching at the District 27 School. Her hospital closed after only a year, but she continued practicing in Hastings, sharing a reception room with Doctors E.C. Foote, E.J. Latta, and W.W. Keith. She is shown in the late 1880s.

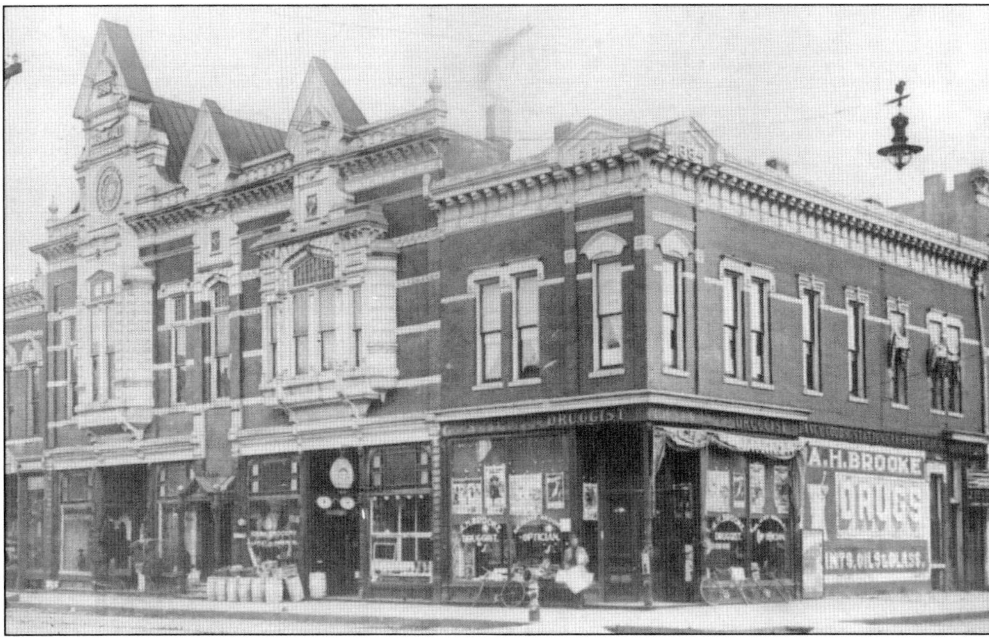

Hastings first Masonic Temple was built in 1886, at 619 West Second Street. The $30,000 structure dwarfed the Brooke Drug Store to the right. In 1913, the building was razed so the second temple could be built. In 1885, the Fraham brothers operated the drug store, where an upstairs office served as the city's first police headquarters. The drug store, which was constructed in 1884, still stands.

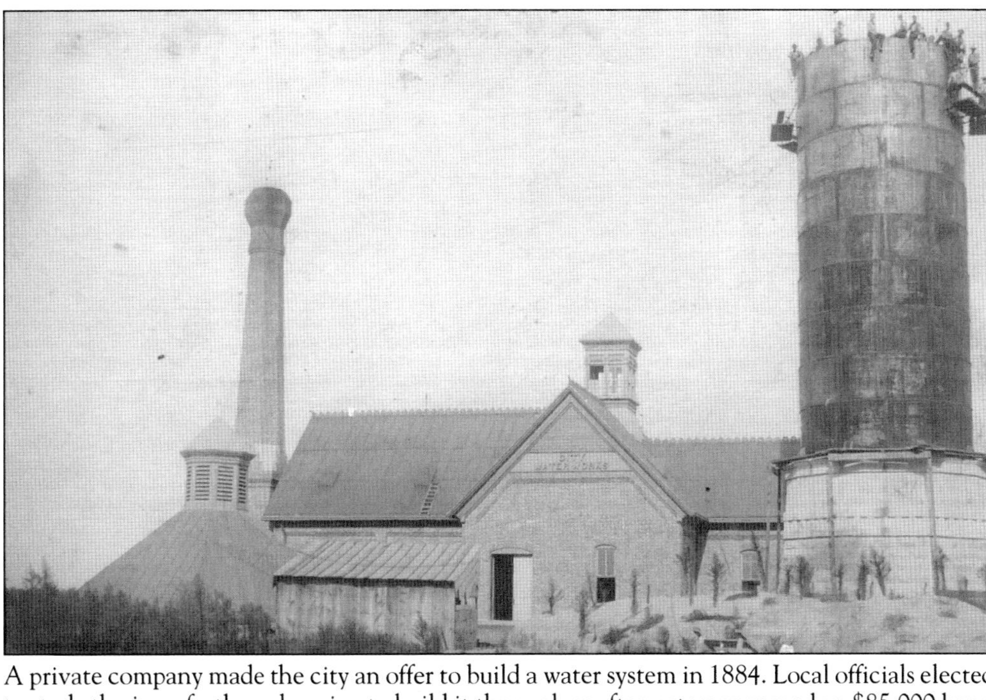
A private company made the city an offer to build a water system in 1884. Local officials elected to study the issue further, choosing to build it themselves after voters approved an $85,000 bond issue in 1886. Work was nearly complete on the standpipe when this photo was taken.

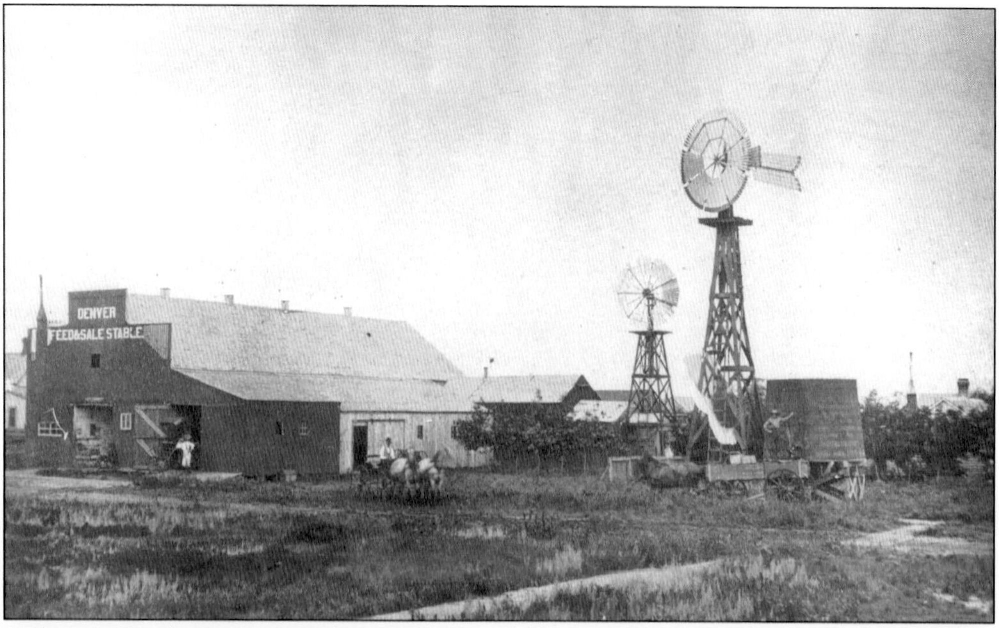


Built in 1878, the Denver Feed and Stable was one of the first livery barns in Hastings. On March 9th of that year a fire destroyed the barn and eight horses. William Cutler Sr. is shown at right near his well and water tank. He sold water for 10¢ per barrel or three for 25¢ before the city water works was established.

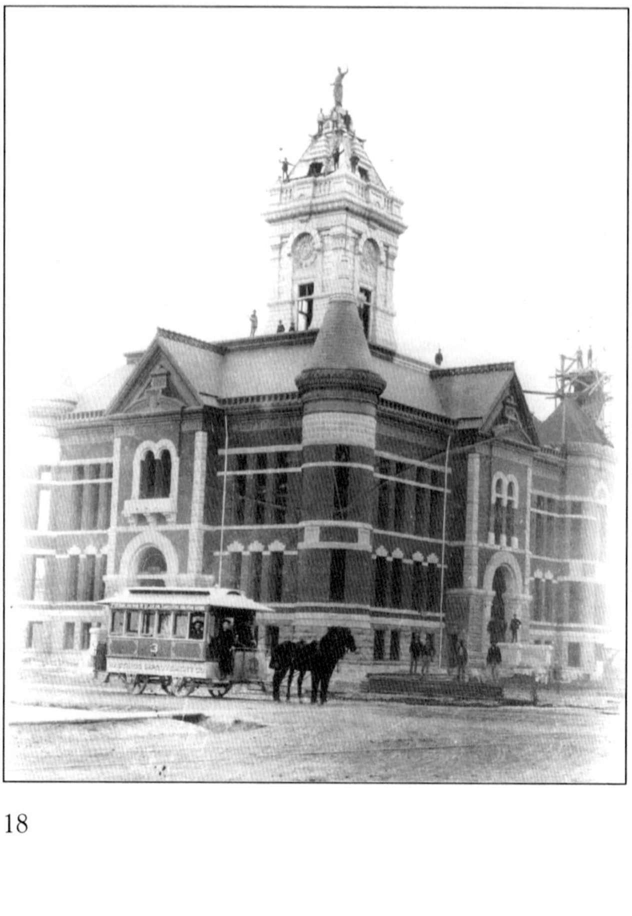

The village of Juniata was the first county seat (1871). Hastings became the county seat in 1878, after hotly contested elections. It was not until 1889 that a new courthouse was built. It was located between Hastings and Denver Avenues, and Fourth and Fifth Streets. The $77,000 courthouse was partially built of Colorado sandstone, topped with a 10-foot statue of the goddess of justice. It was torn down in 1964, after a new courthouse was built.

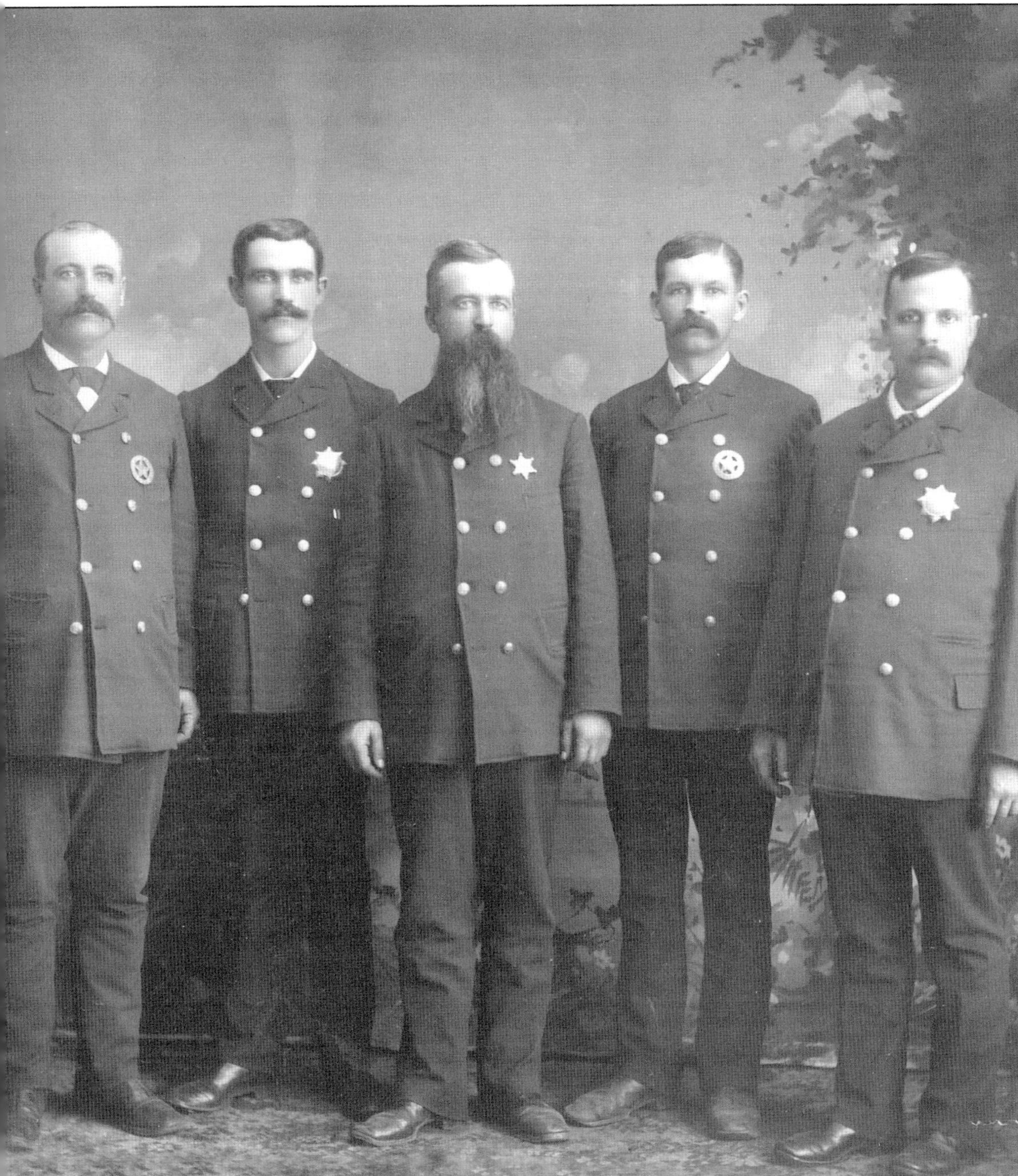

The first city marshal, Alfred Berg, was elected in 1874. This was a time when law enforcement required brute strength rather than education. Marshals were appointed by the mayor after the first election. The marshal, and oftentimes the officers, were replaced each time a new mayor took office. This unfortunate practice occurred well into modern times with police chiefs. The five members of the Hastings Police Department posed for this photo in 1888. From left to right, they are: Charles Wanzer, Archie Burchfield, Chief George Crane, J.M. Tennant, and Nicholas Schilling. The department currently has about 40 sworn officers, including two reserves.

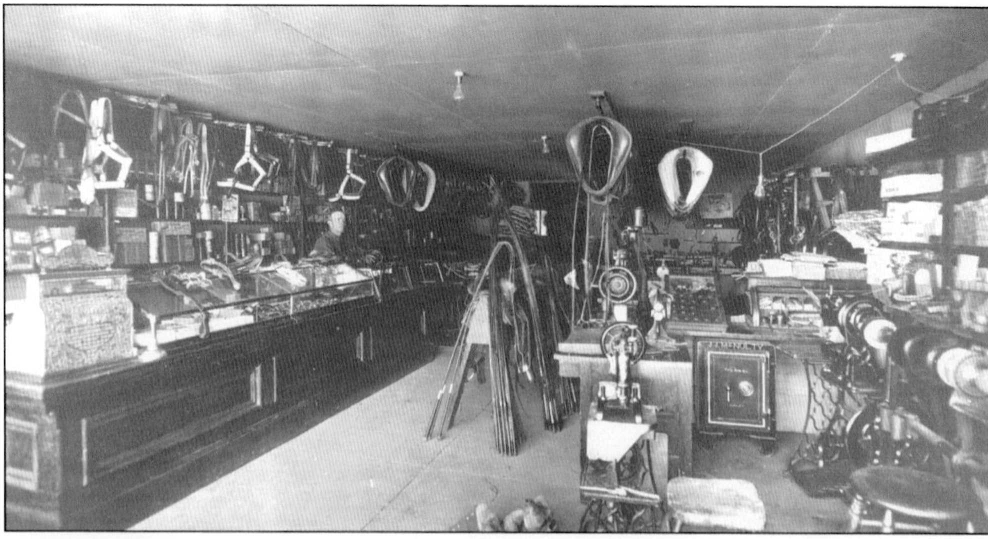

In 1886, William M. Dutton, J.H. Haney, and W.A. McKey became partners in the manufacture of high quality harness and horse collars. The business was known as the J.H. Haney Co., which expanded into a line of automobile parts and accessories. It eventually was named the W.H. Dutton & Sons Co., for the new owners. The business expanded, building a six-story building, and is now the Dutton-Lainson Co.

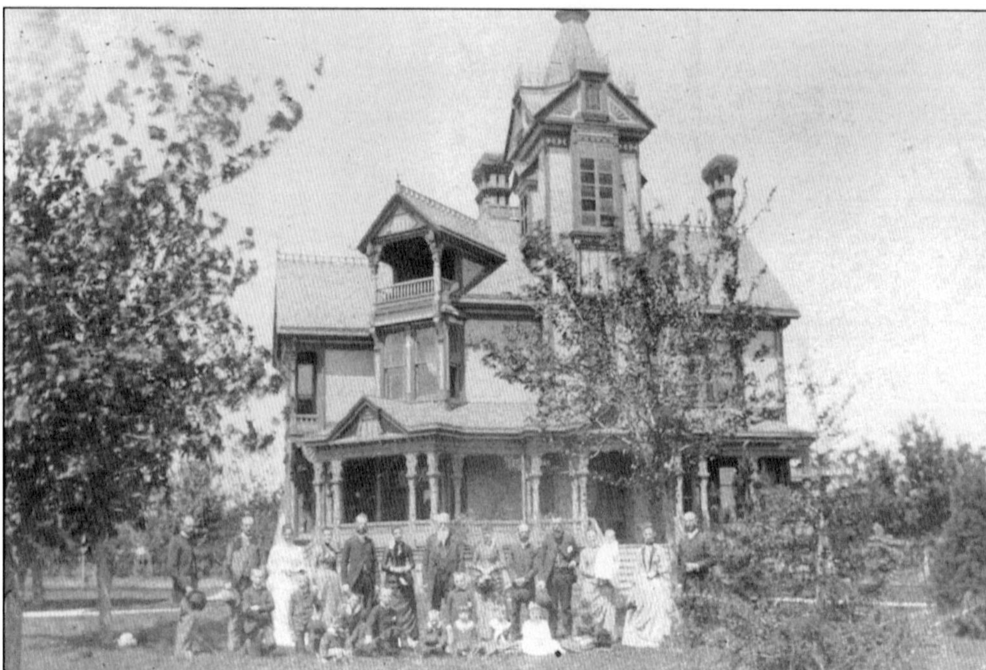

In 1886, the most elaborate house in Hastings was built at Ninth Street and Lincoln Avenue. The owner, James B. Heartwell, chose the highest point, then located north of town, to build his home. The $30,000 home was built of the finest materials, including interior trim of walnut, birds eye maple, cherry, oak, and hard pine. A Chicago craftsman was brought in to build the hand-carved oak staircase. Private horse stables were also located on the full city block owned by Heartwell.

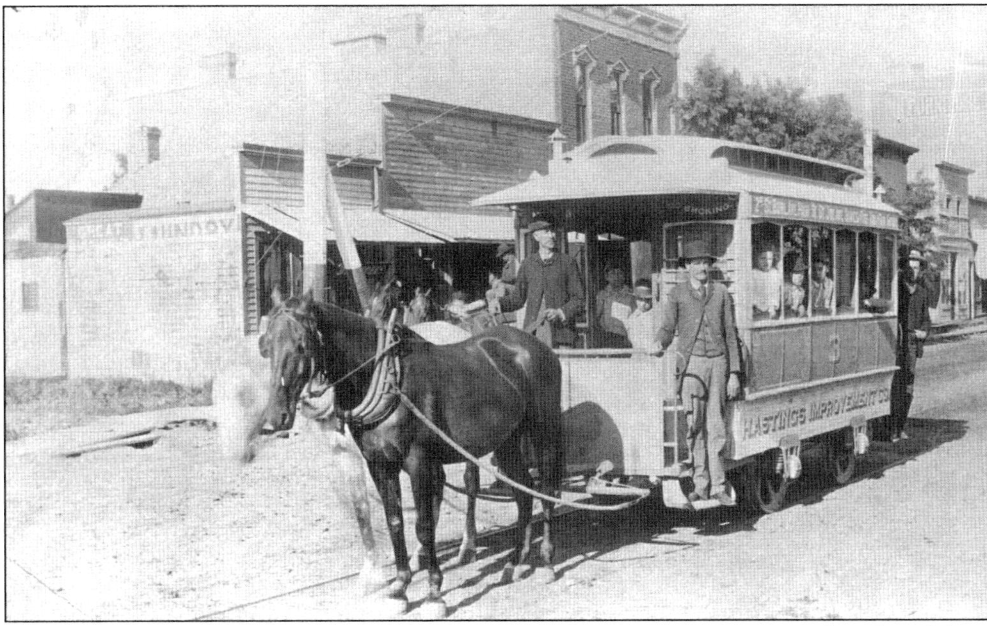


Plans for the first streetcar system arose in the bustling prairie town in 1885, but they did not materialize until two years later. Voters approved franchises for not one, but two companies, the Hastings Improvement Co. and the Citizens Railway Co. The process of claiming streets and laying track evolved into a war that required settlement in court. In 1889, Jonas F. Proffitt (standing on the step), leased the Improvement Company with J.B. Thompson, but shut it down that same year. The Citizens Company operated until 1894.

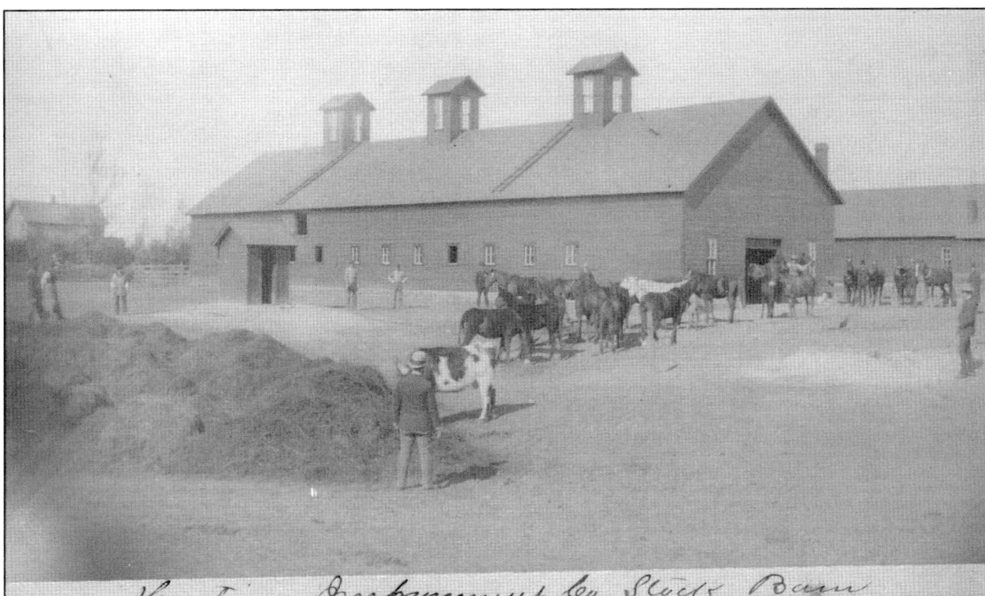


The Hastings Improvement Company stock and streetcar barns were located near C Street and Bellevue Avenue. The car barn could house 25 streetcars, although the company never owned more than 12. The stable had stalls for 40 head of mules and horses, and included a blacksmith shop and oil house.

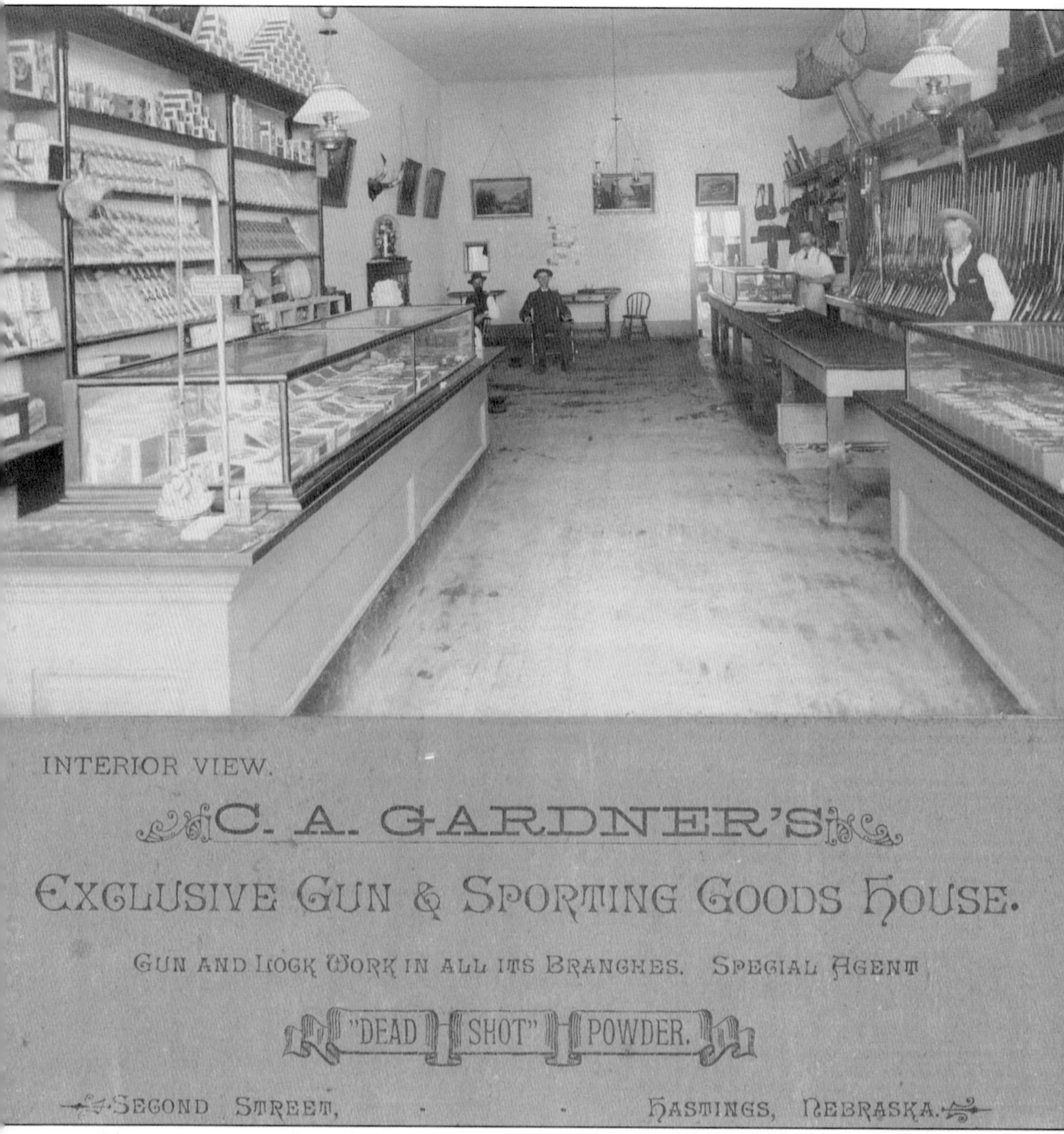


The primary source for guns, ammunition, and sporting goods in 1888 was C.A. Gardner's store, which was located at 515 West Second Street. A large selection of long guns can be seen at right. A customer could purchase a double-barrel shotgun for $8.69, and 100 shells for about $1.40. A fine Winchester Model 1886 lever-action rifle would fetch $14, and a box of 100 .40–82-caliber cartridges about $3. Those looking for close personal protection could lay out 68¢ for a seven-shot .22 caliber spur-trigger revolver. If the customer had the funds, he could buy the best—a Colt's Single Action Army revolver in .45 caliber, for about $12. A box of 50 .45 caliber cartridges was 80¢. A good rod and reel for fishing would set the sportsman back $3.

A local newspaper ran an editorial in August 1873, which promoted the idea of establishing a college in Hastings. Poor economic conditions during the 1870s delayed any progress. The Kearny Presbytery had been approached, and finally in 1882, Hastings College was founded. Ninety-three civic minded men donated $10,050 for land and construction of buildings. McCormick Hall (shown here in 1888) was the first building built. It was repaired after a fire, and still serves on the campus.

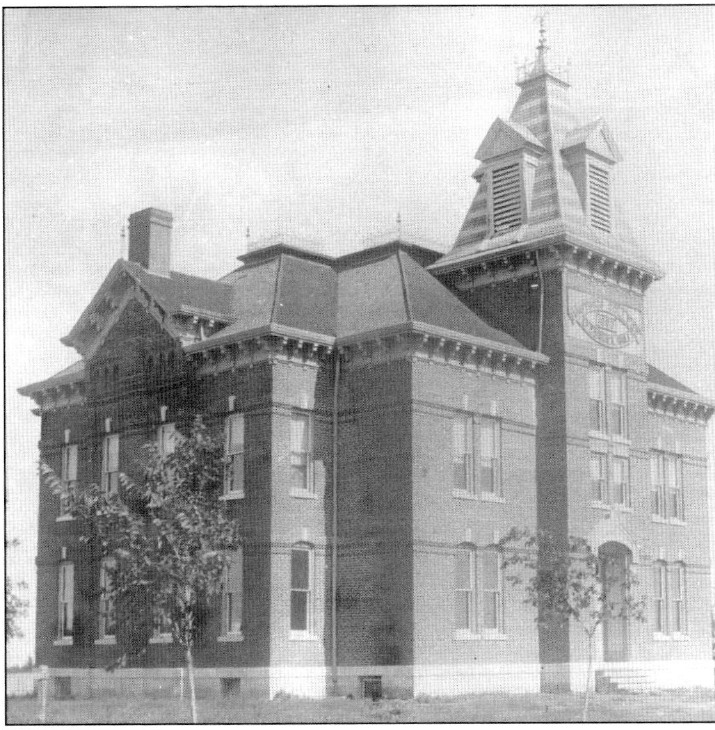

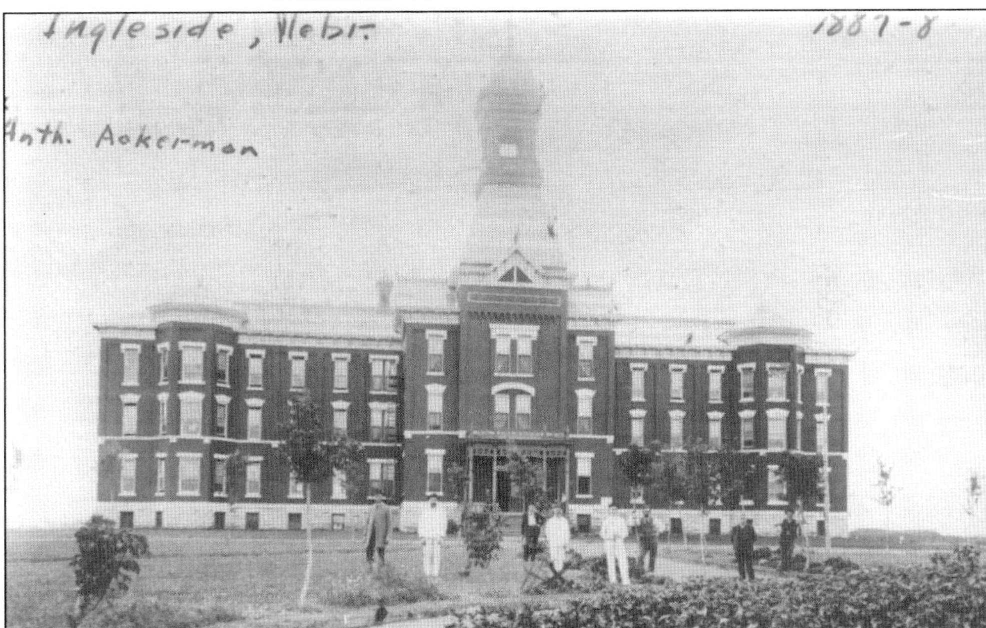


In 1887, the state legislature appropriated $75,000 for construction of the "Hospital for the Incurably Insane," which relieved those in Lincoln and Norfolk. A total of 630 acres were obtained 1 mile west of town. Several buildings were added through the years and the name changed to "Asylum for the Chronic Insane" in 1895; to the "Nebraska State Hospital" in 1905; the "Ingleside Hospital for the Insane" in 1915; and later the "Hastings State Hospital"; and then in 1971, "Hastings Regional Center."

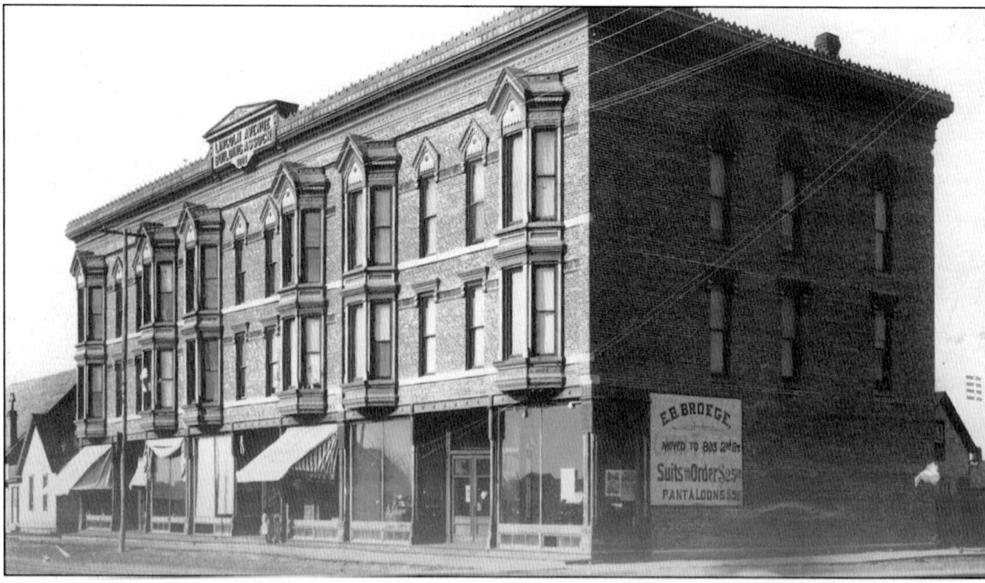


The Lincoln Avenue Block was built in 1887, between Third and Fourth Streets. Various businesses were situated on the main level, while the second and third floors were flats. Shown in this 1890 photo, the building is situated at an intersection of the town's two streetcar companies. Residents and passersby probably witnessed more than one scuffle between the rival companies at the corner!

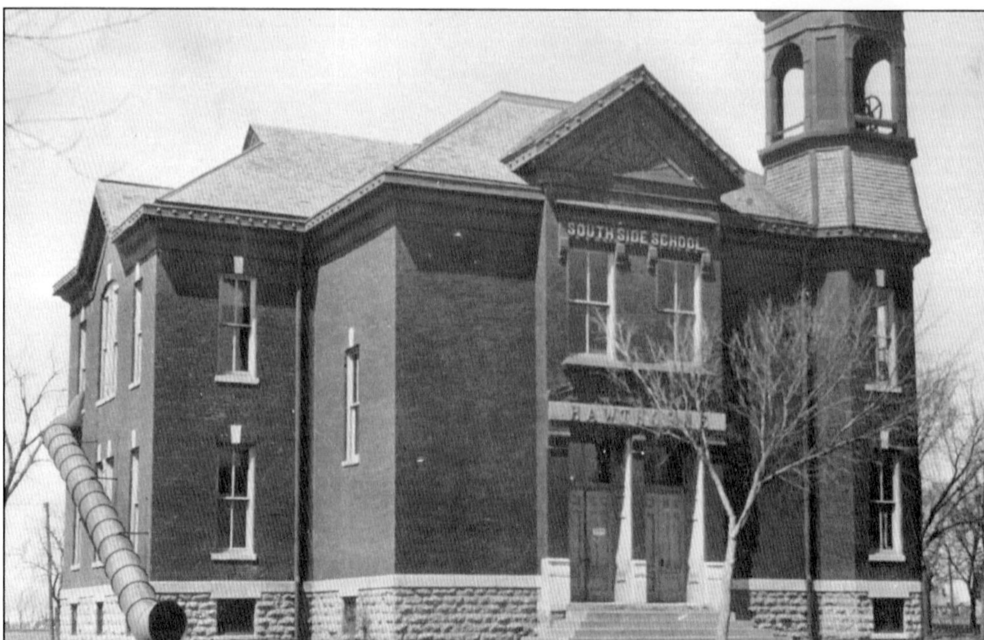


The South Side School, later named Hawthorne, was built in 1888. It was located on Hastings Avenue between G and I Streets. With approval of the city council, it became the home for the first Hastings Museum, which opened January 9, 1927. After the museum outgrew the building, it was sold to G. Bouricius, who operated a battery factory there. Who remembers the big dark tubes used for fire escapes?

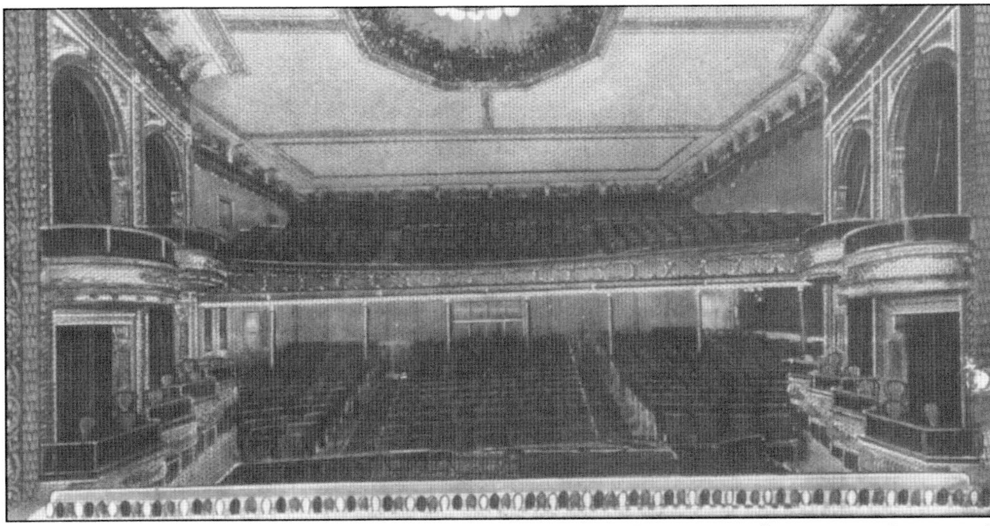

The Kerr Opera House was built in 1884, after formation of a joint stock company. It was well known for being the only theatre building of its type between Omaha and Denver. The stage was 66 feet wide and 38 feet deep, with an orchestra pit in front. Traveling theatre troupes brought culture to town with various stage productions. Notables such as President William H. Taft, William Jennings Bryan, and Theodore Roosevelt appeared there.

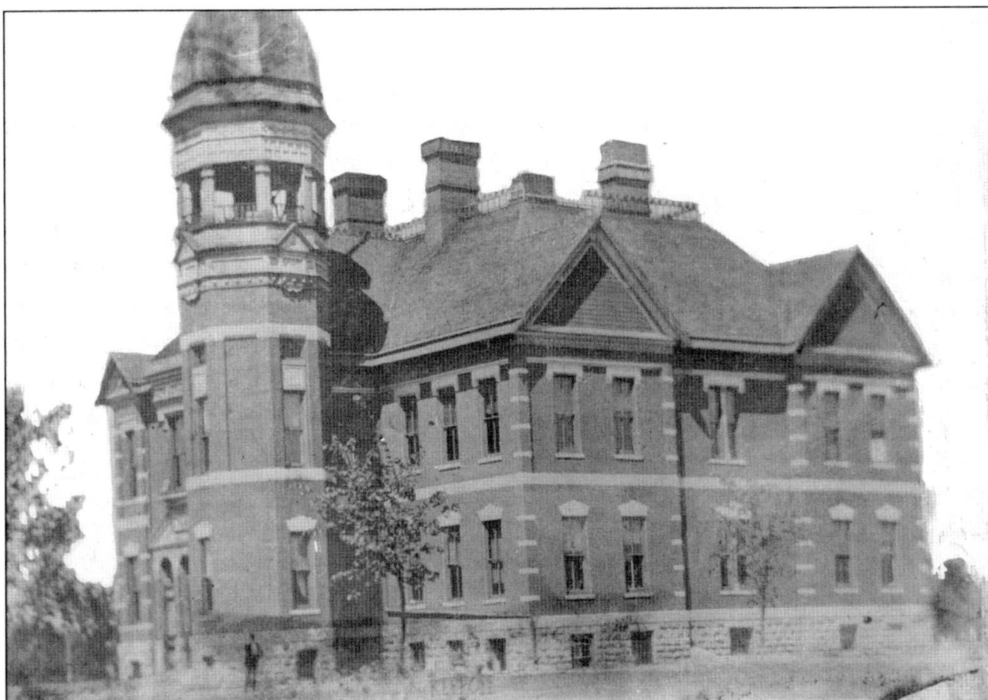

The first high school was built in 1882, between Seventh and High (now called Ninth) Streets, facing Denver Avenue. Fire losses were high in the 19th century, and the school was one of the victims. In 1887, it was replaced by the building shown. Elementary classes were held on the first floor, with high school on the second floor. The first graduates were Clara Green, Leta Horlocker, and Carrie Kimball.

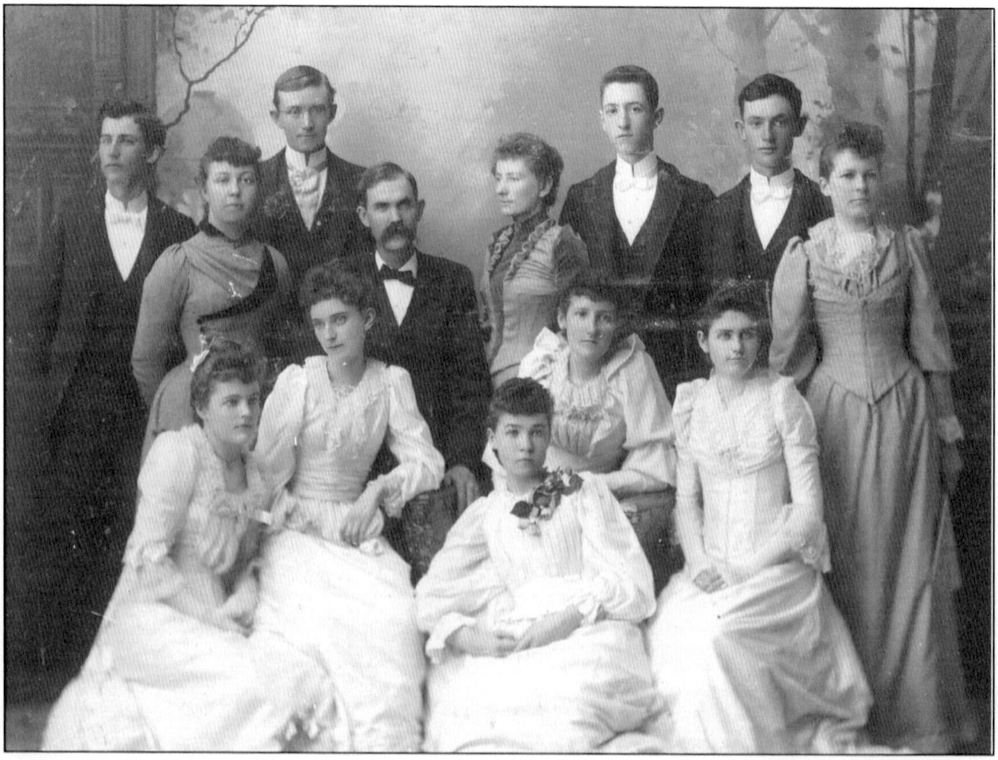

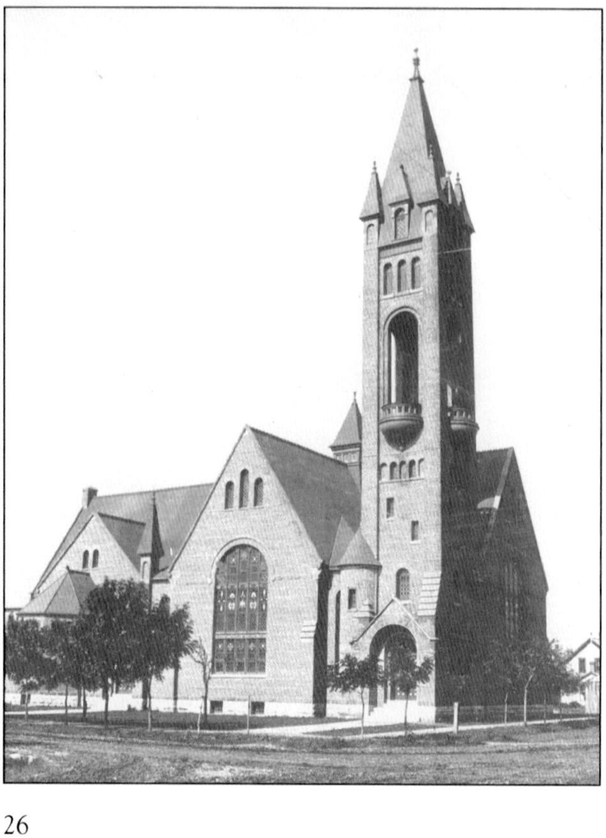

The Hastings Public Schools established a graded system in 1877, with seven grades totaling 176 pupils. Later, more grades were added with 11th, 12th, and 13th being designated as the high school course. Pictured are the teachers and students of the Hastings High School graduating class of 1892.

The Presbyterians moved into their brand new church in January 1891. The Reverend George T. Crissman gave the first sermon in the building, which was located at Seventh Street and Lincoln Avenue. The church, declared "the finest church structure in town," served until a 1910 fire destroyed it. Pastor C.W. Weyer started planning the reconstruction before the last embers were extinguished.

Harry and Ed Mock moved to Hastings from Alma, Nebraska and founded the *Hastings Evening Record* in 1899. It was one of several newspapers in the area at the time. Isaac LeDioyt was editor (bearded man in center), with Harry W. Borley (shown third from the right of seated carrier boys). It was sold to J.S. Ramsey a short time later, and ceased operation in 1901. It was located on a lot that is now partially occupied by the old Strand Theatre building.

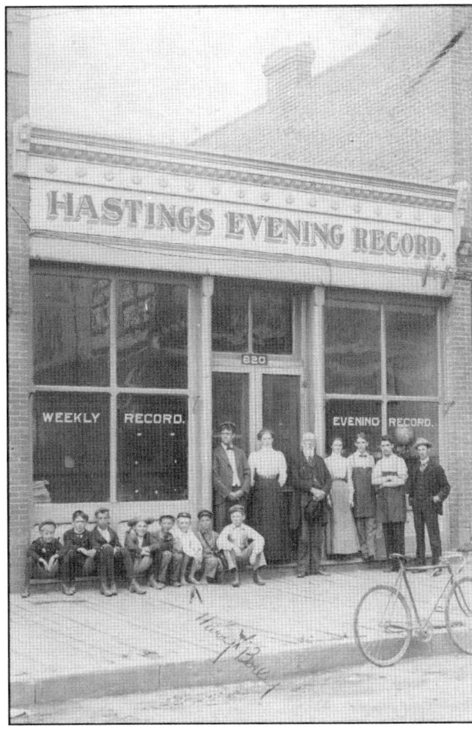


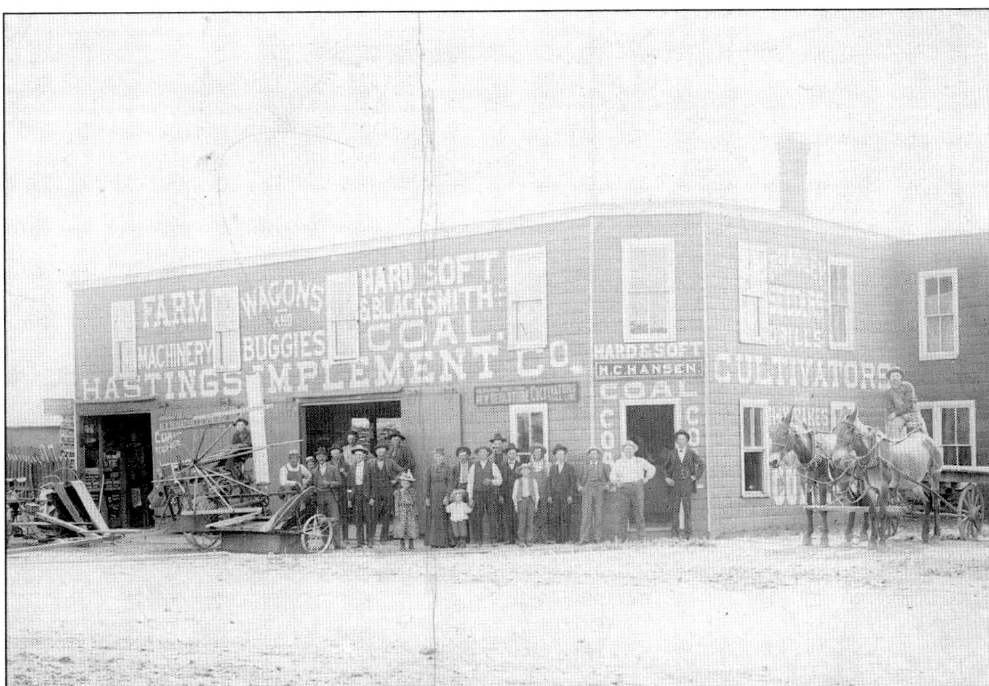


H.C. Hansen purchased this building in 1890, establishing the Hastings Implement Company. Manager E. Hazlett saw the business grow to an average $100,000 in sales per year. During the early years, 100 binders and 60,000 pounds of twine were sold every season, he claimed. While plans were being made to sell the business to a Minden firm, it was destroyed by fire.

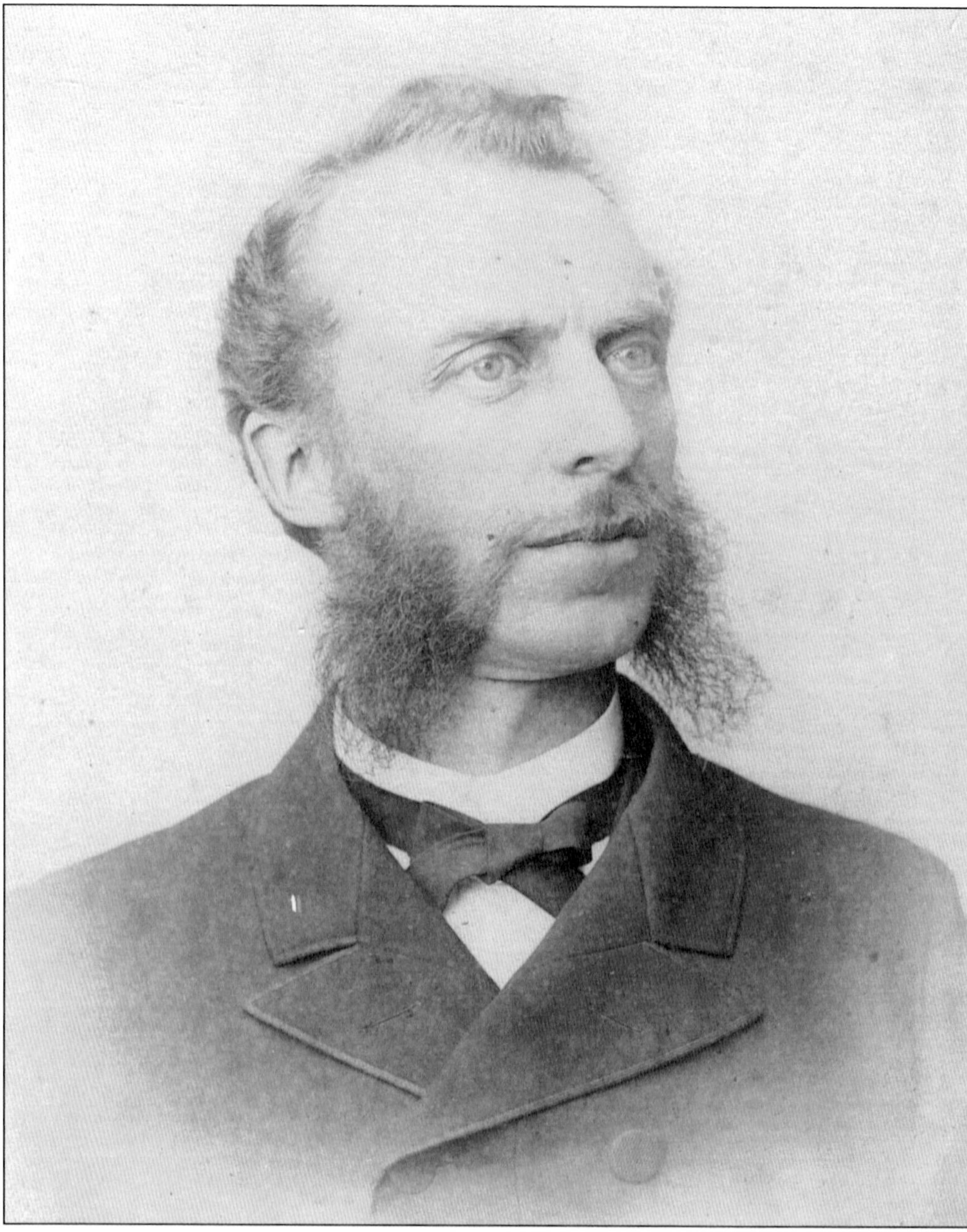

James Benjamin Heartwell was born in upstate New York in 1843. After attending a business college, he began a career in banking and real estate. Heartwell came to Hastings in 1879, but left for California 17 years later after his various enterprises failed during poor economic times. Before leaving, James Heartwell left quite a mark on the town. He had been involved in many areas including, banking, politics, construction of new buildings, was the first president of the YMCA, and participated in the formation of Hastings College. He established a private family park, which later became one of the most popular city parks. The park was part of his 45-acre development called "Heartwell's Park Addition," which included the first golf course in the county and a plat of 57 residential lots. The addition was unique because it was designed by landscape architect A.N. Carpenter of Galesburg, Illinois.

# *Two*

# EARLY 20TH CENTURY 1900–1929

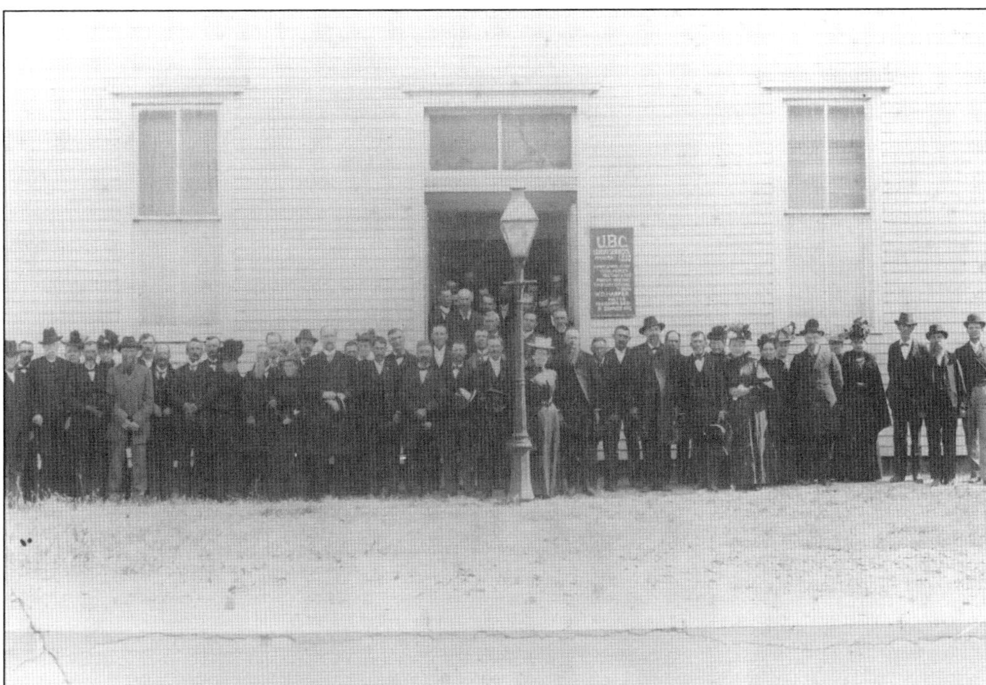

This is the only known photograph of Liberal Hall, which was built by the Free Religion Society in 1878. The name indicated the religious precepts. It was the only public meeting place until the Kerr Opera House and the Bostwick Hotel were built. It was used for a variety of religious services, theatre, and social gatherings, but it is especially noted for being the site where the trial of I.P. "Print" Olive and Fred Fischer was held. The Custer County ranchers were tried for the lynching and burning of two suspected rustlers.

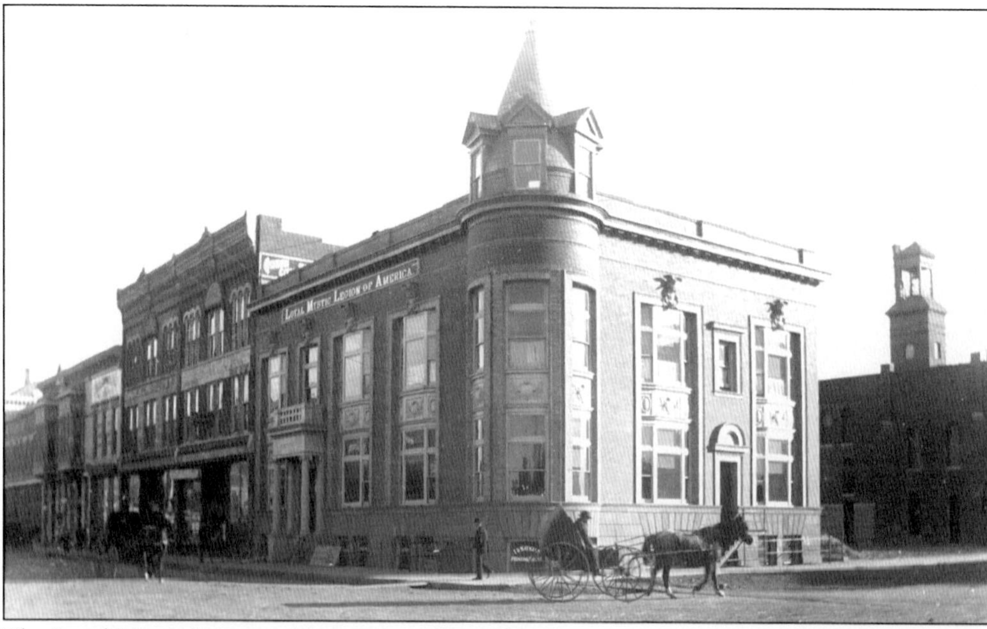


The Loyal Mystic Legion of America, a fraternal insurance organization, was founded in 1892, after articles of incorporation were filed by city leaders, including J.B. Heartwell. The building was completed in 1901, which featured marble, granite, and pressed brick trimmings. The name of the society could be read in the mosaic style flooring inside the entrance. The building was later sold to John Kipp, a cigar maker, and in 1962, it was replaced by a J.C. Penney store. It currently houses the Eakes Office Products store.

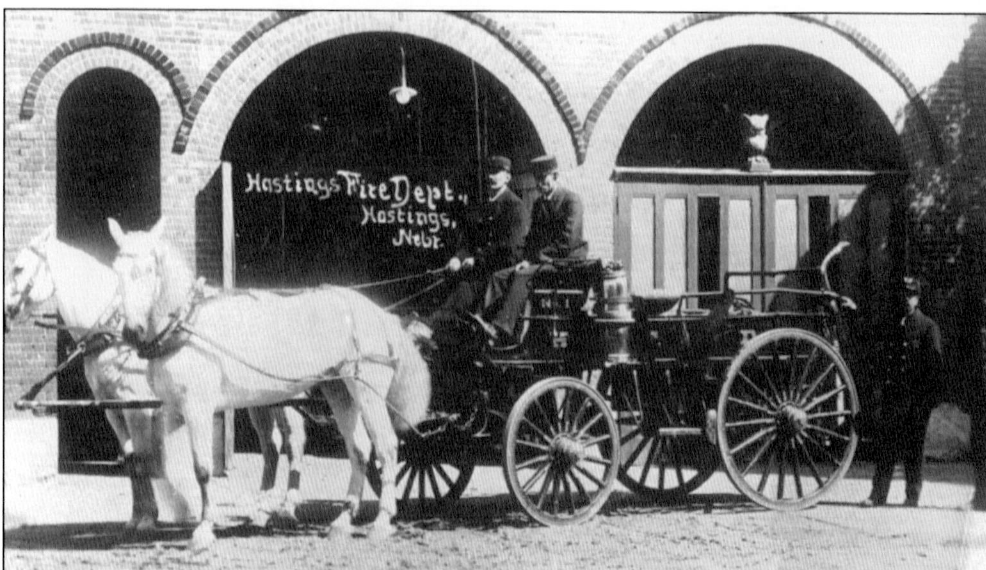


The first fire-fighting apparatus had to be pulled to the scene by manpower. A few years later, horse-drawn equipment was utilized as shown in this 1900 photo, which was taken in front of the old engine house on Burlington Avenue. The mayor suggested as early as 1913 that the city should purchase a motorized truck with which to more effectively fight fires, but the department didn't receive one until 1917.

The Congregationalists of Adams County were the first to establish a church organization in the county and in the city. Early services were held in a number of places, including covered wagons. Their first church was built at a cost of $3,000, and was dedicated in March 1879. The ornately designed wood framed building featured an eye catching bell tower.

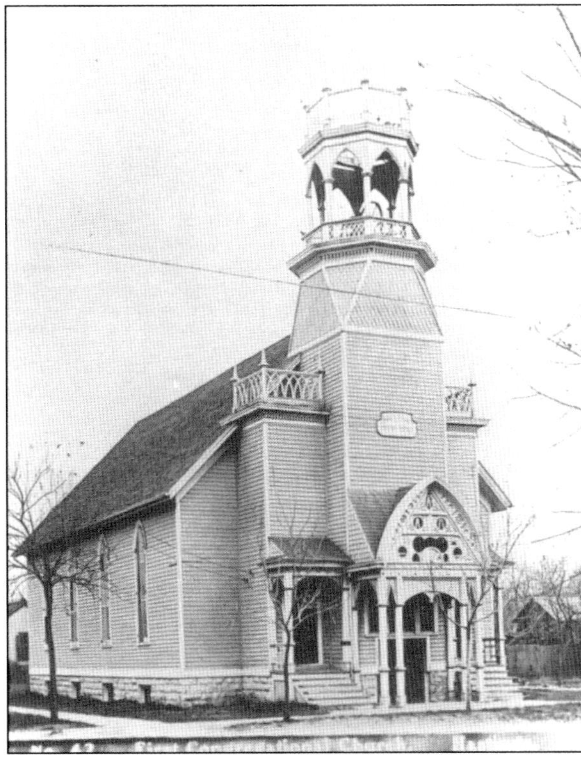

*The Kenesaw Times* was moved to Hastings in 1878, and the name changed to the *Central Nebraskan*. Later, when the paper became a daily, the name was changed to the *Hastings Central Nebraskan*. It was purchased by the *Daily Republican* on January 12, 1889, and continued to publish until 1915 when Adam Breede consolidated it with his *Daily Tribune*. Fred Jasper, Ed Watkins, and George Hensman are shown at work at the *Republican* in 1903.

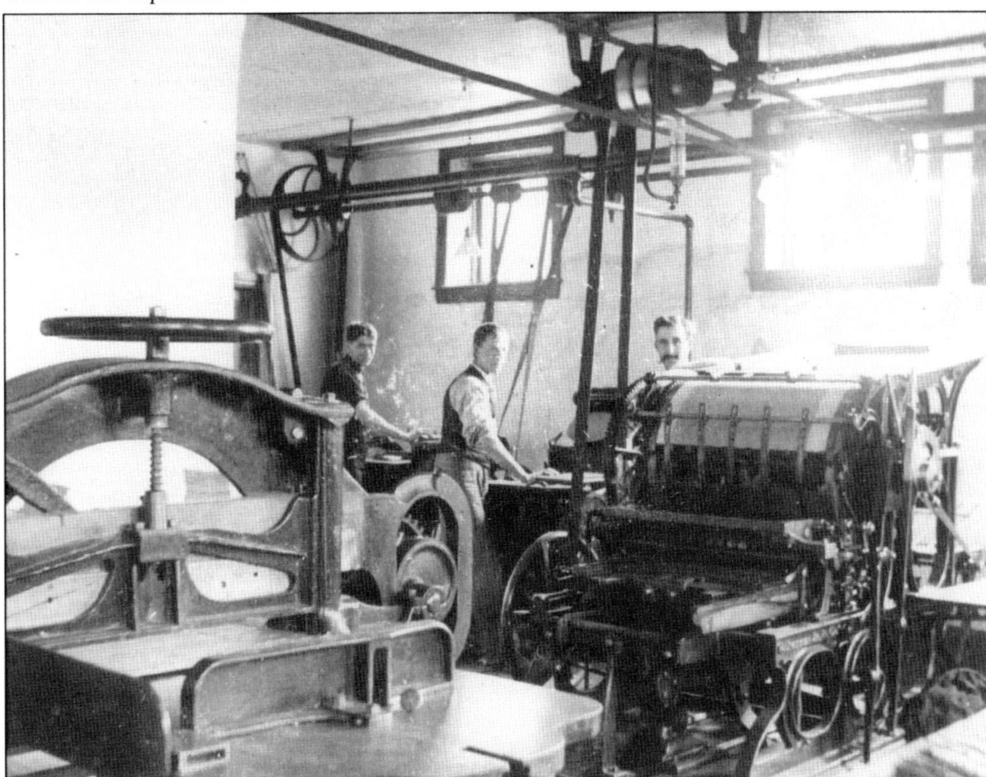

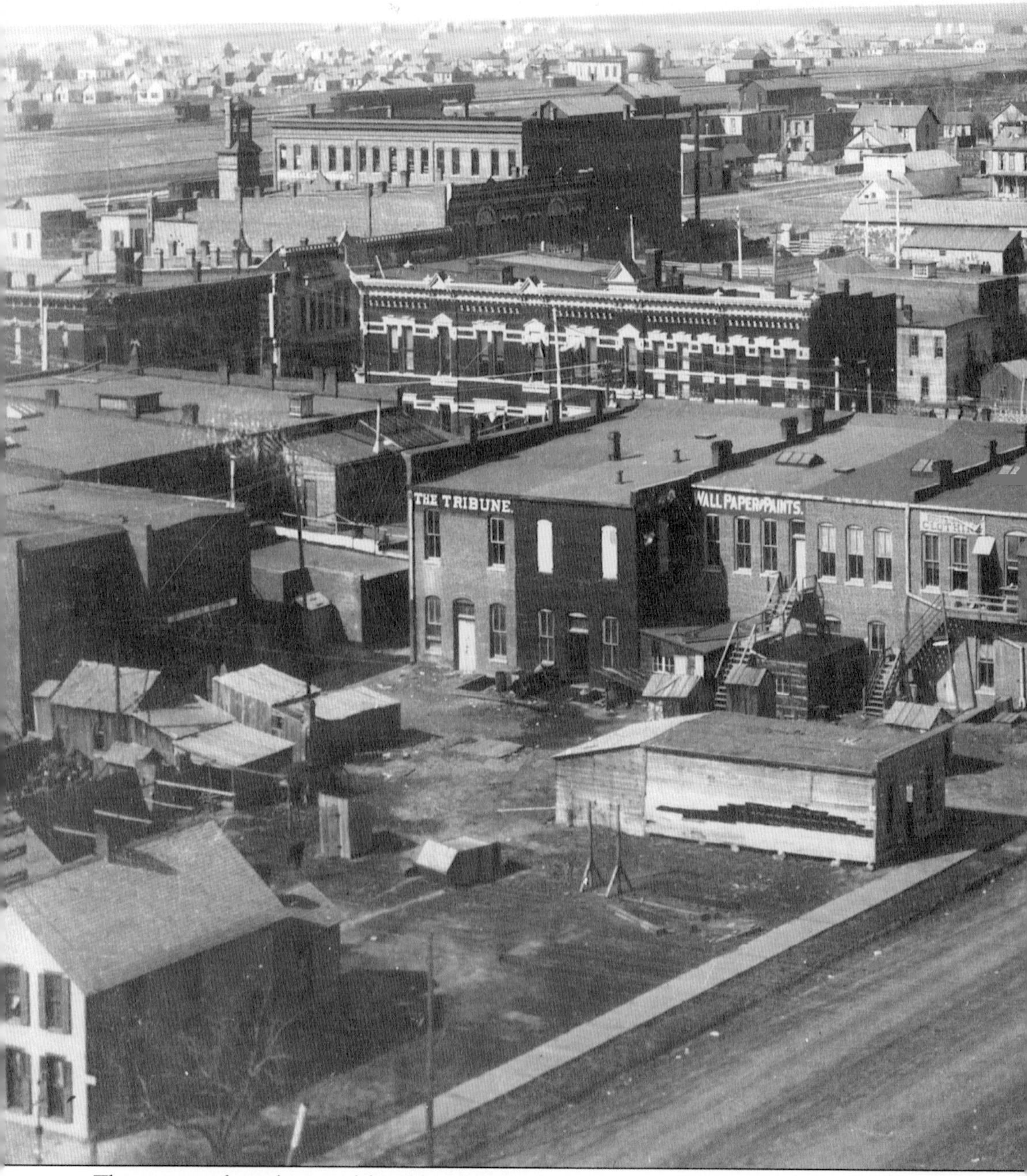


This is a view from the top of the old courthouse looking in a southwesterly direction about 1900. The three-story building to the right was the Madgett flats, and the empty lot in the foreground would be the location of the post office and federal building in 1905. The two-story residence in the lower left-hand corner is the present site of the Kensington (formerly the Clarke

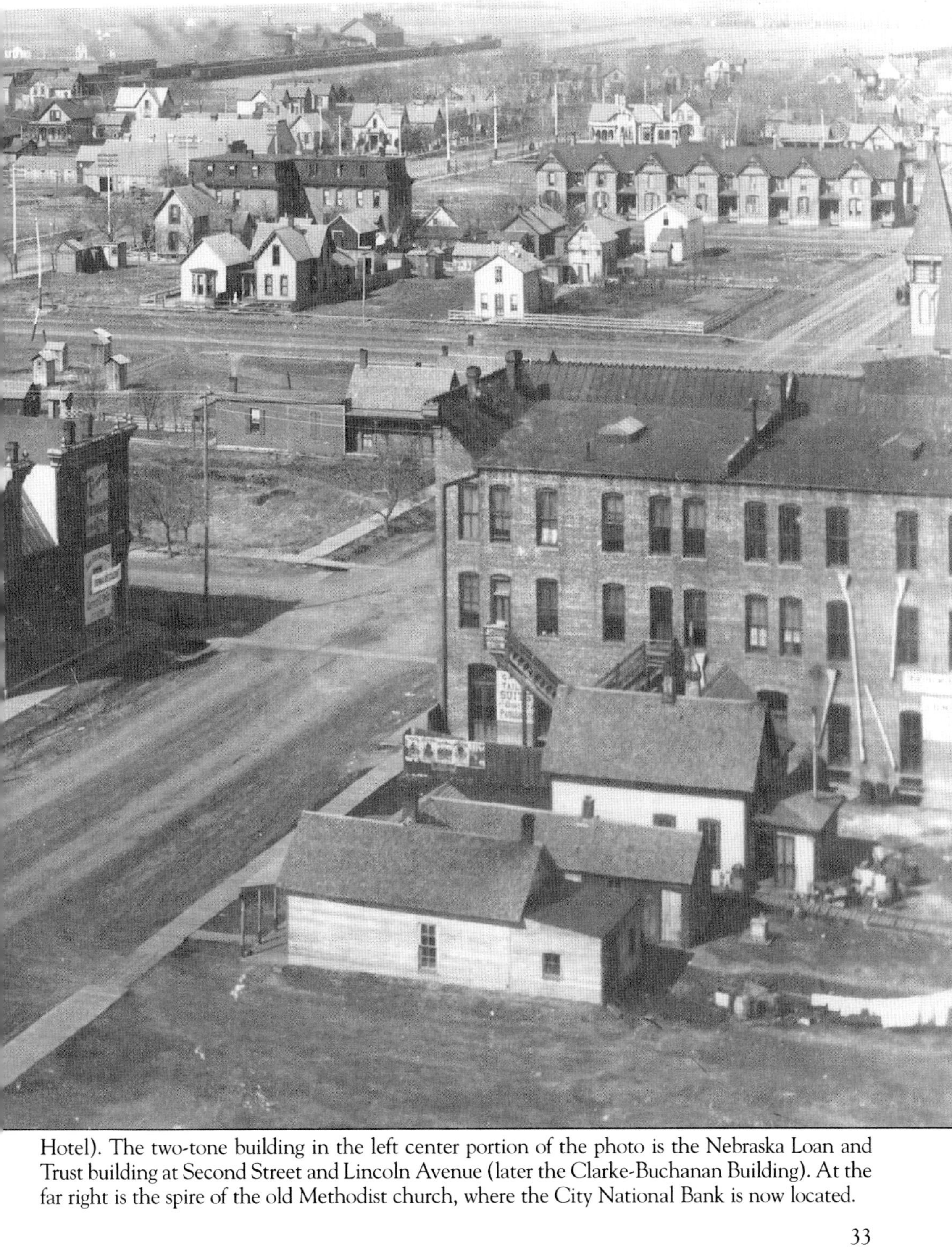

Hotel). The two-tone building in the left center portion of the photo is the Nebraska Loan and Trust building at Second Street and Lincoln Avenue (later the Clarke-Buchanan Building). At the far right is the spire of the old Methodist church, where the City National Bank is now located.

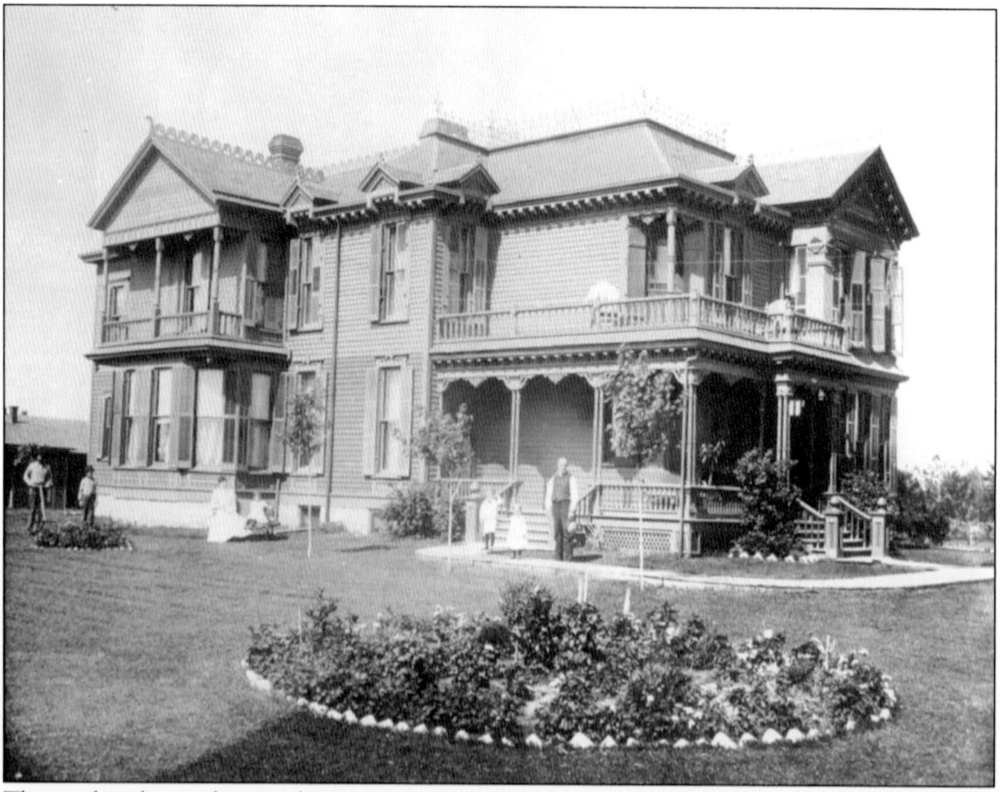

This is the elegant home of prominent Hastings businessman and city council member Ezra Langevin in 1904. Langevin, a native of Canada, came to the city in 1878. He was prominent in the grocery as well as food canning and ice businesses. His restored home still stands at 1000 West Ninth Street, now the proud home of local attorney Stephen Scherr.

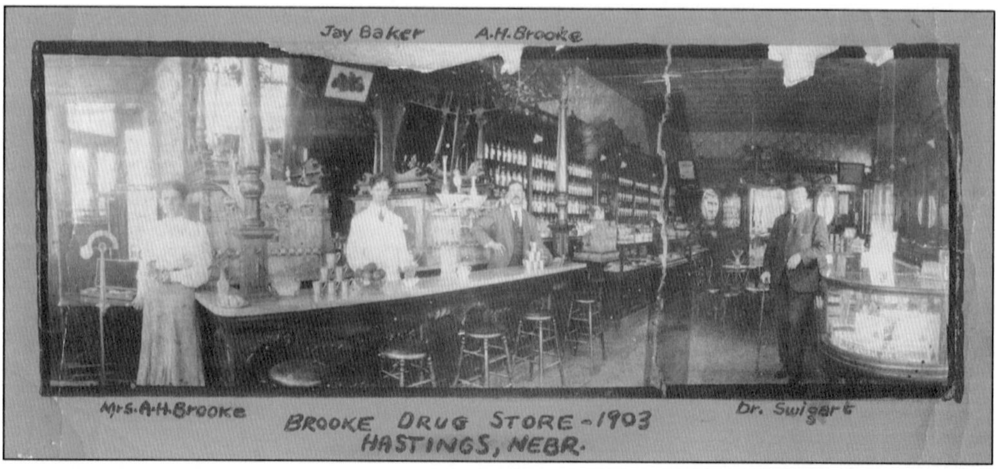


In 1884, Claus and George Fraham erected a building at Second Street and Hastings Avenue, where they operated their apothecary until 1899. A.H. Brooke opened his drug store here in 1905, a classic, which included a marble-topped soda fountain. Brooke's wife was the first woman on the city council. The store later became the Redfield Drug Store, and is now the First Federal Lincoln Bank.

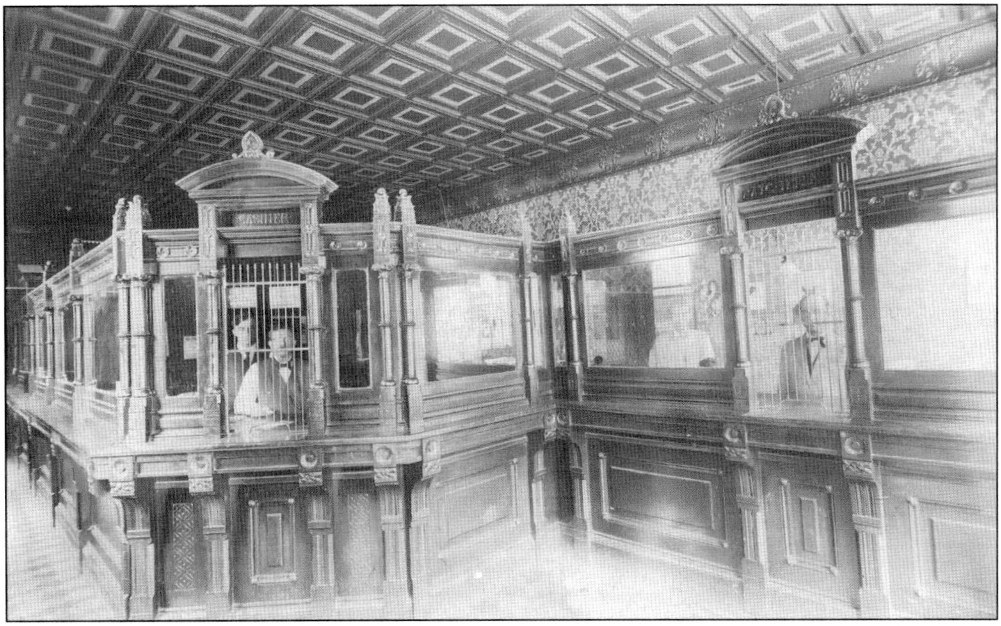

The Exchange Bank moved into the newly finished Cameron Building at First and Hastings in 1883. It was built on the site of Charles Cameron's original mercantile business. The bank re-organized as the Exchange National Bank in 1884, and remained there until merging with the First National Bank in 1926. This interior view was taken about 1905.

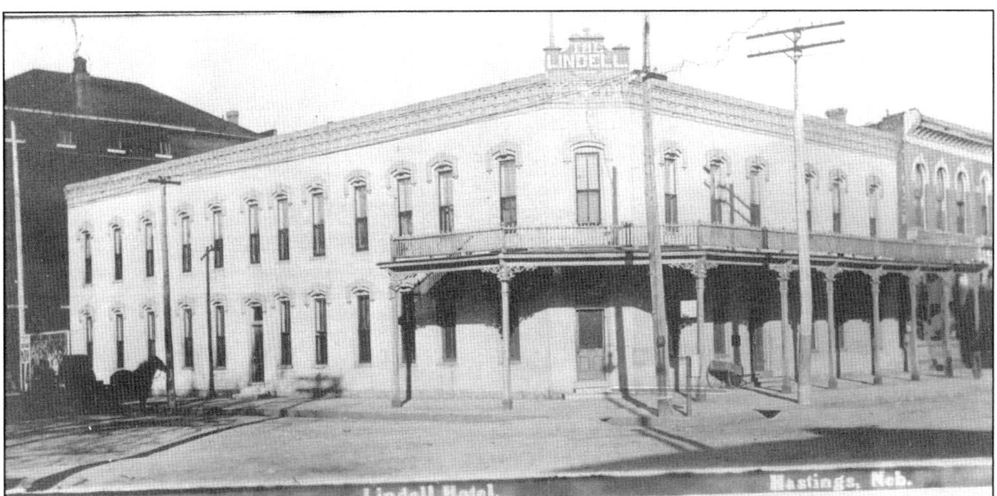


The Lindell Hotel was located on the northeast corner of First Street and Lincoln Avenue. It was built in 1880, by Missouri native Nicholas F. Damron. At the age of 13, Damron was driving a peddler's wagon in southern Wisconsin until moving to Hastings. In addition to the hotel business, he also was involved in the livery and sale business. Mr. J.N. Bowen was the manager at the time this photo was taken in 1905.

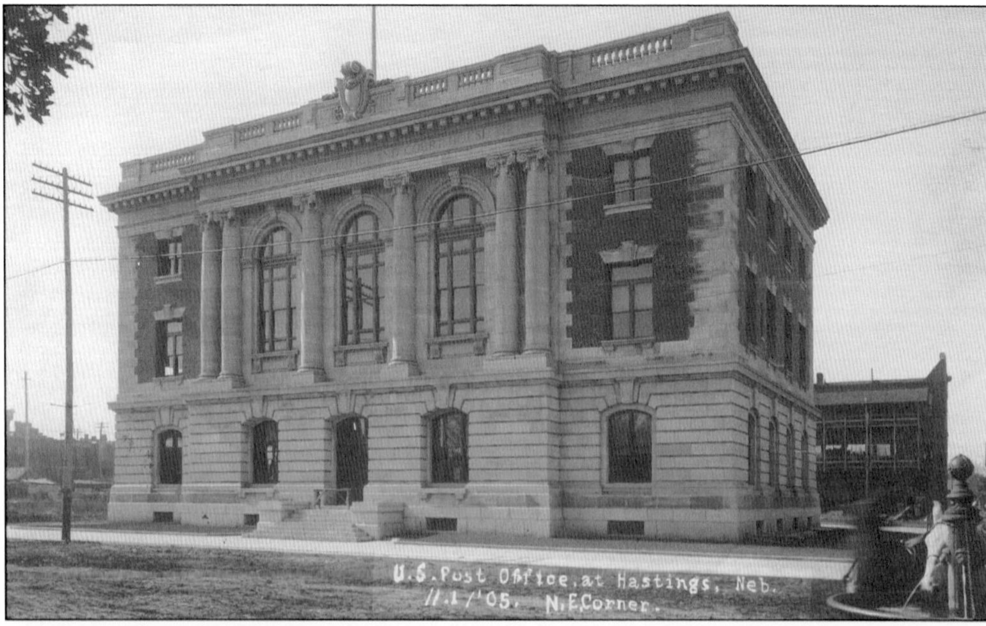


Hastings banker Charles H. Dietrich was elected governor in 1901, serving only a few months before accepting a vacant seat in the U.S. Senate. One of his accomplishments before leaving the Senate was passage of his bill, which allowed for construction of a new U.S. Post Office and Courthouse building in Hastings. Built in 1905, the classic Palladian style structure, complete with Terrazo floors, marble borders, and wainscoting, served at the corner of Third Street and Hastings Avenue until 1963.

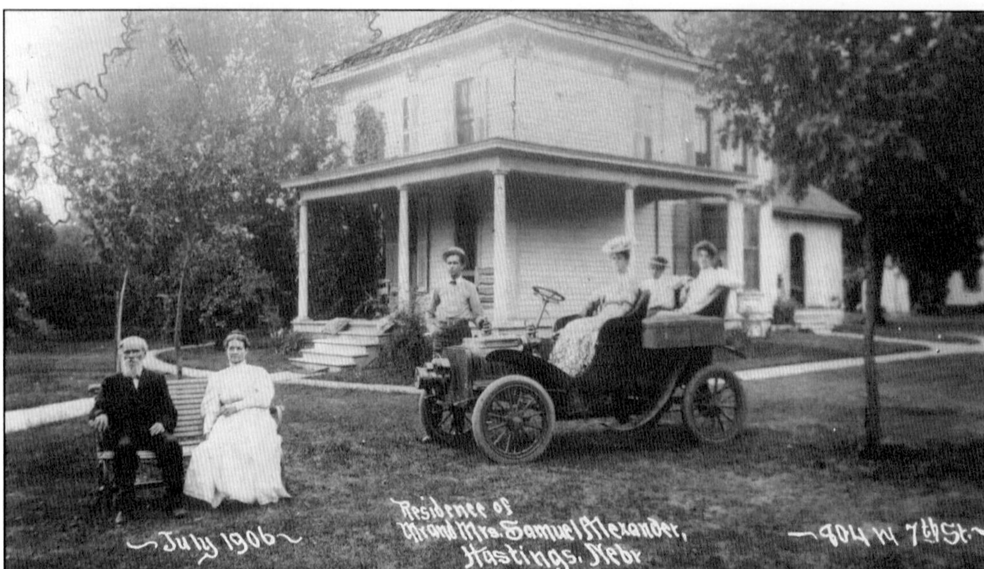


Samuel Alexander, a Civil War veteran from Pennsylvania, moved to the county in 1864, staking a claim where Hastings was later located. He was the town's first postmaster and served as a city treasurer, councilman, and mayor. The family posed for this photo in 1906, at their home at Seventh Street and Lincoln Avenue (now Alexander Park); from left to right, they are: Samuel, wife Harriet, and daughter Rachel, in the auto's front seat.

Charley Jacobs brought the first auto to Hastings in 1901. By 1910, the city had many new car dealers selling a variety of brands, including REO, Metz, Cadillac, Maxwell, Chalmers, and Carters. By 1921, there were 4,000 motor vehicles licensed in the county! The Jones & Brandes Company, located at 715 West First Street in 1906, were dealers in REOs, Maxwells, and Premieres.

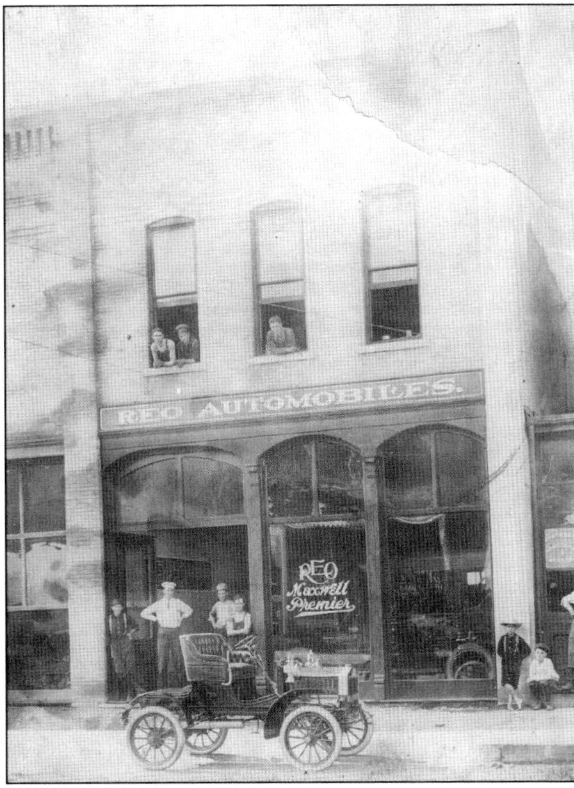


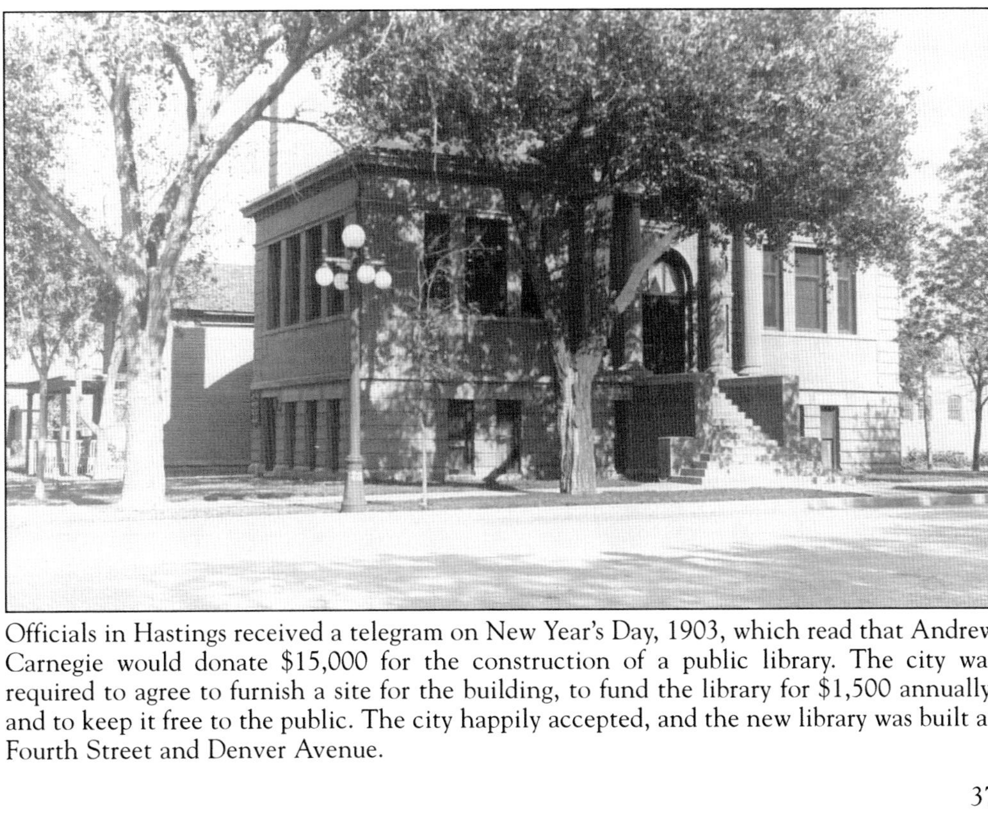

Officials in Hastings received a telegram on New Year's Day, 1903, which read that Andrew Carnegie would donate $15,000 for the construction of a public library. The city was required to agree to furnish a site for the building, to fund the library for $1,500 annually, and to keep it free to the public. The city happily accepted, and the new library was built at Fourth Street and Denver Avenue.

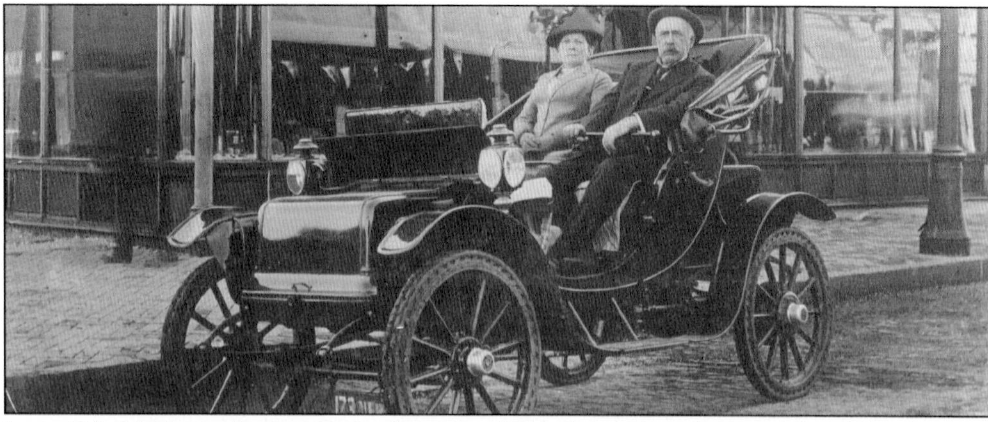

James P.A. Black was born in Pennsylvania in 1854. At age five, he arrived with his family at the Omaha Indian Reservation in Nebraska, where his father taught school. James attended school with the Native Americans and later graduated from the Peru Normal School. He became a lawyer and banker, moving to Hastings in 1904. Two years later, the Blacks were showing off their new electric automobile, the first one in town.

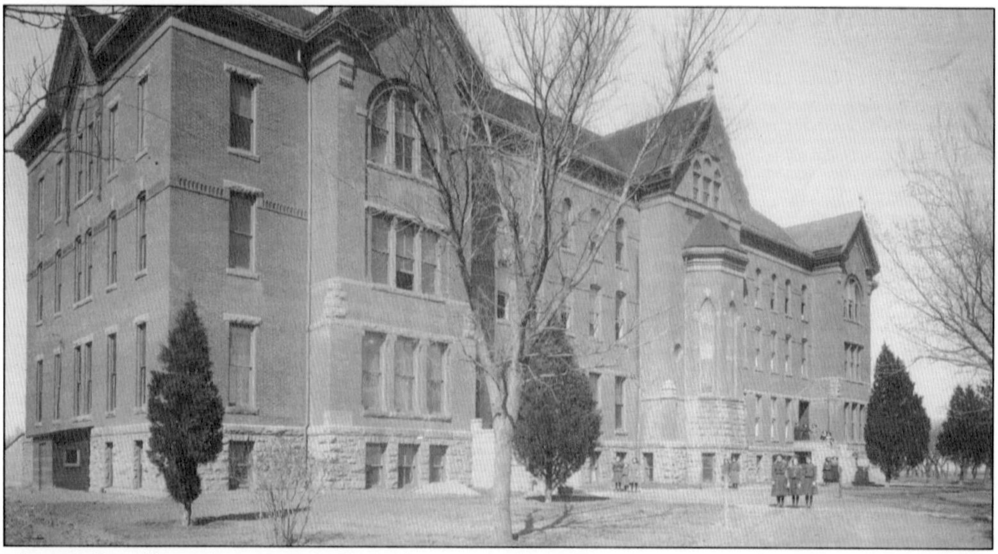

Thomas Farrell, a prominent Catholic businessman, sold a 10-acre parcel at the northeast edge of town in 1889. The land was purchased by the Sisters of Visitation, where a Catholic girl's boarding school was built. The $40,000 building consisted of a convent, the sisters' chapel, and student academy. The Academy of Visitation operated only for six years, closing due to non-payment of the mortgage. It was vacant until 1908, when the efforts of Rev. William McDonald of Hastings put the building to use again. The Commercial Club and the town's Catholics raised $8,000 to purchase the property, which was given to the Sisters of Saint Dominic of Saint Catherine, Kentucky, for $1. The school became the Immaculate Conception Academy, which received state accreditation in 1912. The Academy was forced to close due to low enrollment during the Depression, with the last graduation being held in 1932. The property was sold to the Crosier Fathers, who opened a college and seminary for men. In the 1970s, the Crosier Renewal Center was established in the newer additions to the building. The Crosiers occupied the building until the turn of the 21st century. Now being remodeled, the Crosier Park Professional Center will soon house various offices. It is scheduled to re-open in November 2001.

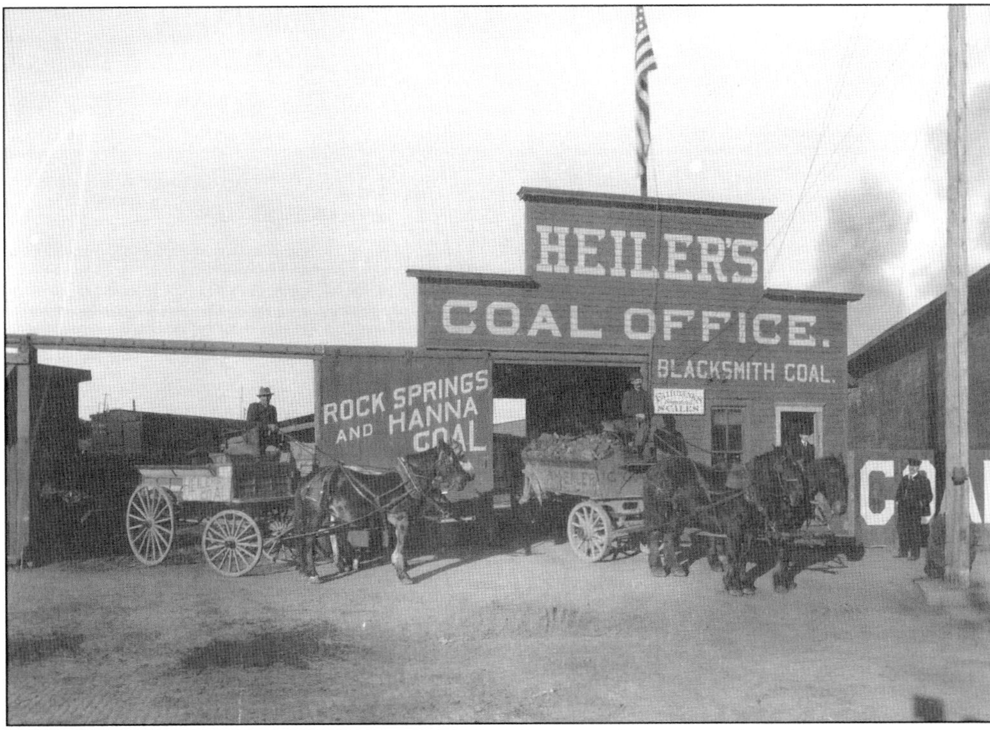


For many years, coal was a primary source of fuel for home heating and cooking as well as many commercial applications. Coal was an important retail trade with several dealers competing for business. Heiler's was one of eight dealers in 1906, when this photo was taken. The company operated out of their South Denver Avenue offices from 1897 to 1907.

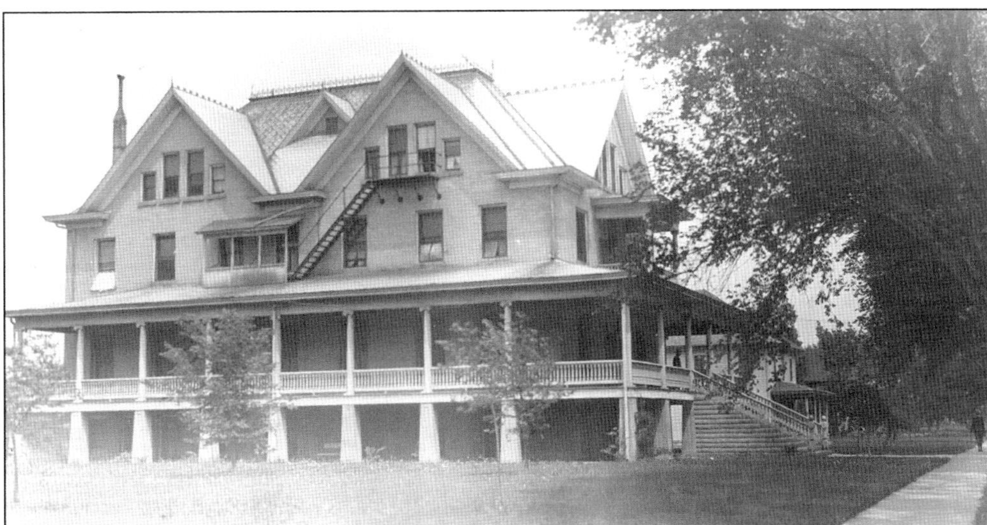

The Seventh Day Adventist Conference moved their headquarters from Lincoln to Hastings in 1907. Property was purchased on East Ninth Street, where buildings were constructed to accommodate nursing and children's classes, a store, and a hospital. The Nebraska Sanitarium was dedicated in 1908, and served as the only hospital in town for several years. By the late '20s, it was used as a business college, and during World War II it was converted into apartments.

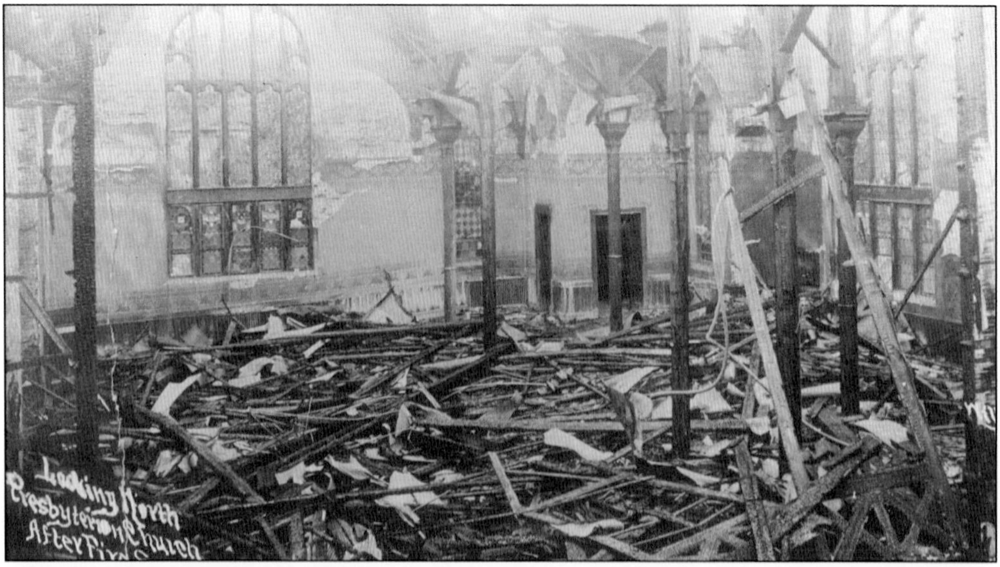


Fire was the scourge of most frontier towns, and Hastings was no exception. On September 14, 1879, a fire claimed 33 buildings in the main business district, from the Burlington Railroad tracks to Second Street and between Hastings and Lincoln Avenues. Sexton Fred W. Raney was killed while trying to save the church records during the First Presbyterian Church fire in September 1910.

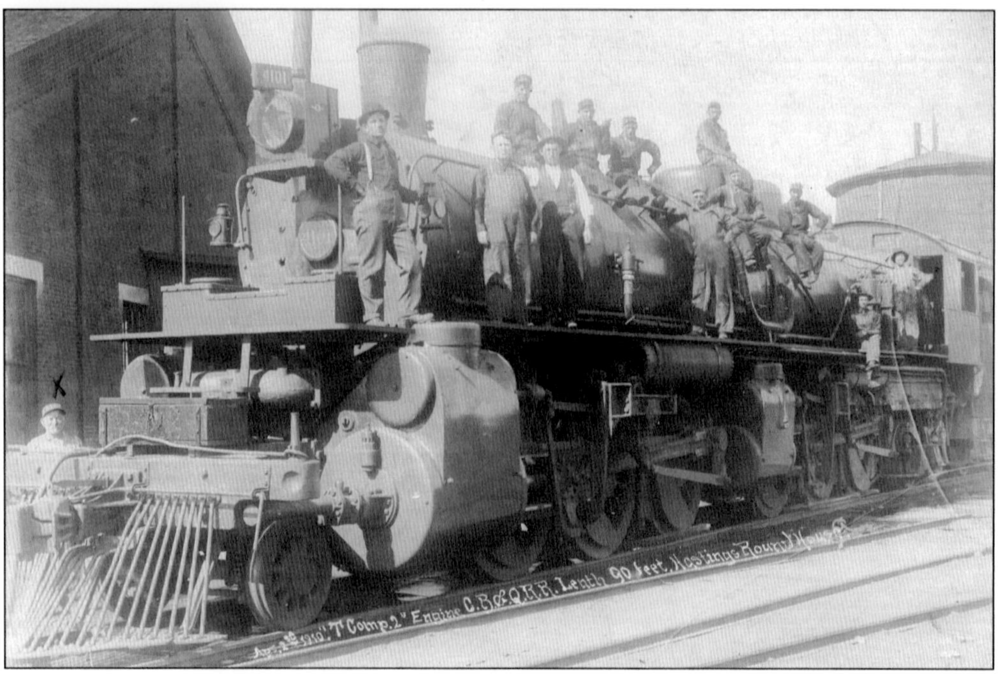


The Chicago, Burlington, and Quincy, and the Burlington and Missouri River Railroads consolidated in 1880, thereafter known as the CB&Q. It merged with the Great Northern in 1970, becoming the Burlington Northern Railroad. Recent years have seen another merger, this time with the Santa Fe Railroad. In 1910, CB&Q crewmen posed in the yard with a "T-Comp 2," engine which was 90 feet in length.

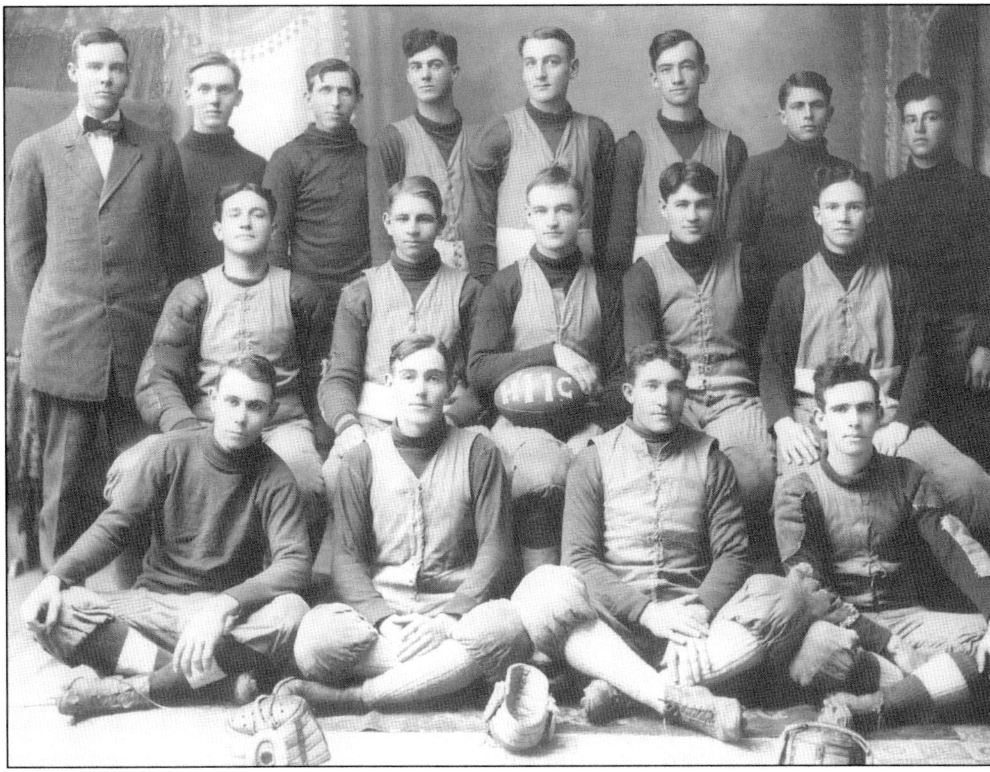

During the 1888 school year, Hastings College had its first football team, joining the already established baseball team. The first game was against Doane College, but unfortunately a compromise had to be reached before the end, as Hastings played Rugby football and Doane played National football. Pictured is the 1911 team, from left to right: (front row) Dan Schlick, Bill Crosson, Jay Livingston, Bedford Johnson; (middle row) Clarence Yager, Luke Parker, ? Smith, Ruben Dunlap, Archie Marvel; (back row) Ben Bracken, Wm. Hargelroad, Dan Gretzinger, ? Churchill, ? Smith, Ray Crawford, Chris Bitner, and Warren Davidson.

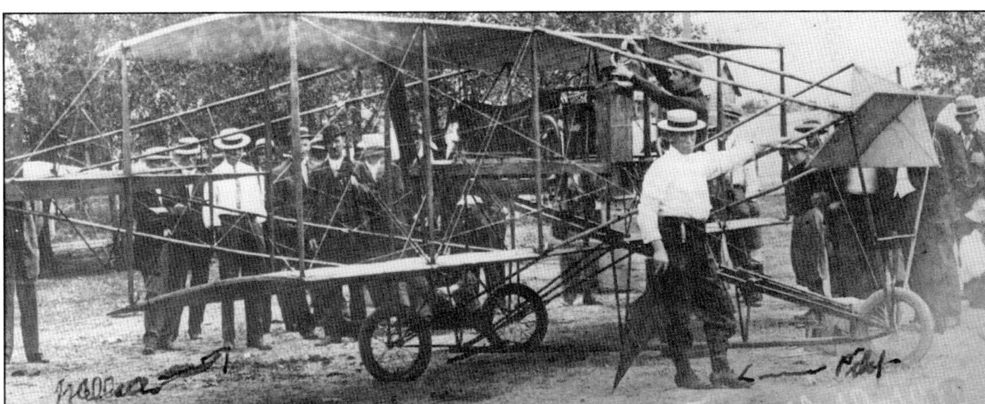

On July 18 and 19, 1911, a huge crowd gathered at the Hastings College campus to witness the first airplane ever seen in this region. Jimmie Ward, pilot of the Curtiss *Shooting Star*, made four flights each day for the mesmerized crowds. His flights ranged from 2,500 to 5,500 feet, where he performed a series of spirals, dips, and glides for the onlookers.

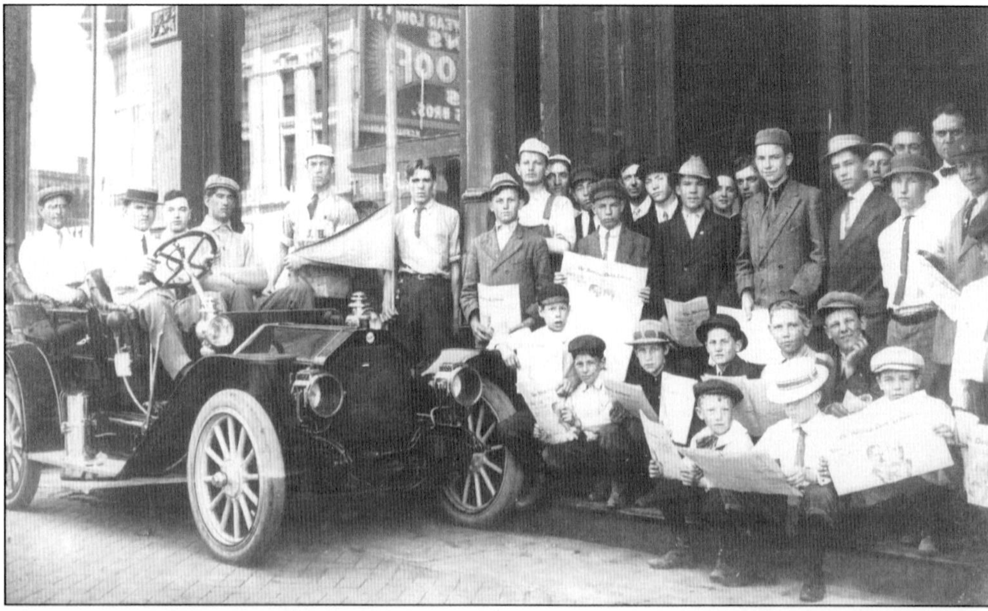

The *Hastings Tribune* editorial, circulation, and composing room staff posed for the photographer in 1911. Adam Breede, (tall man, far right) was a colorful, ambitious, and self-educated man. He purchased the *Independent-Tribune* from H.P. Brown in 1894, and renamed it. The newspaper was published weekly until 1905, when Breede changed it to a daily.

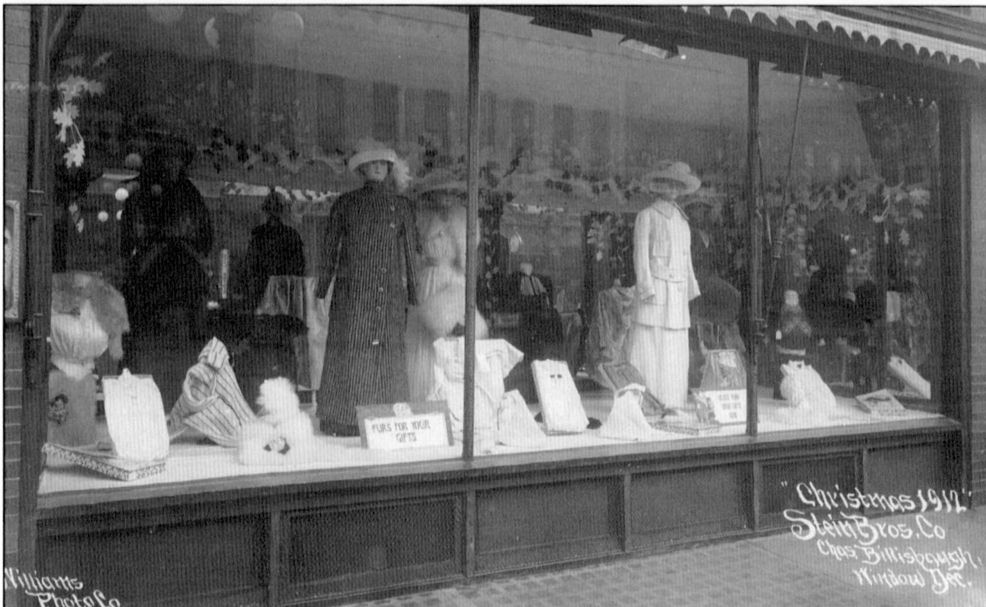


The Stein Brothers mercantile business originated in Harvard, Nebraska, in 1872. By 1905, the brothers operated a store in downtown Hastings on Second Street. Stein's offered a huge selection of merchandise, which ranged from groceries and furniture, to clothing, tools, and gifts. Their buyers traveled to Europe to purchase stock directly from manufacturers. Christmas window displays always attracted attention. A victim of the Depression, it closed in 1933. From 1934 to 1968, Montgomery Wards occupied the building.

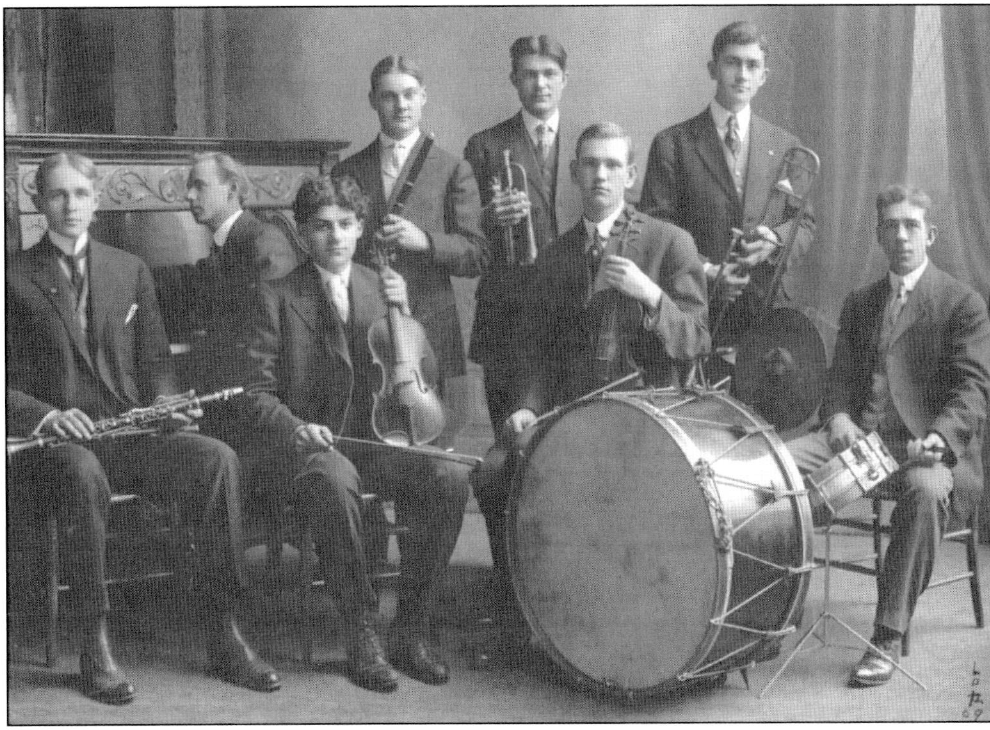

Music played an important role in the culture of Hastings. One of the earliest groups was called the Cornet Band, who played at various public events including Fourth of July celebrations. A later group, Rose's Orchestra, performed from 1908 to 1913. Shown here, from left to right, are: William Sorensen, A.H. Lotz, Joe Spellman, Harry Johnson, Earl Bruce, Guy Rose, Earl Bratney, and Knute Davies.

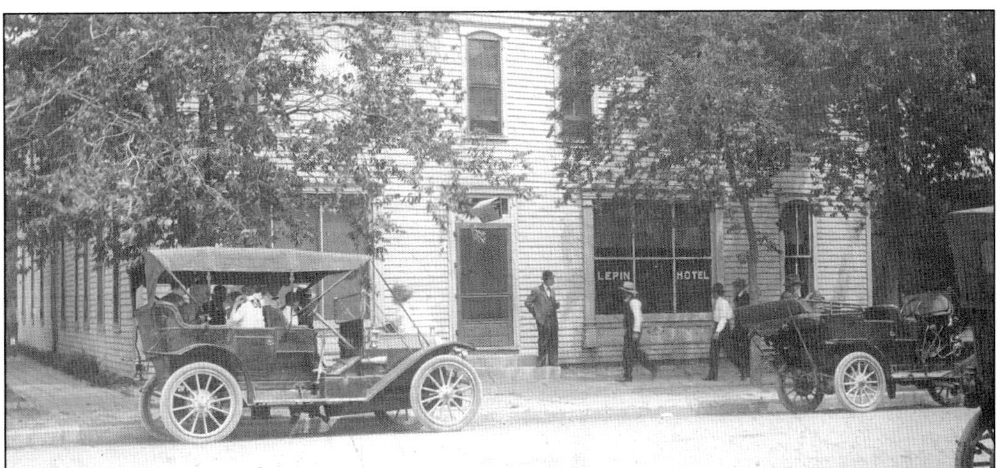


Herman Lepin immigrated to America from Germany in the 1850s. He worked in the mercantile business until arriving in Hastings in 1873, as an agent for McCormick's harvesting machines. A few years later, he engaged in the hotel business but lost his establishment to the fire of 1879. He built the Lepin Hotel at Second Street and Lexington Avenue in 1880. The fine three-story hotel survived until 1931, when it was razed to make way for an auto service station. *The Hastings Tribune*'s press building is currently located on the site.

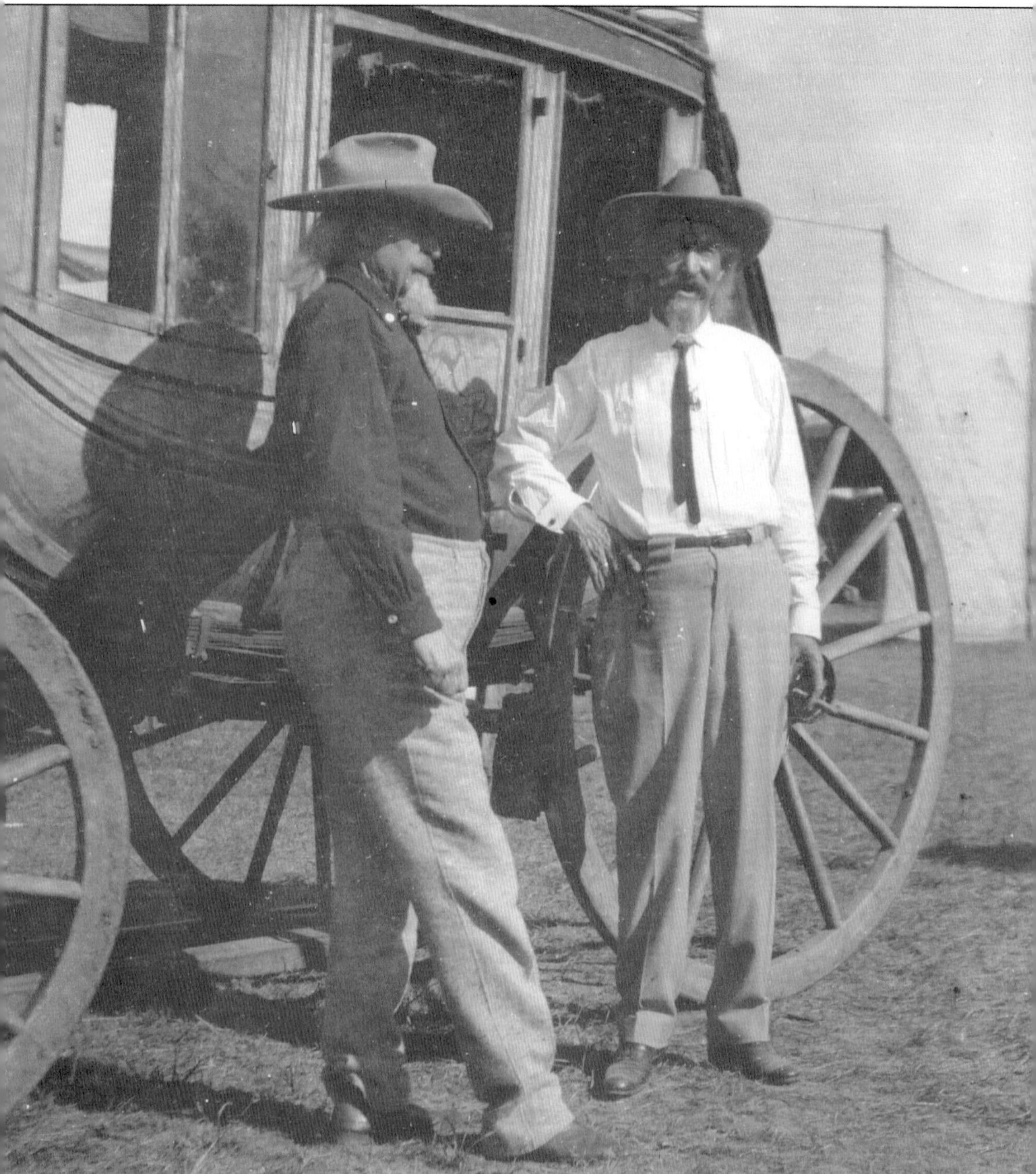

Curtis Alexander (right) was a colorful Hastings personality. The Indiana native was a Civil War veteran, horseman, city councilman, state senator, and served on the staff of three Nebraska governors. He was photographed in Hastings talking with his friend, William F. Cody, during one of Cody's Wild West Shows. Alexander was known for his uncanny resemblance to Buffalo Bill, and reportedly took Cody's place during a pre-show parade here. Buffalo Bill would usually join the Alexanders at their home for dinner when he came to Hastings.

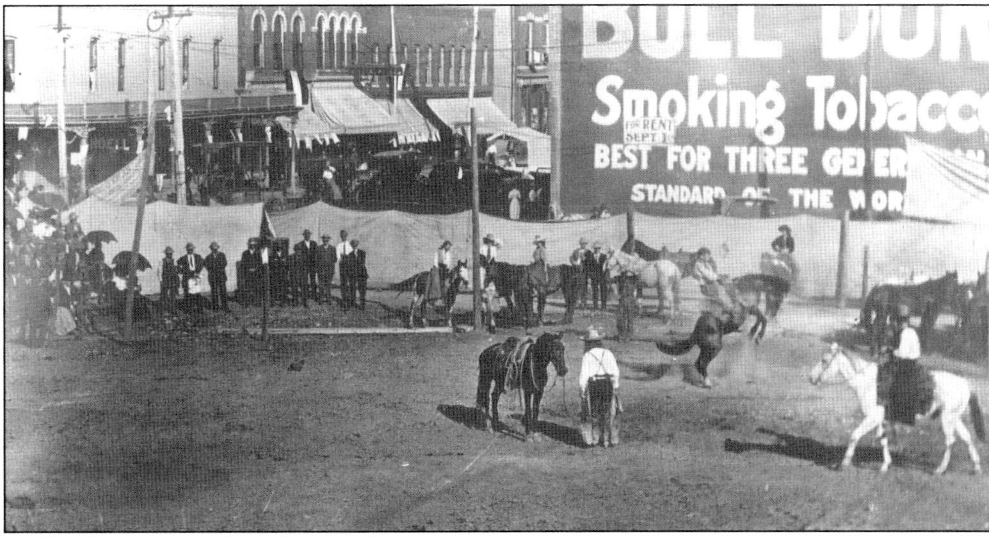


Between 1896 and 1913, Buffalo Bill's Wild West Show appeared in Hastings five different times. The first visit was on October 13, 1896, where the entire Wild West Show and Congress of Rough Riders appeared. Included in the world famous show was the renowned woman sharpshooter, Annie Oakley, who performed for the large crowds. She stunned the audience as she used mirrors to shoot targets behind her, and those thrown in the air. No one had ever seen a woman handle guns like she did! The photo shows a rodeo being held at the southwest corner of First Street and Lincoln Avenue during one of William F. "Buffalo Bill" Cody's visits.

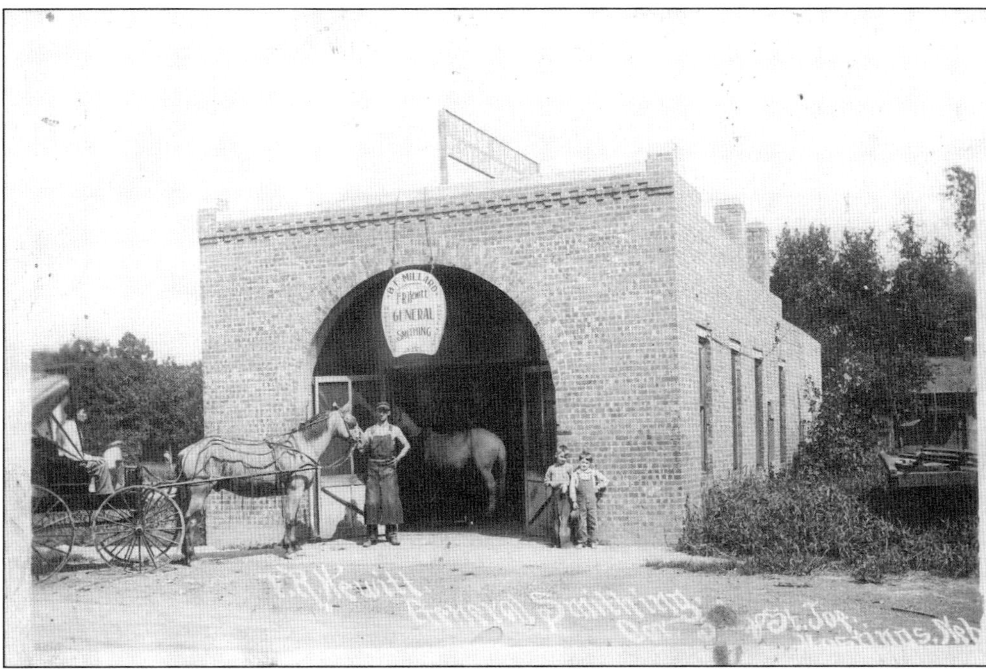


The horseshoe shaped sign in this 1913 photograph reads, "B.F. Millard, F.R. Hewitt—General Smithing—Hastings, Nebraska." The Millard-Hewitt blacksmith shop was located at 508 West Third Street, at the corner of Third and St. Joseph Avenue. More than 500 Nebraska blacksmiths converged on the city in 1916 for a state convention.

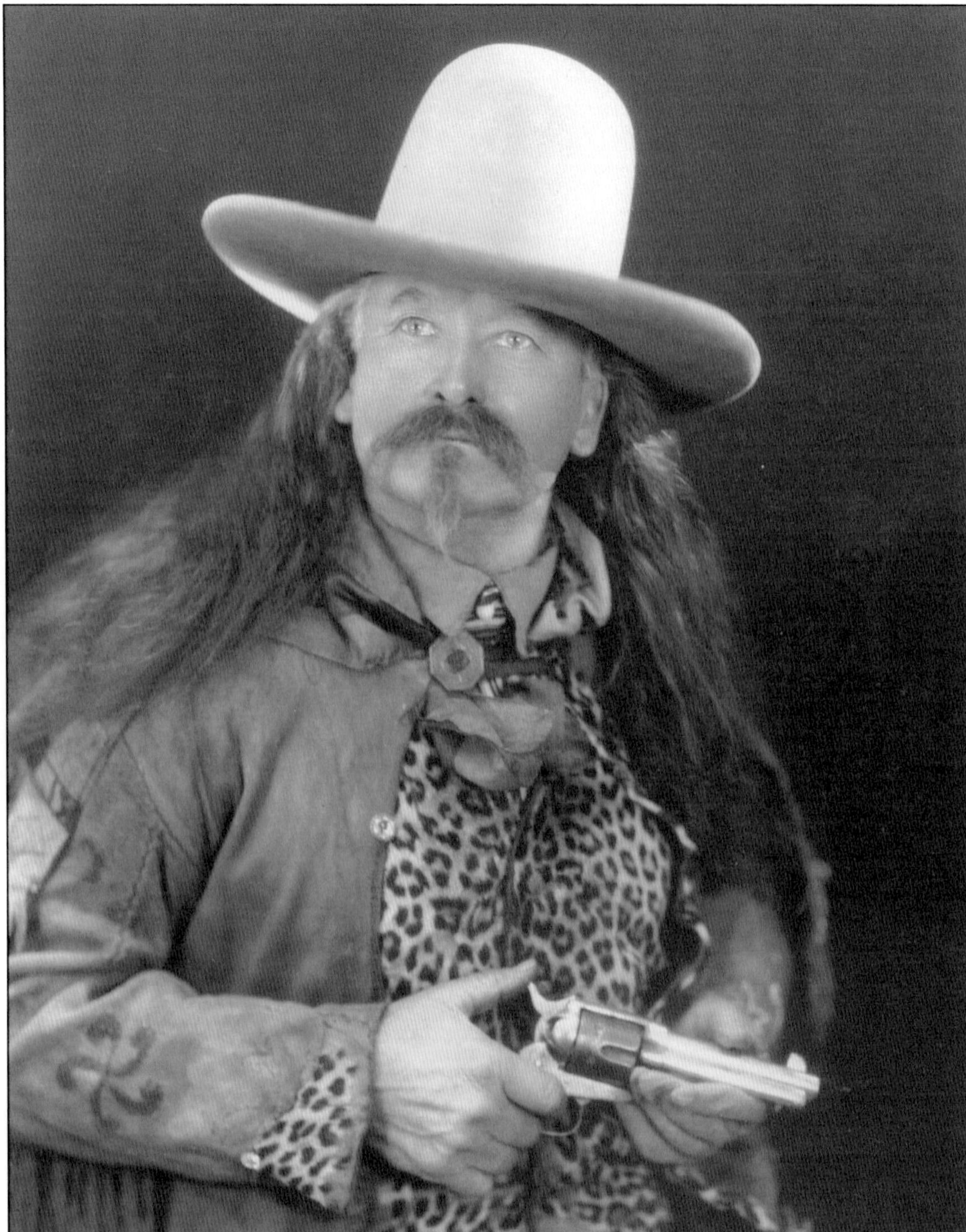

At age four, Bonde R. Pearson and his parents came to America from Sweden. Changing his name to "Barney," Pearson went west where he bought and sold wild horses. He married Sarah (Sadie) Thrifty in 1891, while living in Colorado. Later, they moved to Hastings where Barney hit the headlines in 1906. Standing outside his own house, he fired a shotgun through the picture window, in front of his wife and three others, killing Walter McCulla. After he was acquitted on murder charges and the divorce was finalized, he headed west again. Upon his return to Hastings, he went by the moniker, "Idaho Bill," and sported a flamboyance akin to Buffalo Bill himself. A personal friend of Teddy Roosevelt, Pearson was asked to ride to the Burlington Railroad station with him during a campaign stop.

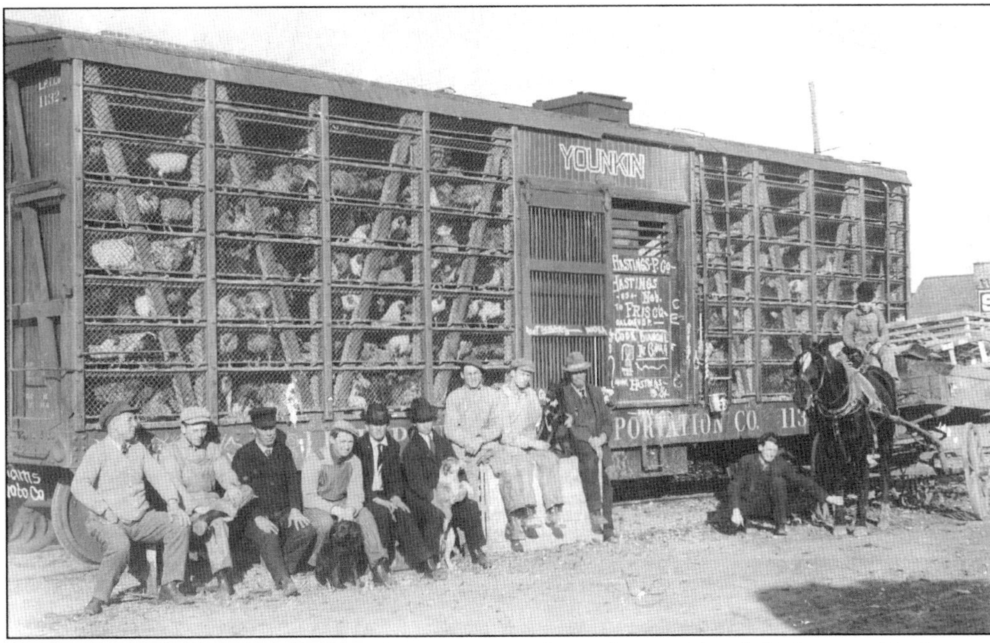


Employees of the Hastings Poultry Company pose for a photo with a "chicken car" in January 1913. The company, owned by J.T. Oder, was a major supplier of chickens to San Francisco, Chicago, and New York for 25 years. The specially built railroad cars, leased from the Live Poultry Transportation Company, accommodated over 4,000 caged chickens. Chickens were shipped live because of lack of refrigeration. Attendants traveled in each car during the five-day trip to either coast, so the birds could be fed and watered. Living quarters for a "car man" included a bunk, desk, and heating stove.

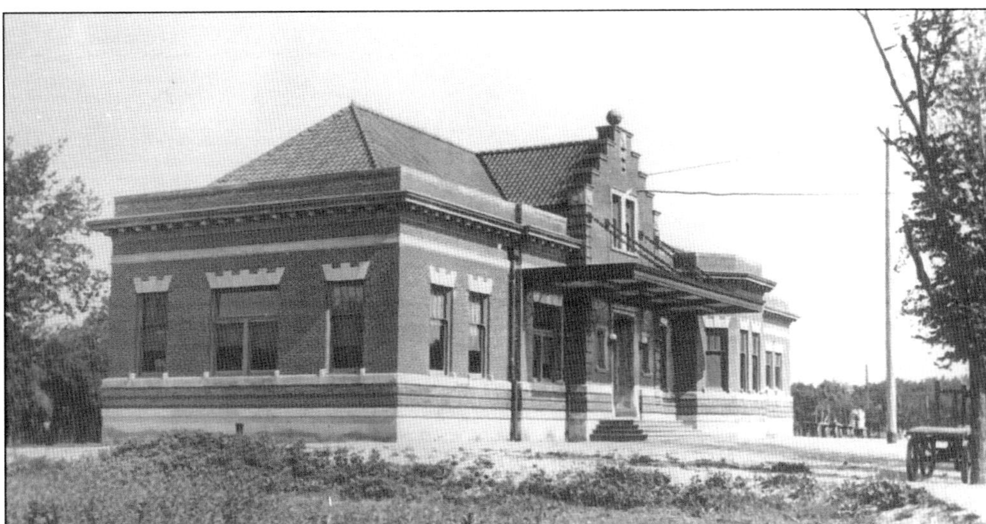

The Union Pacific Railroad depot was dedicated on April 24, 1914, by UP and St. Joseph & Grand Island Railroad officials. The Union Pacific was the first transcontinental railroad to cross Nebraska, reaching Grand Island (25 miles north) in 1866. Even though the Burlington & Missouri River was the first rail line in Hastings, most of the land on which the city was built was UPRR grant land.

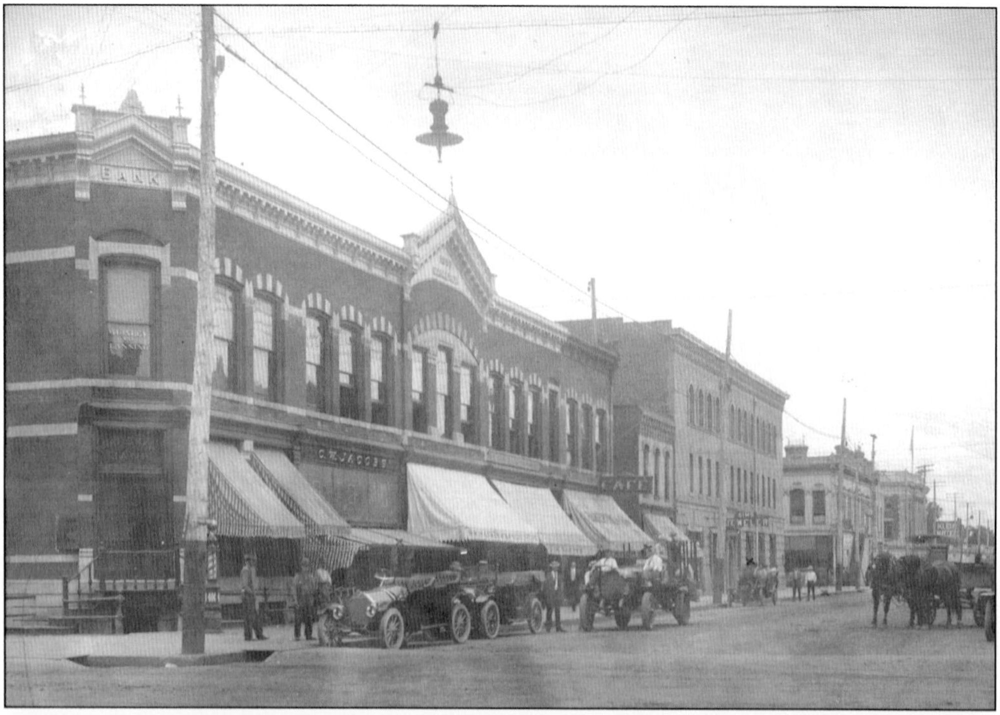

This is a view of Hastings Avenue (which was considered Main Street) looking north from First Street in 1914. The Exchange National Bank is at the far left in the corner of the Cameron Building, which was built in 1883. Other businesses at the time include a harness shop and cafe. Today this block includes a beauty shop, ethnic stores, and a coffee/art shop. Horses were being edged out by automobiles as the transport of choice by this time.

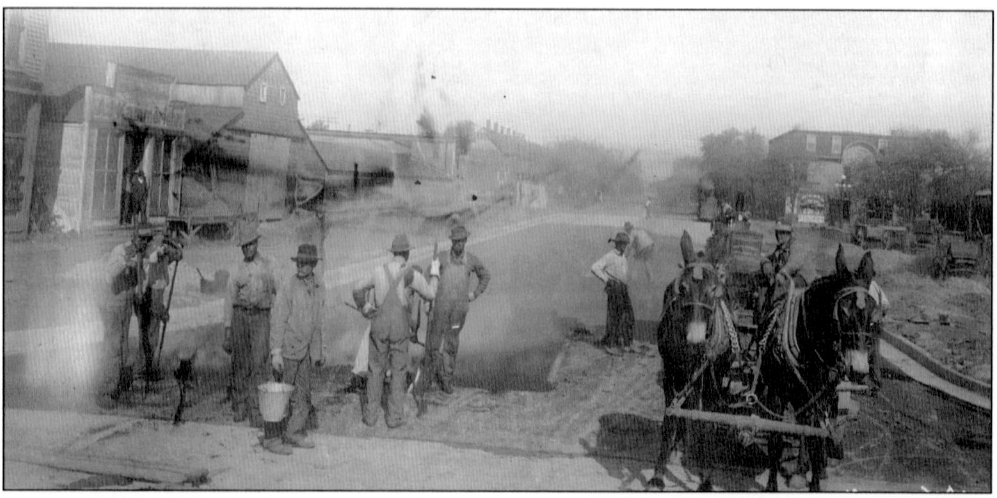

Paving of city streets began in 1891, with the first project on Second Street, reaching from St. Joseph west to Burlington Avenue. This 1916 photograph shows a paving project underway on Lexington between First and Second Streets in 1916. The Watts and Amerman Paving Company had contracted with the city for the project. Most of the paving took place between 1915 and 1920. Hastings had 27 miles of hard surfaced streets by 1919. Note the Lepin Hotel at Second and Lexington.

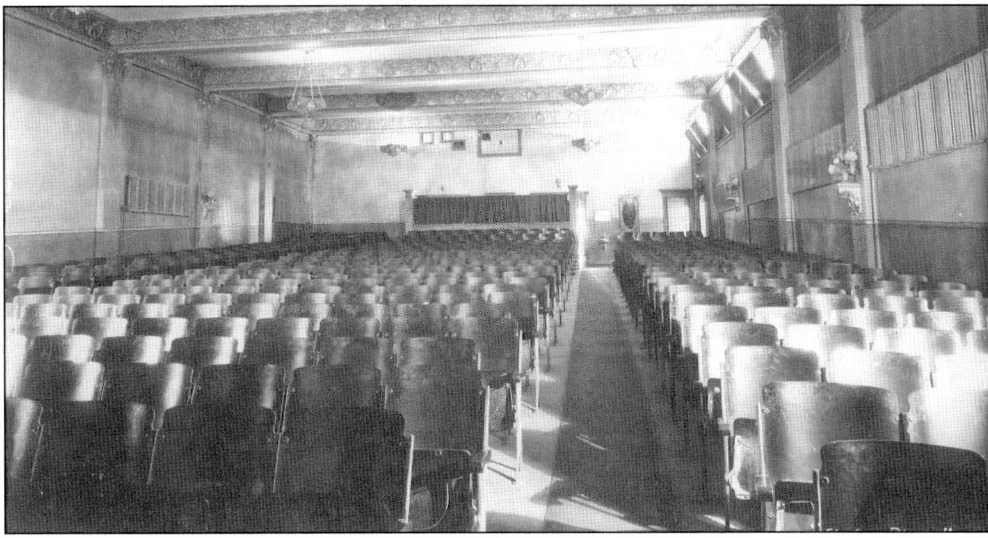

In 1915, William Brach hired local architect C.W. Way to design a two-story moving picture theatre and office building on his property. Completed in 1916 at a cost of $40,000, the new theatre featured an enameled white terra cotta front. The lobby was decorated with tiled floors and marble walls. The Brach Theatre opened in October, and a crowd of 1,400 people were packed into the 700-seat facility. The first film shown (a silent film) was *The Light at Dusk*. In 1951, Fred Teller purchased the Strand Theatre, as it had been named since the '20s, and operated it until its closing in 1984. It has since been renovated into an office complex called the Strand Center.

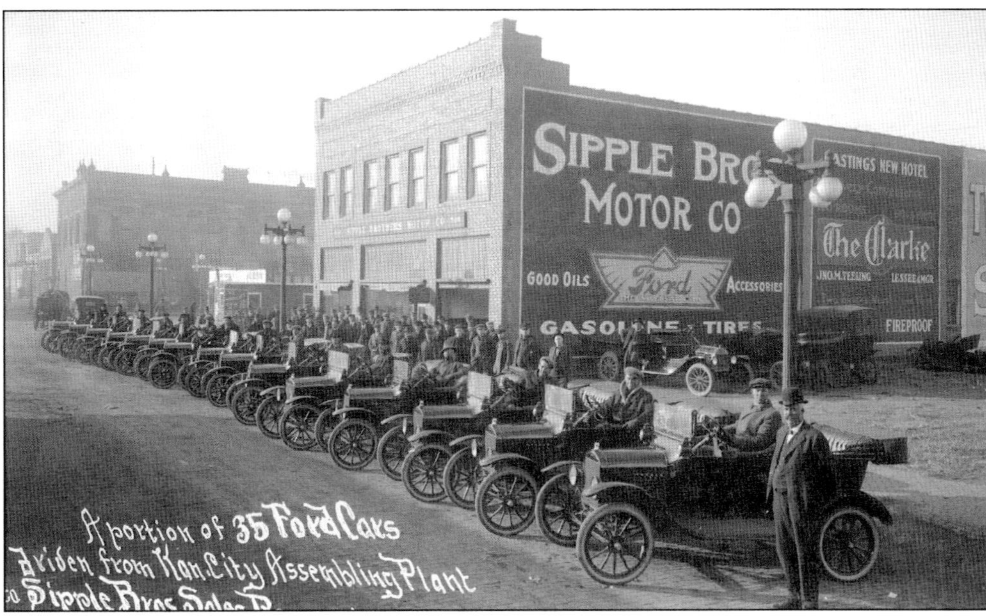


Ray Sipple left his fathers ranch in Boone County and arrived in Hastings in 1914. Ray and his brother Earl entered into a partnership and established the Sipple Brothers Motor Company, dealers in Ford and Oldsmobile autos. Their business included parts and repairs as well. In November 1916, a shipment of 35 Ford Model Ts were driven to the dealership from the factory in Kansas City. By that year, there were 1,172 automobiles on the tax rolls.

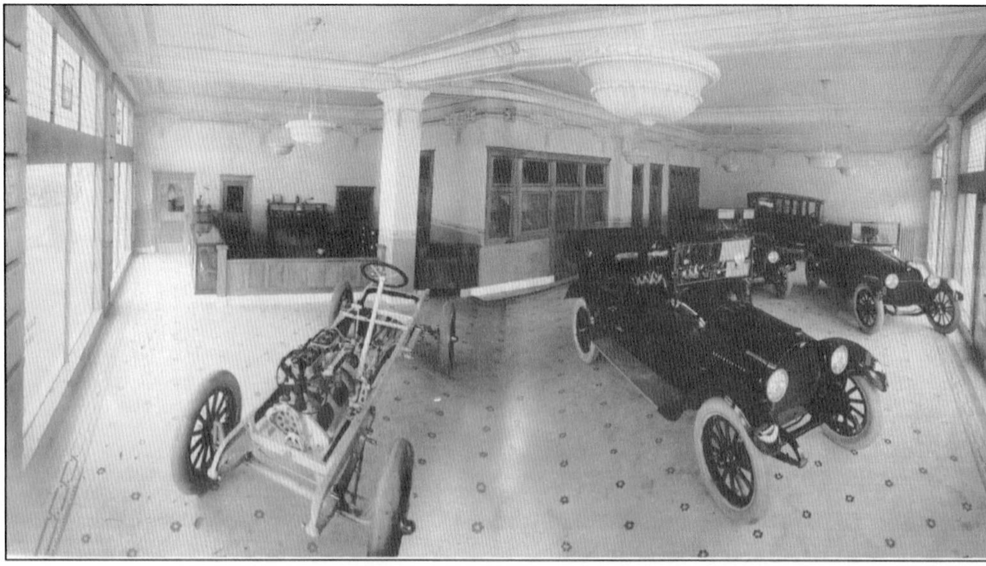

A.H. Jones and E.A. Brandes partnered in another auto dealership in 1907. By 1916, the A.H. Jones Company constructed this cement, brick, and terra cotta showroom and garage at the corner of Third Street and Lincoln Avenue (the current location of the City National Bank). Jones was a dealer in REO and Cadillac automobiles and switched to Chrysler-brand products in later years.

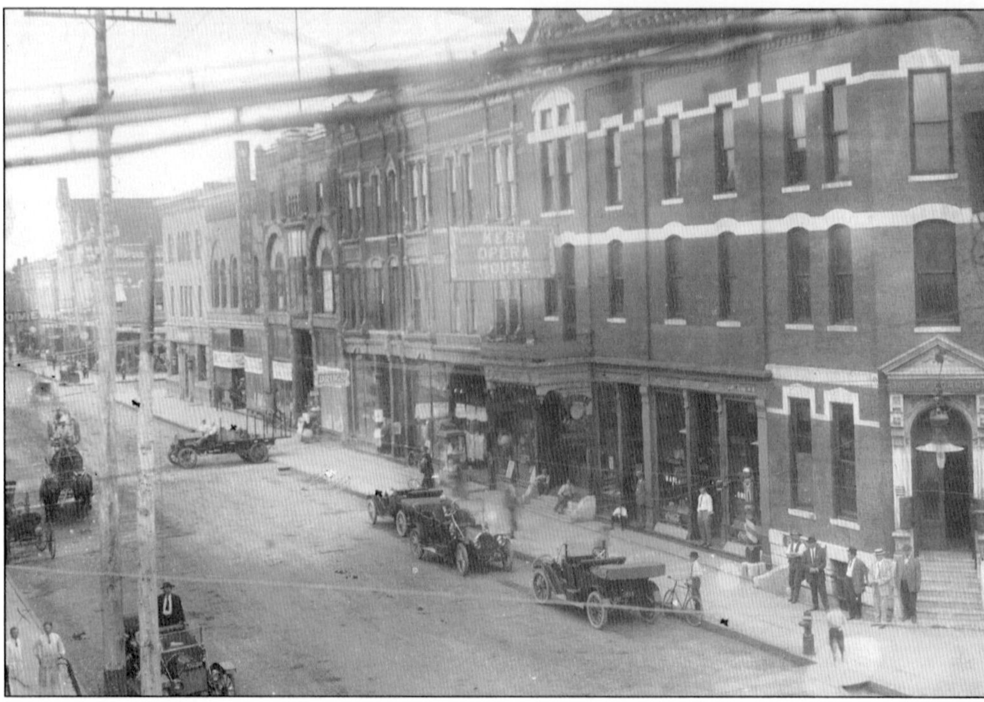


Shoppers and businessmen alike take a break from their activities for the photographer in 1916. The view is looking east on Second Street from Lincoln Avenue. The massive Kerr Opera House was closed down in 1928, and stood vacant for many years. In 1948, it was announced that the Kerr would be replaced by a new J.M. McDonald's clothing store. The McDonald building is now home to Hogan's Sporting Goods.

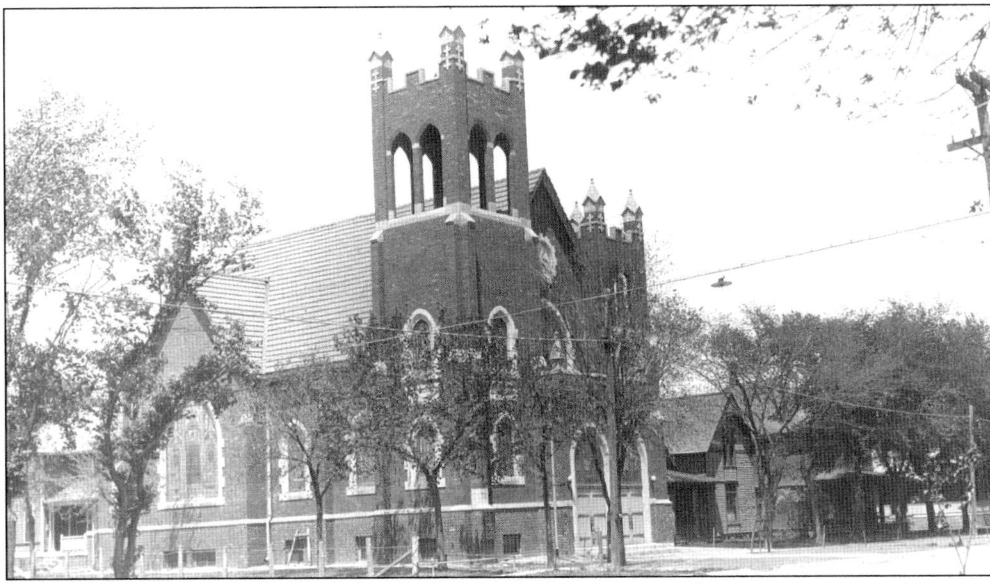

The First St. Paul's Lutheran Church was established in Hastings after an organizational meeting was held in September 1878. A small, white frame building located at Fifth Street and Burlington Avenue served as the church building until this brick structure was dedicated on July 23, 1916. Services had been in German prior to this time, when they switched to English.

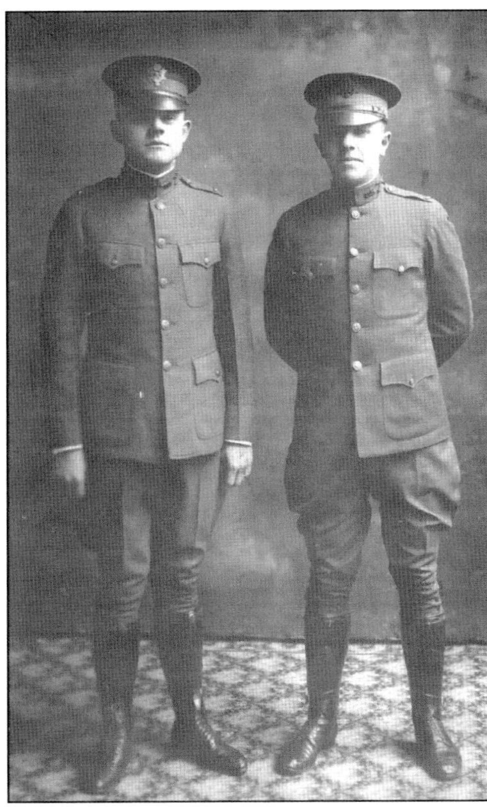

As a result of attacks on our shipping, the United States declared war on Germany on April 6, 1917. By August 1918, Hastings College had become one of 500 American colleges to have a Student Army Training Corps. U.S. Army First Lieutenant Sheehan and Second Lieutenant Gundling were in charge of the corps and its military training program.

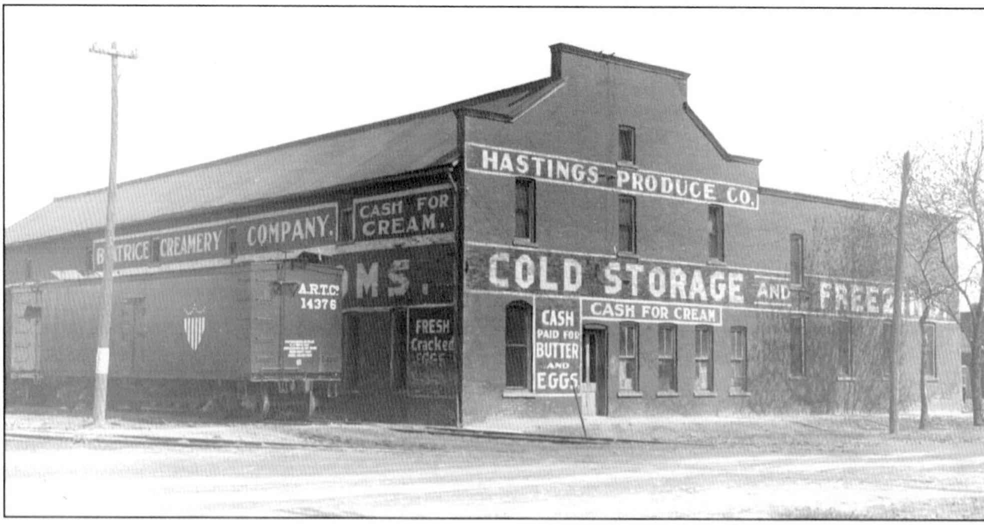


D.B. Ayers and A. Berg built a large stable at 109 South Burlington Avenue in 1887. The Hastings Produce Company purchased the building in 1898, where it was said "840,000 dozen" eggs could be stored. The company shipped eggs and butter as far away as Boston and San Francisco. The building, shown here in 1918, later became a Jack & Jill grocery store, and then a mini-mall.

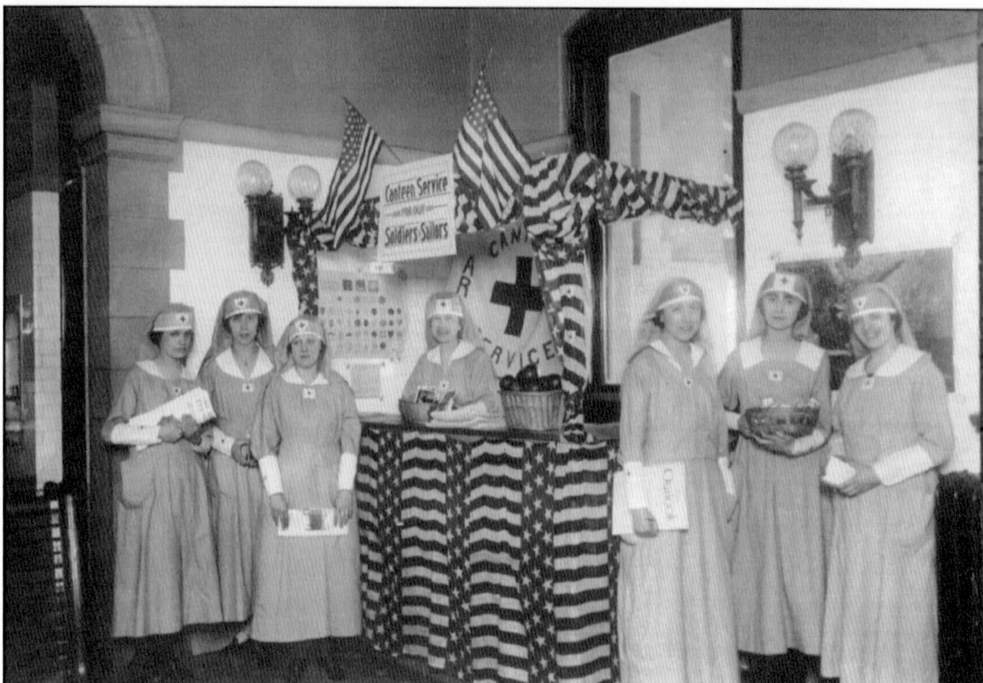


During World War I, members of the local Red Cross operated a canteen at the Burlington Railroad station at First and St. Joseph Avenue. Soldiers and sailors who passed through were offered candy, chewing gum, and magazines to enjoy. They are, from left to right: Faye Klein, Marguerite McIntosh, Alfreda Clark, Mrs. William Lowman (sponsor), Hazel Klein, Clara Chick, and Mary Steele.

Adam Breede was said to have purchased the *Tribune* for $1 down in 1894. The *Hastings Tribune* has been a daily since 1905, and now is published by Don Seaton. This photo was taken in Paris while Breede was a war correspondent during World War I. In the 1920s, he traveled the world hunting big game, bringing back many trophies—which were donated to the University of Nebraska. Breede died in 1928, from the effects of black water fever contracted in Africa.

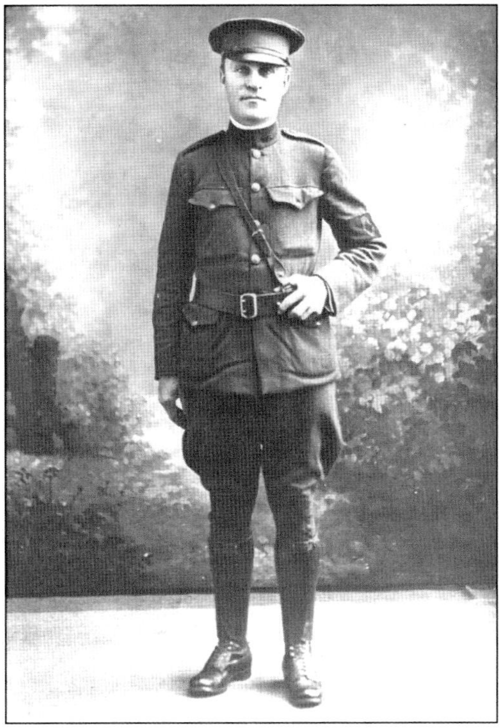

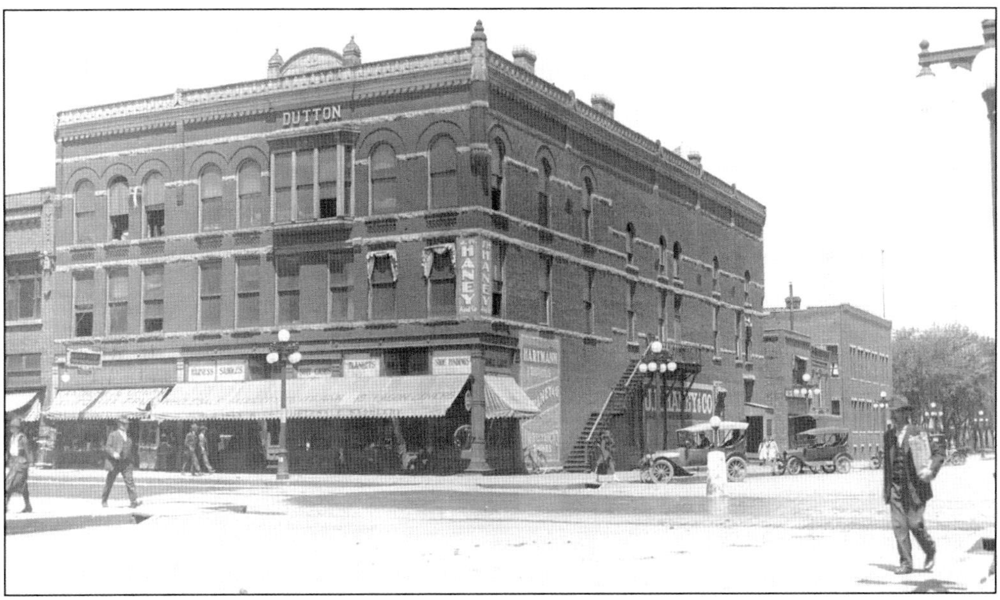


Harness makers William M. Dutton and J.H. Haney had this two-story building constructed in 1891, "at the time when Hastings was afflicted with as bad a dose of the blues and feeling the general depression about as bad as any city west of the Missouri," a local paper stated. The community was proud of the Dutton-Haney block as it was called. In 1920, it was sold to the Gaston Music Company, and for the next 50 years it was known as the Gaston Building. A battle to save the historic building failed, and it was torn down in 1998. The new Brown's Shoe Fit store was built on the site.

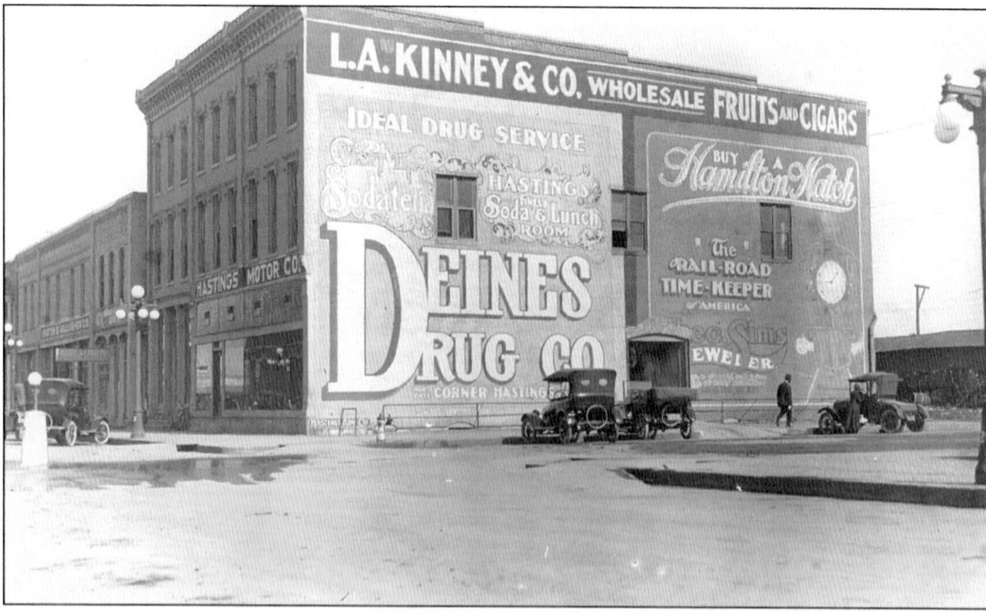


L.A. Kinney & Co., shown here in 1919, was one of the four largest cigar manufacturers in Hastings. More than 10,000 cigars per day were made in the city at the time. The Hastings Motor Company was also located in the building, which was at the southeast corner of First Street and Lincoln Avenue. Cash-Wa Candy Company, a wholesaler of candy, tobacco, paper and food products, has operated in the building since 1967. Cash-Wa has been operated by Delmar and Wilma Pederson since the business opened in 1946, about a block south of the current location.

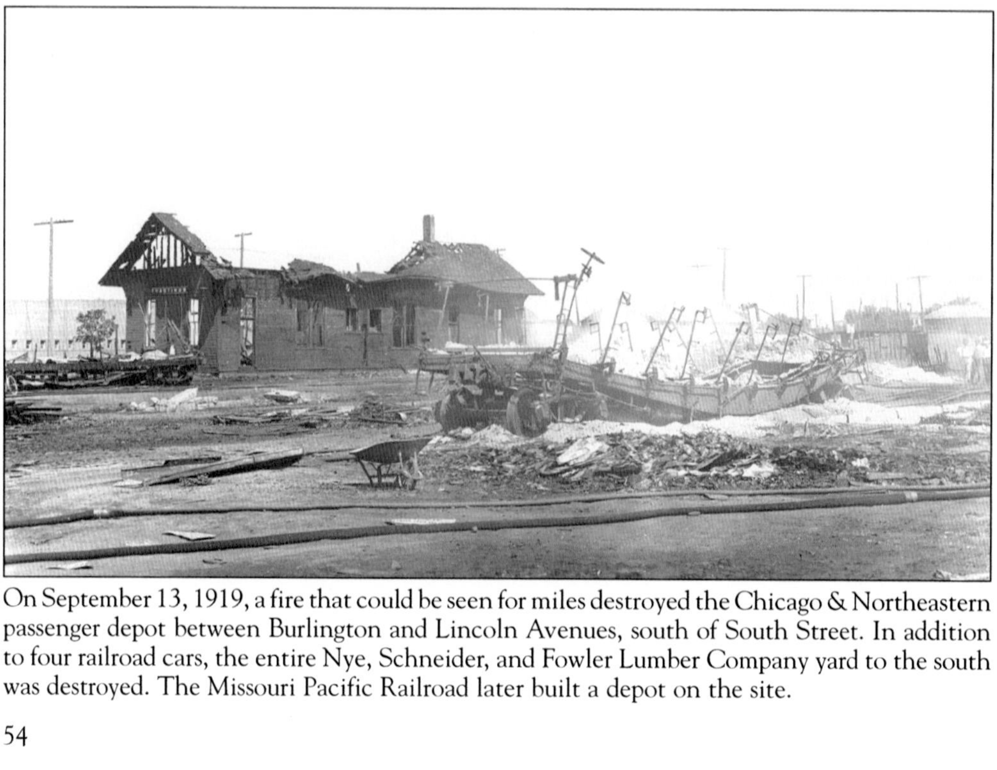

On September 13, 1919, a fire that could be seen for miles destroyed the Chicago & Northeastern passenger depot between Burlington and Lincoln Avenues, south of South Street. In addition to four railroad cars, the entire Nye, Schneider, and Fowler Lumber Company yard to the south was destroyed. The Missouri Pacific Railroad later built a depot on the site.

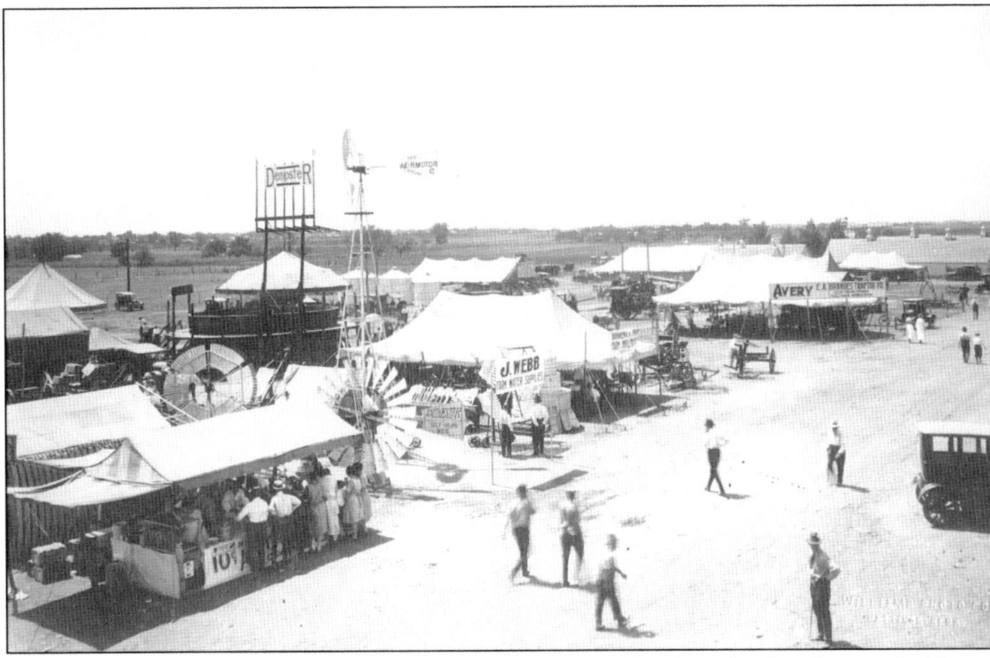


The county fair has been held almost every year since 1873, when the first fair was held near Pauline in southern Adams County. This glimpse of the 1922 fair shows a midway full of agricultural displays and lunch stands. The Hastings Senior High School currently occupies the grounds. The dirt racetrack is partially visible in the background.

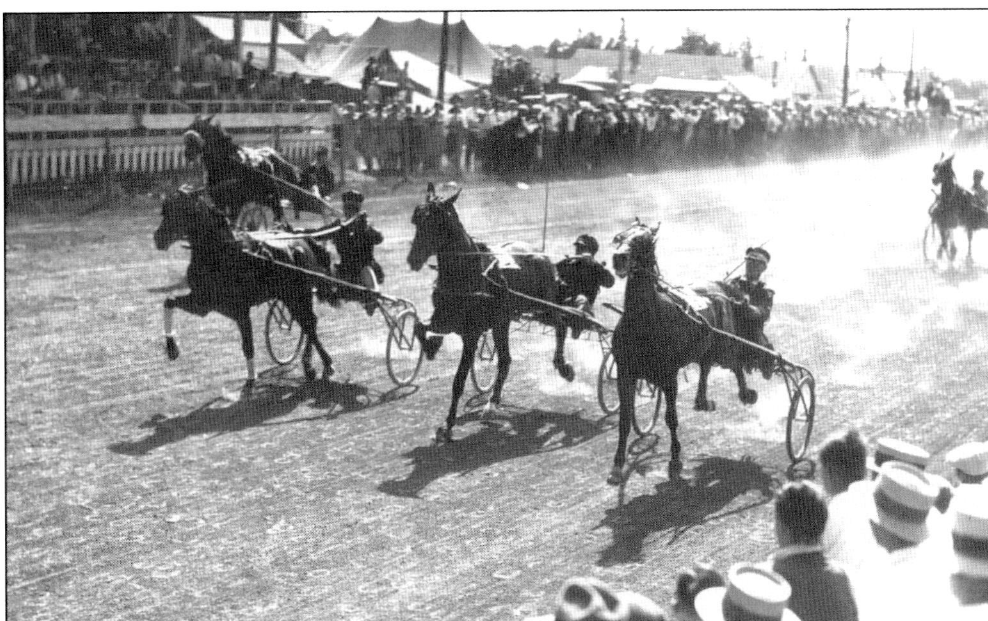

Harness racing was a very popular attraction at the county fair in the 1920s. The Adams County Agricultural Society was a member of the American Trotting Association, who sanctioned the events. Over $2,600 in purse money was offered at the races in 1924. The schedule of events included a "mule race."

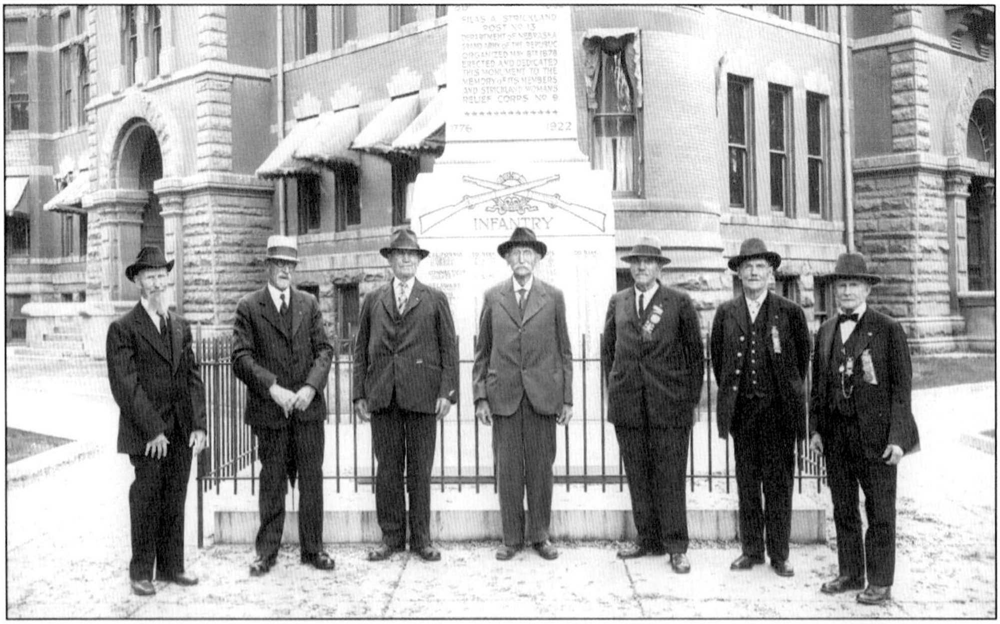


Members of the Silas Strickland Post of the Grand Army of the Republic, pose with their new monument at the courthouse in 1923. The granite obelisk served as a memorial to Union troops killed in the Civil War. It was 46 feet high and surmounted with the figure of a Union soldier at the top. By this time, only about 15 members of the post were still living. The obelisk is now located at Parkview Cemetery.

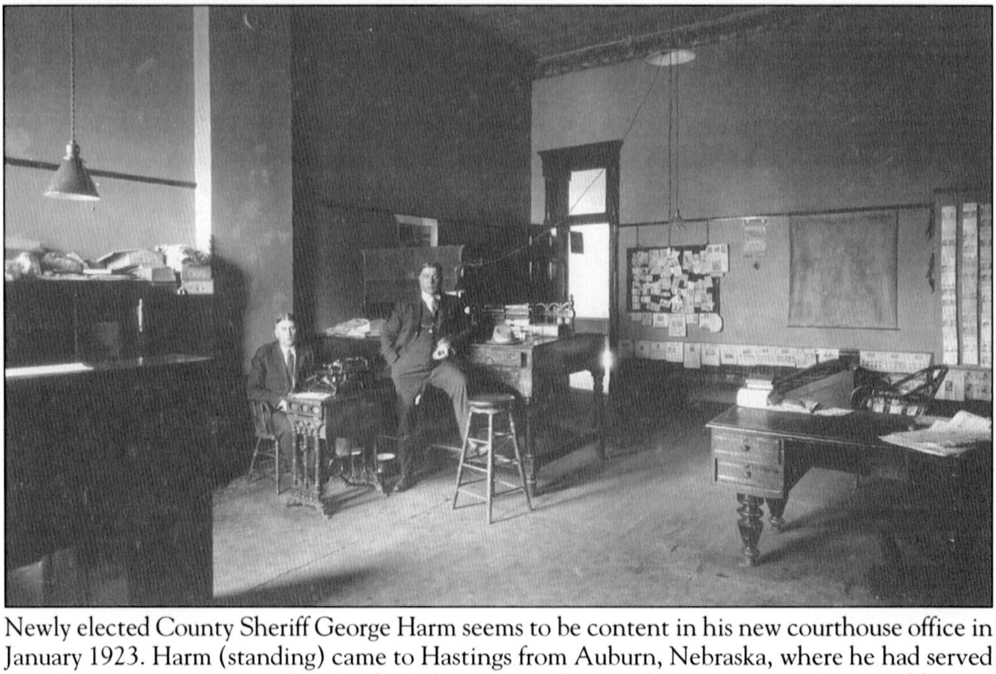

Newly elected County Sheriff George Harm seems to be content in his new courthouse office in January 1923. Harm (standing) came to Hastings from Auburn, Nebraska, where he had served as a deputy state game warden. He had also previously served as Hastings police chief for two years before becoming sheriff. His campaign posters read, "My opponent has had three and half terms, and has received over $20,000 from taxpayers."

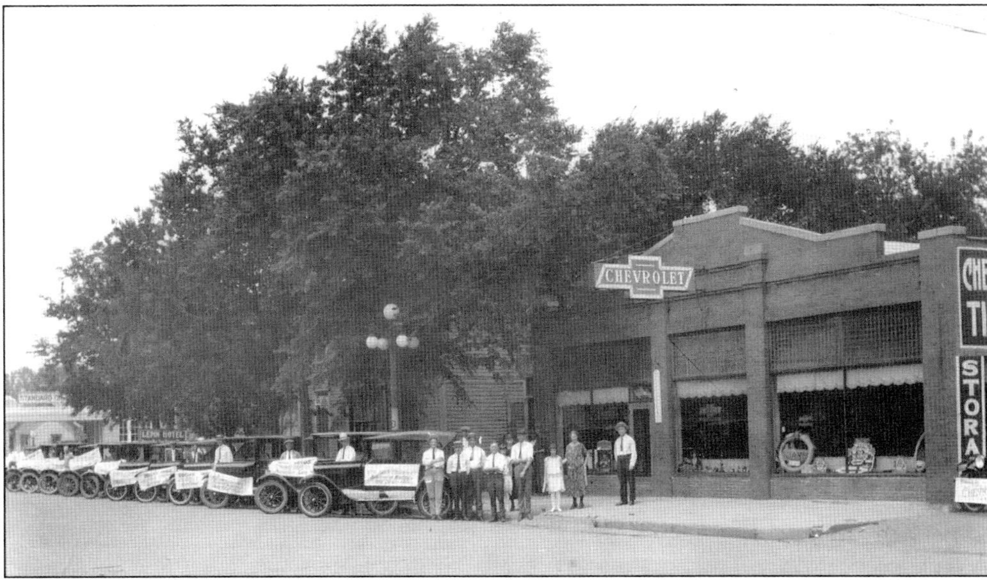


Chester J. Lienhart retired from the pharmacy business in 1921, selling his stores in Norman, Heartwell, and Funk. From 1922 to 1930, he owned and operated the Hastings Chevrolet Sales Company, located next to the Lepin Hotel. A new shipment of 1923 Chevrolets are posed here with employees. The signs read, "261 New 1923 Chevrolet Deliveries since October 22, 1922." In 1932, he established the Lienhart Motor Company, dealers in Buick, Oldsmobile, and Chevrolet autos.

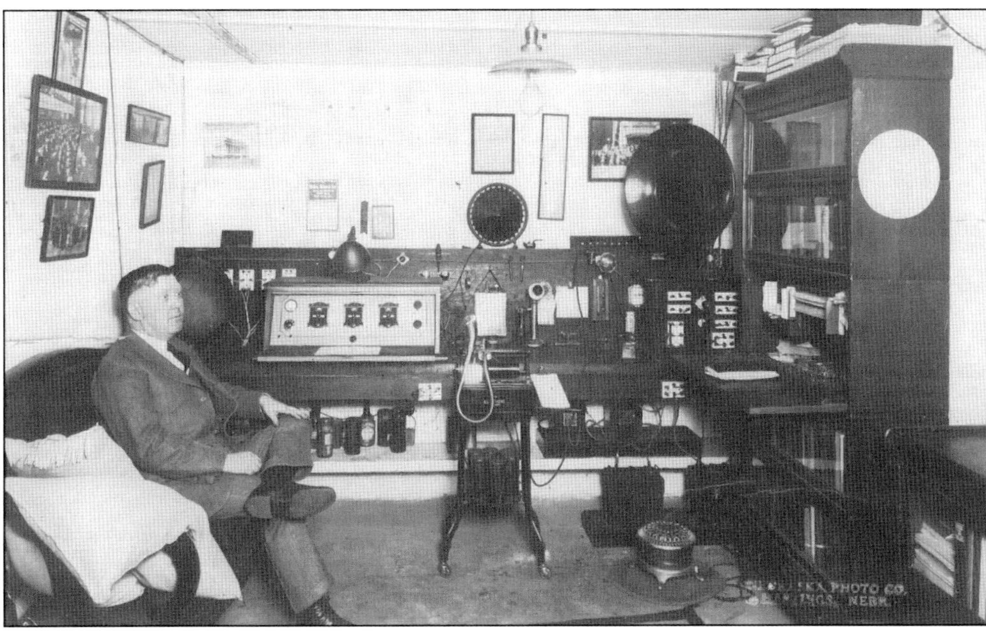

In 1923, Hastings became known all over the country and as far away as Australia and South Africa. The cause of this notoriety was the first broadcast from the KFKX radio station. The experimental re-broadcasting station of the Westinghouse Company was originally located in the Gaston Music building. In July 1925, KFKX was moved to the Clarke Hotel, ceasing operations only two years later when it was sold to the National Broadcasting Co.

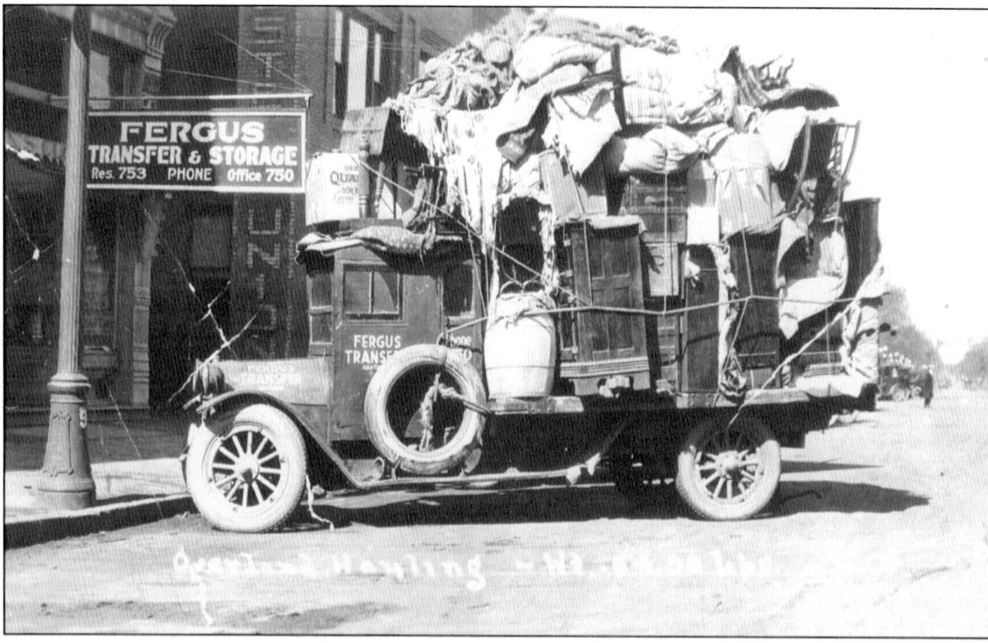


In 1915, George Fergus purchased the first motorized freight-hauling vehicle in town. The Indiana native owned and operated the Fergus Transfer and Storage Company, which was located at 111 North Denver Avenue when this 1924 photo was taken. By the way the truck is loaded, it is safe to assume they wanted to make only one trip on this job!

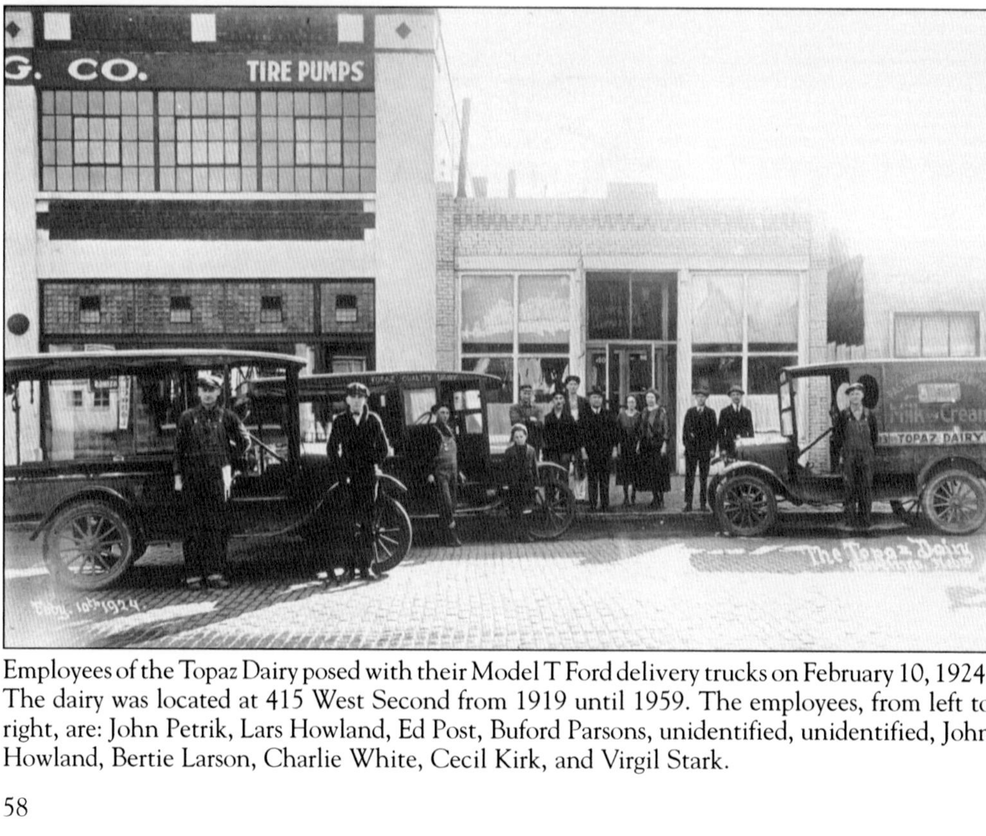


Employees of the Topaz Dairy posed with their Model T Ford delivery trucks on February 10, 1924. The dairy was located at 415 West Second from 1919 until 1959. The employees, from left to right, are: John Petrik, Lars Howland, Ed Post, Buford Parsons, unidentified, unidentified, John Howland, Bertie Larson, Charlie White, Cecil Kirk, and Virgil Stark.

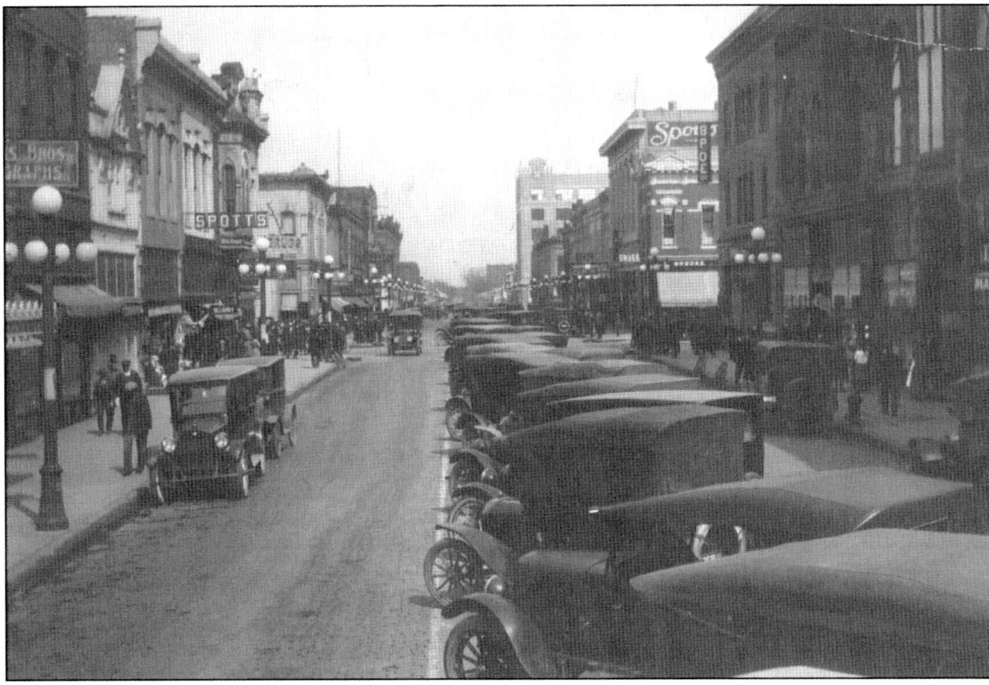


This serene view of West Second Street looking east from Lincoln Avenue portrays the scene where reckless drivers were catching the ire of the city. On November 5, 1915, the *Tribune* reported that, "an officer went over Second Street last night and placed white circles at the points where it is desired to have traffic follow exact routes. . . a material aid in the handling of traffic." Police Chief Brannigan, in answer to suggested plans of action stated, "Intermittent campaigns against speeders are unfair, and are not effective in establishing the careful driving habits which we seek to establish." Times have changed.

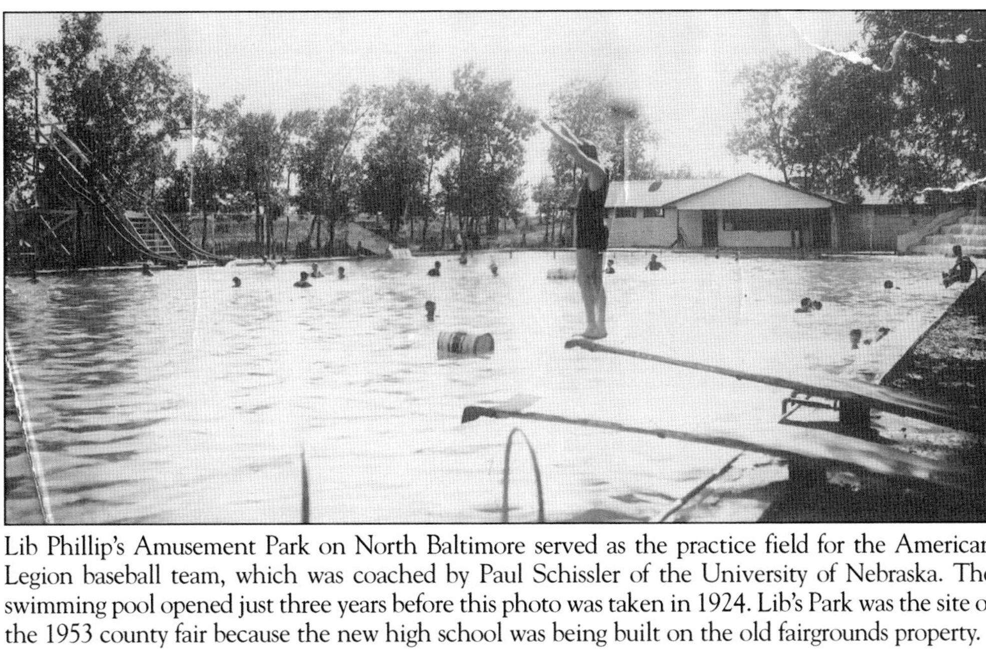

Lib Phillip's Amusement Park on North Baltimore served as the practice field for the American Legion baseball team, which was coached by Paul Schissler of the University of Nebraska. The swimming pool opened just three years before this photo was taken in 1924. Lib's Park was the site of the 1953 county fair because the new high school was being built on the old fairgrounds property.

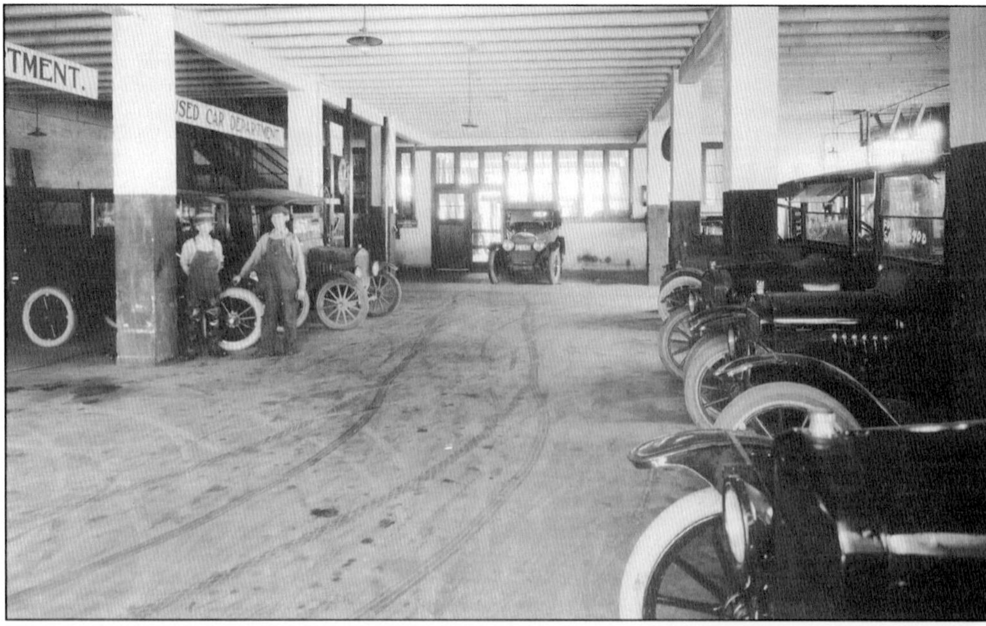


After buying out the Sipple Motor Co., the McClelland-Dunn Motor Co. was established in 1920. The new business was a dealer in Ford and Lincoln automobiles. They bought the three-story building at First Street and Denver Avenue, which became known as the Ford Building. In 1925, a brand new Ford Model T Runabout could be purchased for $260. In 1948, the McClelland Farm Equipment Co. was organized at 119 North Lexington and later moved to South Burlington. The old Ford Building currently houses the Knights of Pythias lodge.

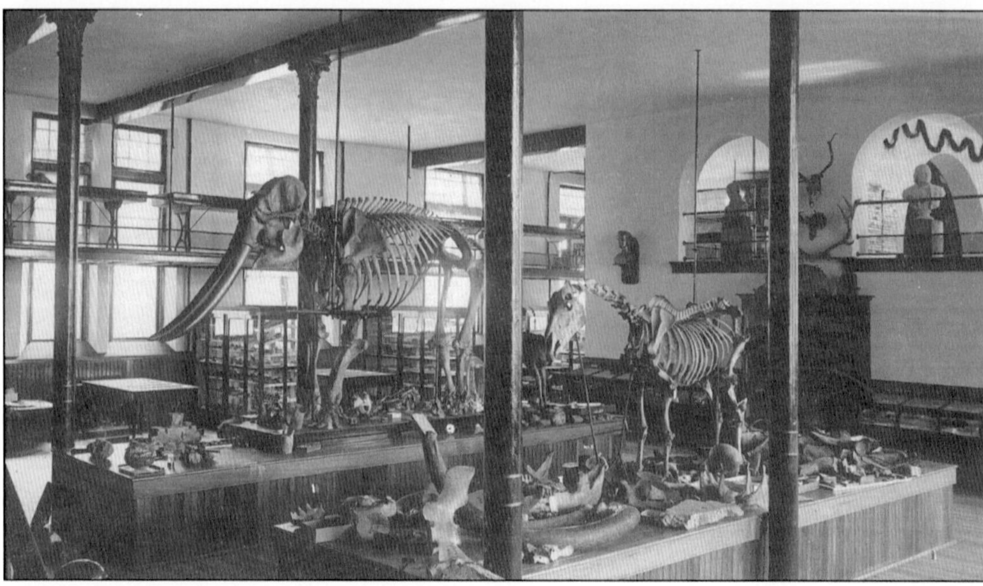

The Hastings Museum was not established until 1926, but the Hastings College library museum housed the notable Walter J. Kent collection of fossils, animals, and other items. Professor Kent, a recognized expert on fossils, served as curator in addition to his teaching duties. In 1913, A.M. Brooking moved his ornithological collection to the museum, as did others. These collections were to be the nucleus of the House of Yesterday (later the Hastings Museum).

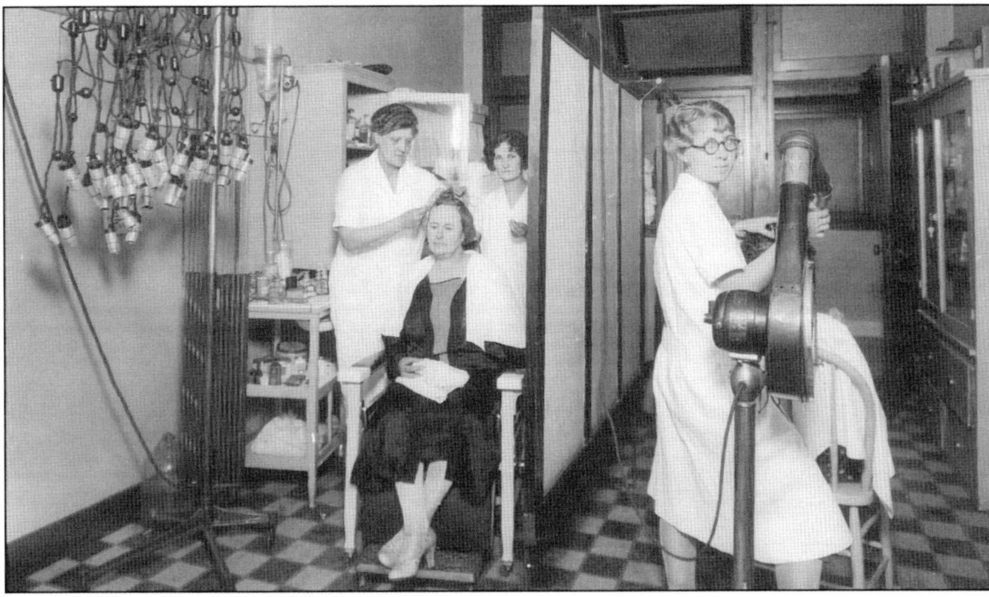

The Marinello Beauty Parlor was located on the second floor of the Strand Theatre in 1925. Employees Emily Koon, Leah Alexander, and Minnie Likely are shown with a customer. The equipment of the time appeared to be somewhat intimidating. By 1931, there were nine beauty shops in town, several of which operated for more than 30 years. Because of tough times in the 1930s, at least one beauty shop stayed open day and night to catch any available customers.

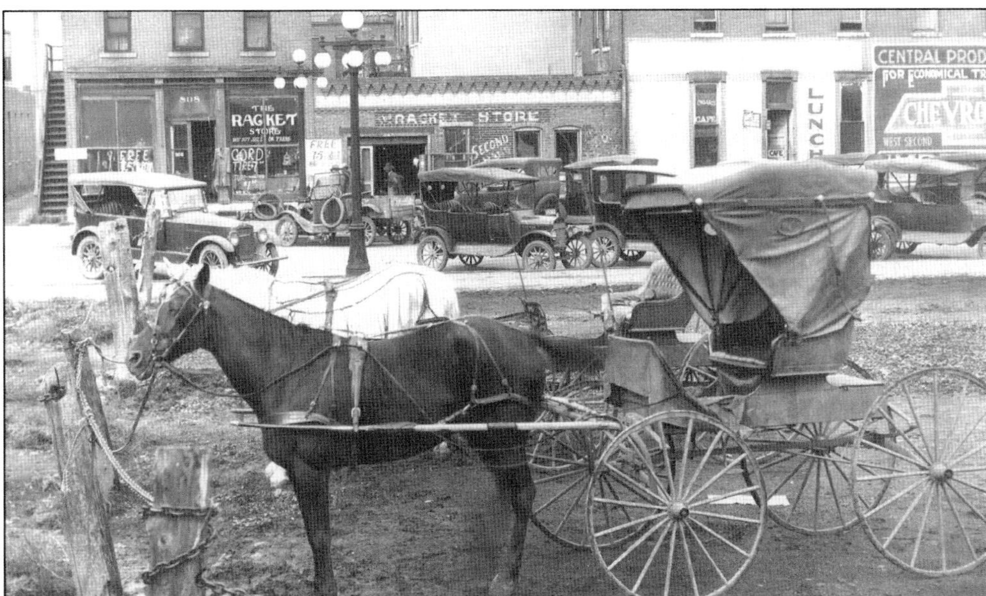


A stark contrast in modes of transportation still existed in Hastings well into the 1920s. This vacant lot on the south side of First Street between Lincoln and Burlington Avenues provided an off-street area in which horse-drawn conveyances could be secured, while the motorized types could be "tied up" at the curbside. In 1921, a new state license plate system went into effect, which placed the licensing of vehicles in the individual county's hands. Adams County received the number pre-fix of "14," as it was 14th in the state in the total number of autos.

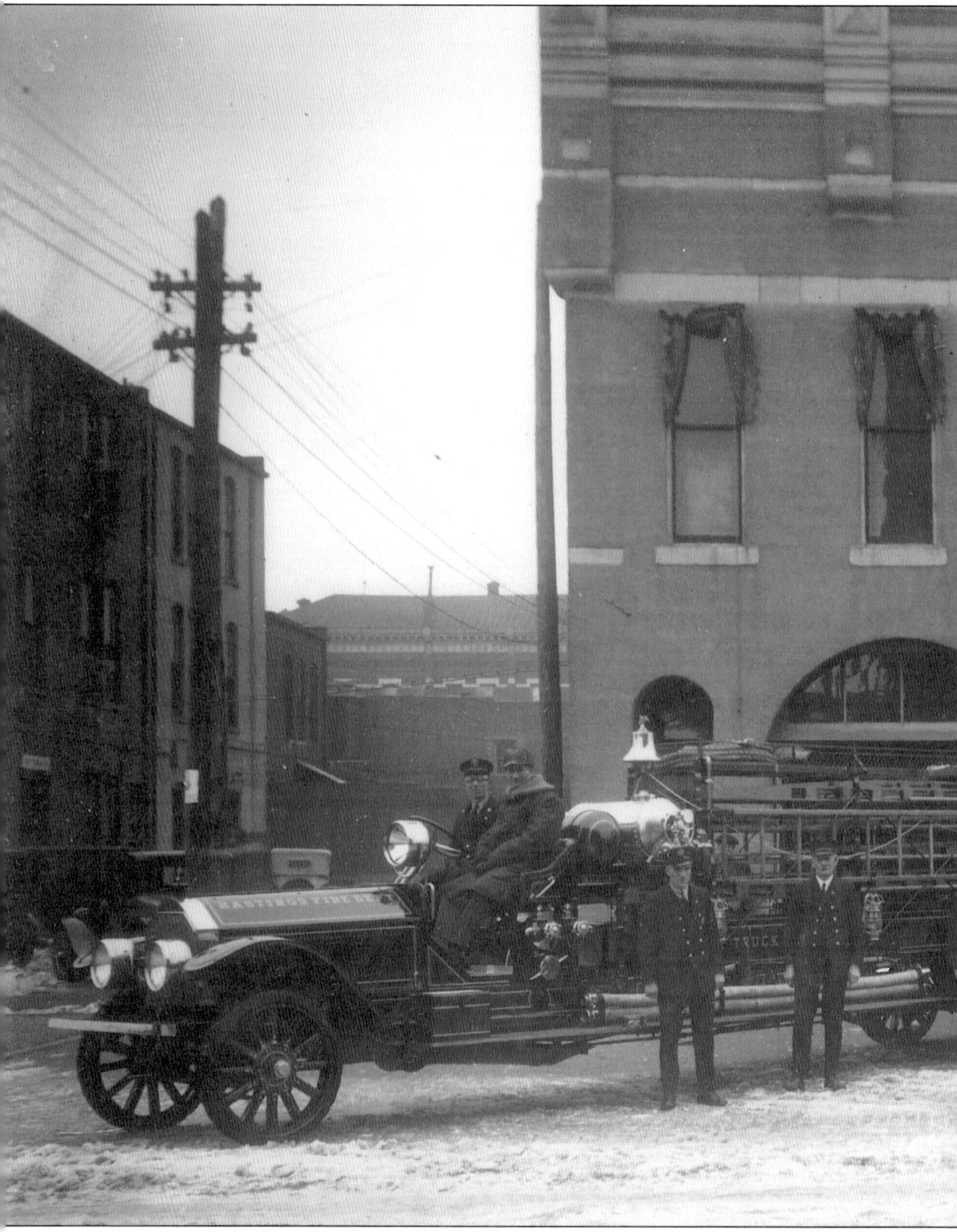


Hastings firemen pose with equipment in front of the engine house on North Burlington on a cold day in December 1925. This photo was taken about two weeks after the huge Bostwick Hotel fire, which seriously injured volunteer fireman Robert J. Van Fleet. Van Fleet later

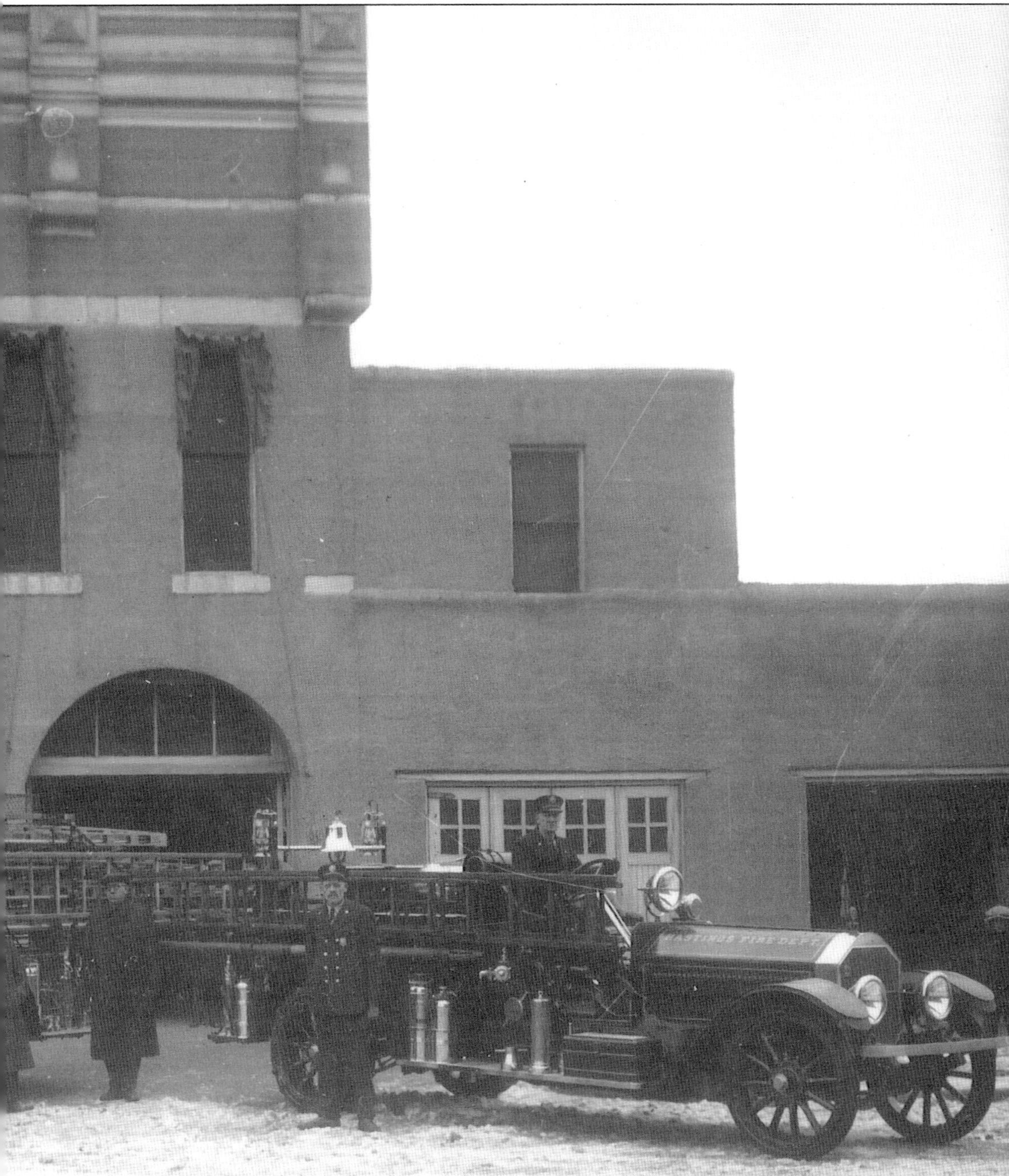


served as fire chief for 30 years. The 1918 American LaFrance engine on the right is now the centerpiece of a display dedicated to the department in the Hastings Museum.

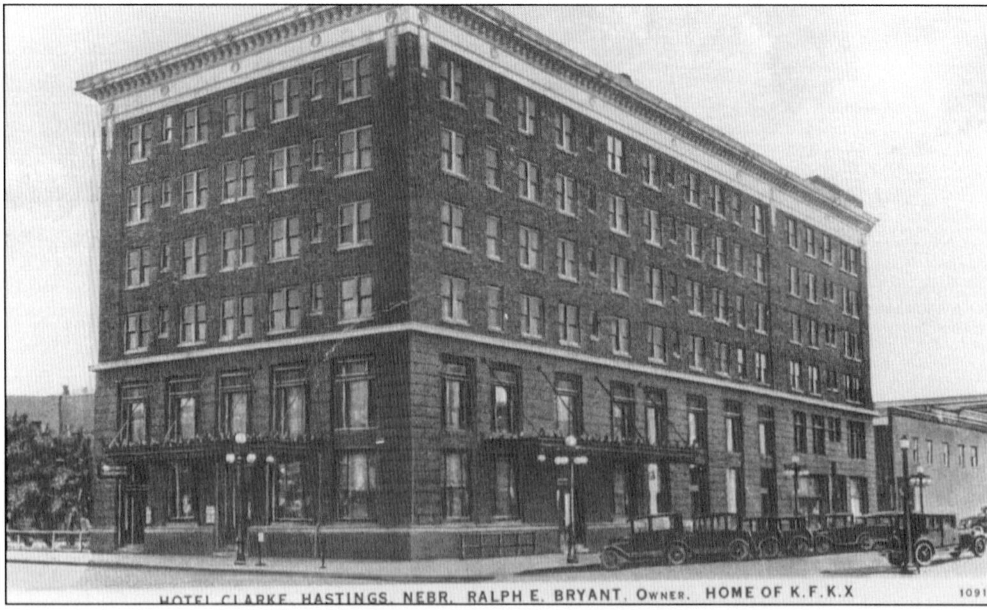


The Clarke Hotel at Third and Hastings was dedicated in February 1914. It was named after Alonzo Logan Clarke, then president of the First National Bank. The hotel is an elegant Renaissance Revival style building, which was placed on the National Register of Historic Places in 1987. A number of famous persons have appeared at the hotel, including former President William Howard Taft, musician John Phillip Sousa, John F. and Edward Kennedy. The Clarke closed in 1987, but opened the next year after a $1 million renovation project. It is now the Kensington, an assisted living residence.

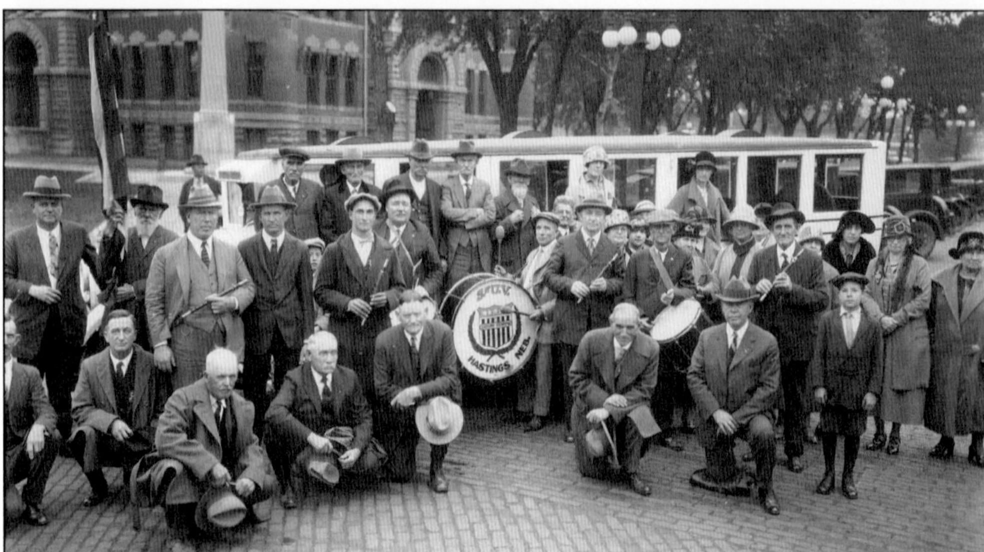


The Sons of Veterans of the United States was formed by the Grand Army of the Republic in 1881, who desired that their heritage would continue. The Sons' name was changed in 1925 to Sons of Union Veterans of the Civil War, which is a patriotic education society. In 1954, the SUV was officially incorporated by an act of Congress. The Drum Corps of the Hastings branch of the SUV is shown near the courthouse in 1926.

What started as William Dutton's harness-making business in 1886, continued to grow and change with the times. The need for a large facility was soon realized, and in 1917, Dutton hired C.W. Way to design a new six-story, Sullivan-esque style structure at Second and St. Joseph. Finished in 1920, it was named the Victory Building to commemorate America's victory in World War I. With the promotion of Harry Lainson to president, the business has been called the Dutton-Lainson Company ever since. The building was named to the National Register of Historic Places in 1987.

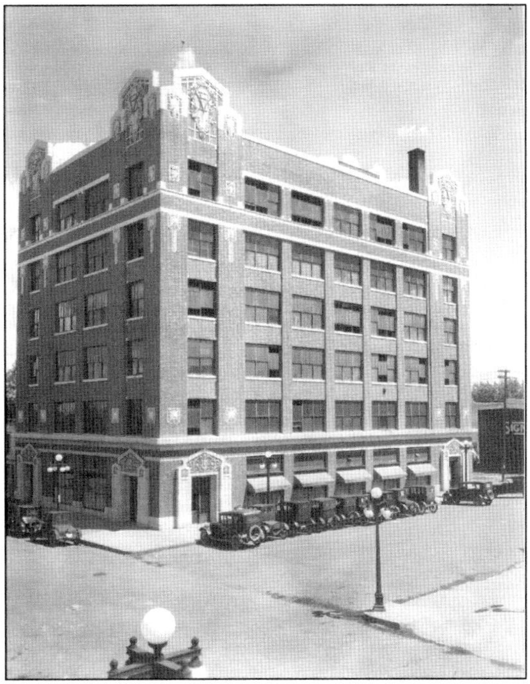

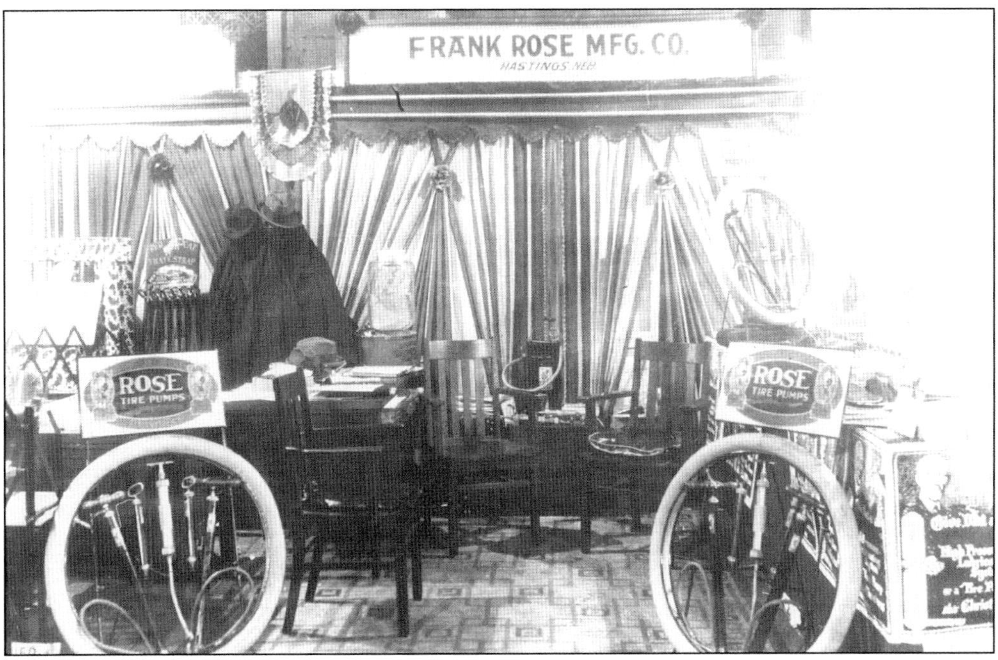


In March 1926, 34 companies exhibited their products at the Made-in-Hastings Exposition at the city auditorium. The Frank Rose Manufacturing Co., displayed its auto accessories, including their famous pneumatic tire pump. The Dutton-Lainson Co. later took over the Rose enterprises, adding its line to an already impressive offering. In 1941, Dutton's manufacturing switched over to producing 37mm projectiles for wartime. Today, Dutton-Lainson manufactures over 800 different products, and is one of the largest manufacturers of hand winches in the world.

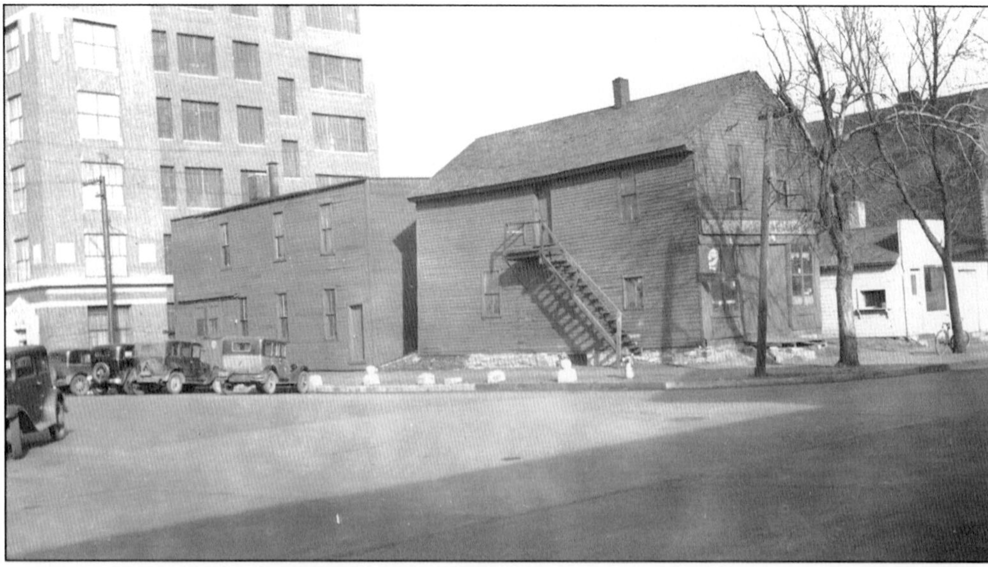

This two-story wood frame building just south of the Victory Building was razed in 1945, to allow for expansion of warehouse space for the Dutton-Lainson Co. The structure was believed to have been one of the few survivors of the great fire of 1879. It was credited with various uses during its long existence including first and second post office, hotel, drug store, carriage and wagon repair shop, as well as carpenter shop.

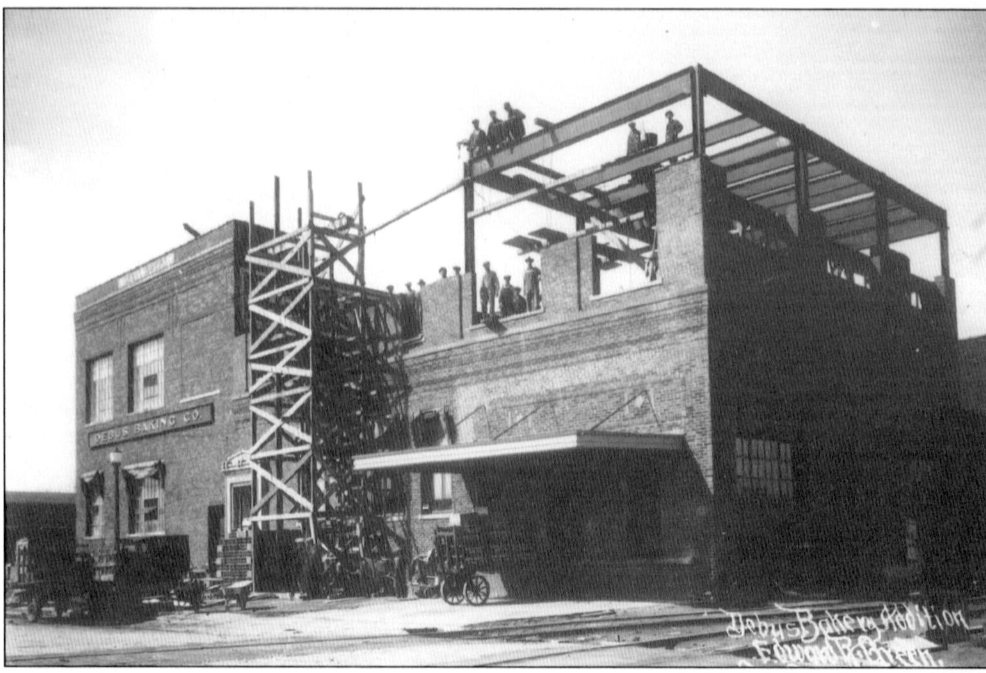


Sander Debus, a baker from Exeter, Nebraska, came to Hastings and built a $45,000 commercial bakery in 1922. The facility could bake up to 8,000 loaves of bread daily. An addition had to be built to their North Colorado Avenue structure five years later. In late 1951, the company constructed a new larger building at Elm Avenue and Highway Six. Now called Metz Baking Company, it produces Old Home-brand bread products.

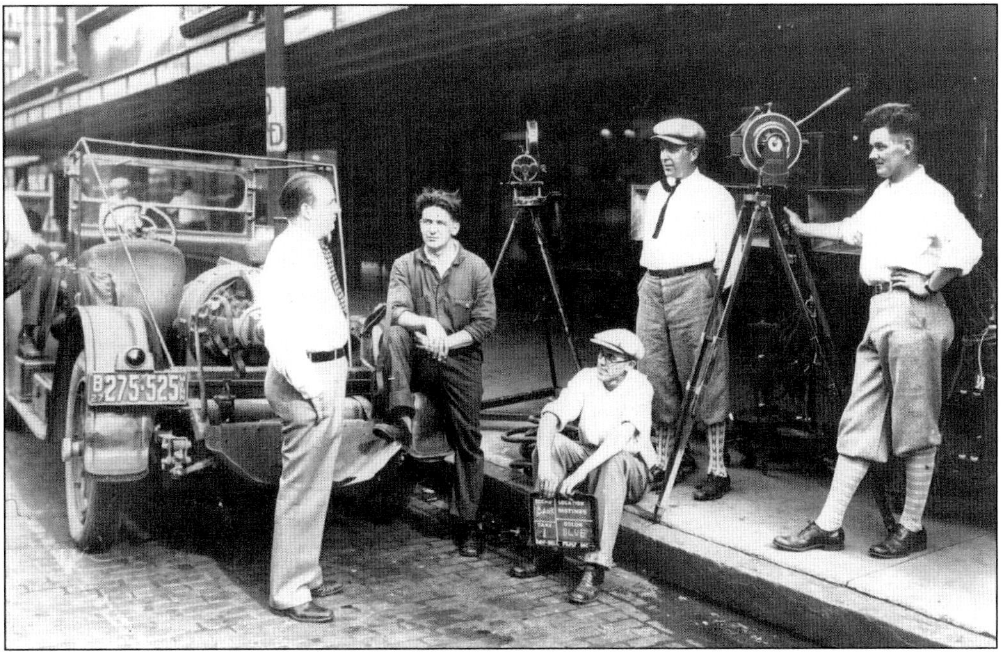

Adam Breede, original owner of the *Hastings Tribune*, conceived the idea of a silent film being made utilizing local actors. The result was the film *The Live Dud*, whose story was based on World War I, Armistice Day, and a bank robbery, was shown at the city auditorium on July 25, 1927. The film crew, shown from left to right, is pictured in front of Stein's department store: R.H. Ray, Ray St. Martin, Elvan McClenahan, R.F. Joseph, and C.E. Bell.

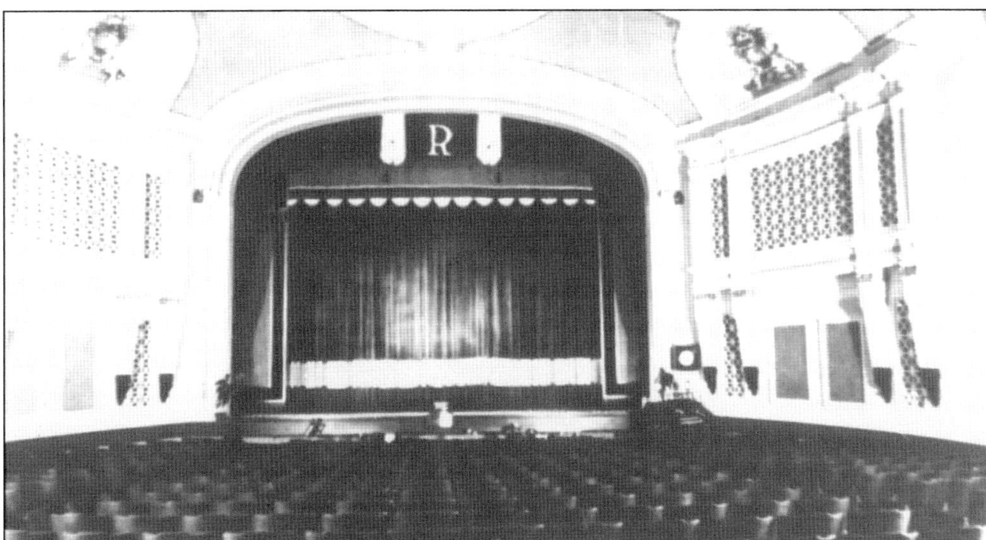

The Rivoli Theatre, at the west end of the Alexander Hotel, opened in 1927. The staff on duty for the March 25 opening were: Homer Garvin (manager), Jonas Daugherty (projectionist), Lola Neff (cashier), Ray Neff (head usher), and Richard Reid (doorman). In 1955, the marquee from the Rocket Theatre in Des Moines, Iowa, replaced the original. Fred Teller, who operated the Strand and Drive-In theatres, acquired the Rivoli in 1967. Although it closed in 1984, it has since had two additional screens added to make it a triplex, which still operates today.

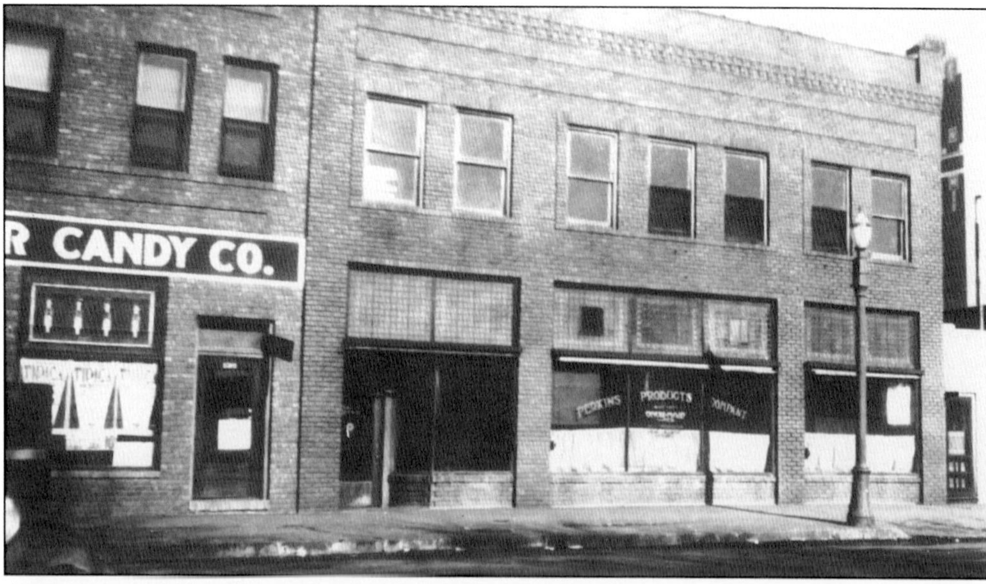


A major source of pride in Hastings comes from the fact that it is the birthplace of Kool-Aid. Edwin and Kathryn (Shoemaker) Perkins moved to the city from Hendley, Nebraska, in 1920. In April 1922, the Perkins Products Company opened for business in this unpretentious building at 508 West First Street. Edwin developed Kool-Aid in 1927, which in a short time became his only product. The company moved to Chicago in 1931, and was sold to General Foods in 1953.

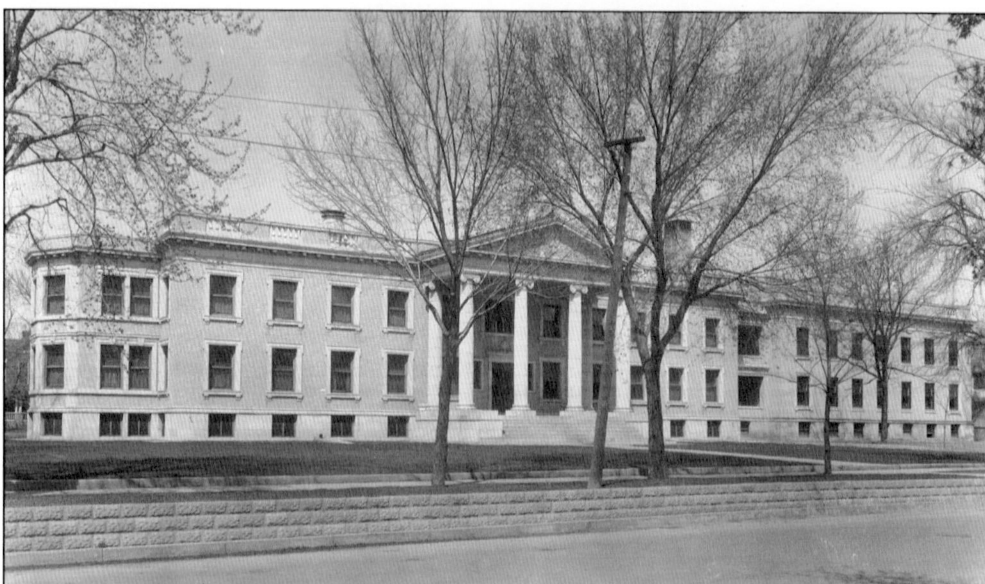

William Holmes Lanning gave decades of public service to the city—including serving as mayor. The Lannings' daughter Mary was born on September 18, 1888, and was their only child. From an early age, Mary was interested in a life of social service. At the end of her first year at Smith College in Massachusetts, she returned home for Christmas 1909. While home, she fell ill and died at 21 years of age. The Lannings decided to establish a hospital in her memory. The Mary Lanning Memorial Hospital is pictured as it looked in the late 1920s.

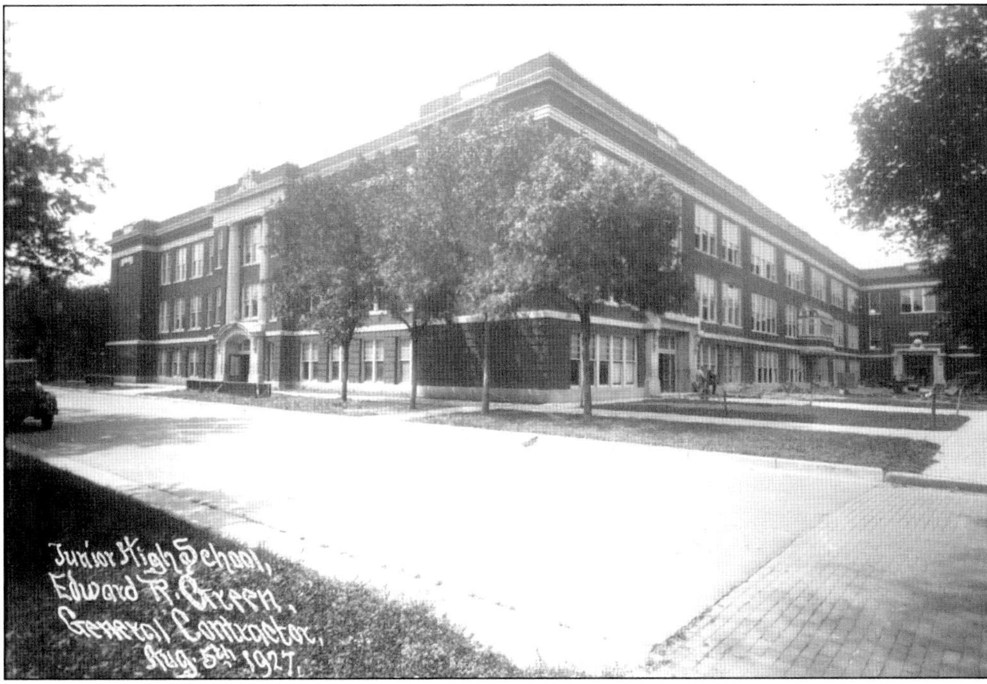


On October 16, 1916, voters approved school bonds for the construction of a junior high building, which began shortly before the United States entered World War I. The new school meant the adoption of a 6-3-3 school program, which was instituted as soon as the building was finished. All furniture, with the exception of the students' desks, was made in the manual training department by a dozen boys working under the direction of C.H. Sharpe. An addition to the building was constructed in 1927.

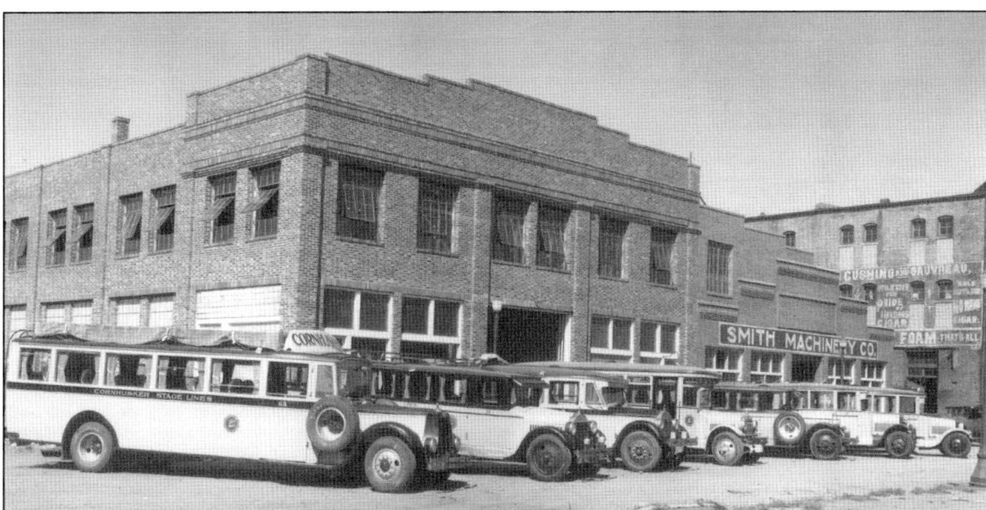


The Cornhusker Stage Lines became the first bus service in the city in 1925. Located at 918 West First Street, two different routes around town were offered every 20 minutes, at 10¢ per ride. In June 1927, Oliver Townsend merged the Platte Valley Coach Lines of Columbus with the Hastings company, changing the name to Yelloway-Cornhusker Bus Lines. The area of service was expanded to 240 towns in Nebraska and eastern Colorado.

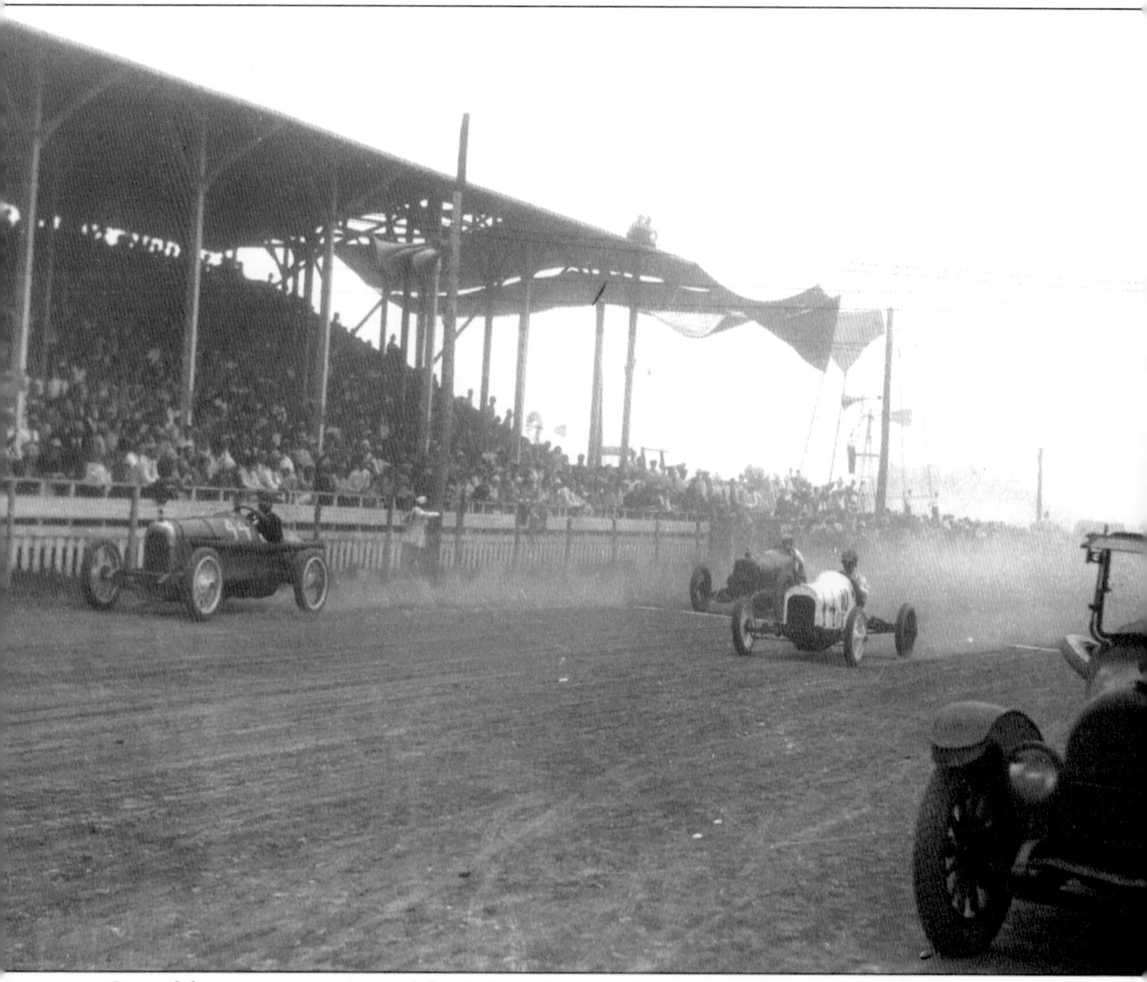

One of the main attractions of the Adams County Fair was auto racing. The first races were held on August 12, 1924, in front of an overcrowded grandstand. Nationwide champions included Irvin "Speed" Hoffman of Wisconsin, Buddy Putnam of Connecticut, and Johnny Waters of Missouri. The dirt track roared until 1934, when it fell victim to hard times. A new era of racing began after World War II, and evolved into a stand-alone attraction. Racing took another hiatus in the late 1950s, only to start again for its last run, which lasted from 1966 to 1975.

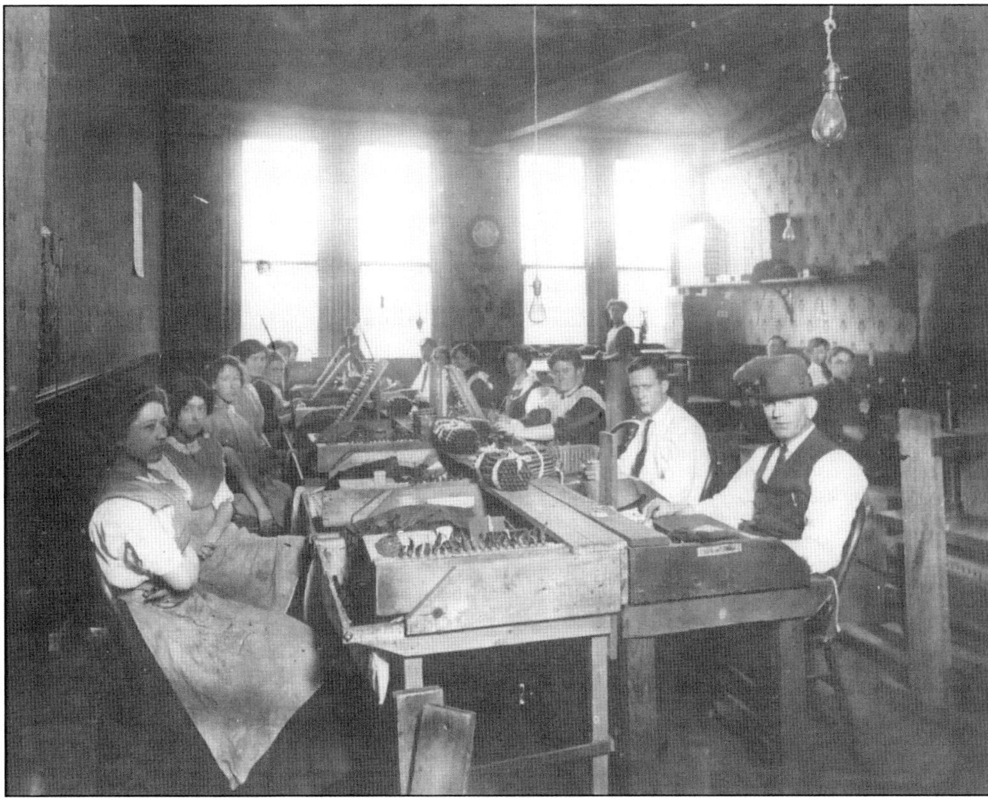

In 1909, John W. Kipp established the Kipp Cigar Company, which was located at 817 West Second Street. By 1919, he employed 125 people who were producing four million cigars per year, which were sold in Nebraska, Kansas, and Colorado. Between 1878 and 1947 (when Kipp went out of business), 39 cigar factories existed in Hastings.

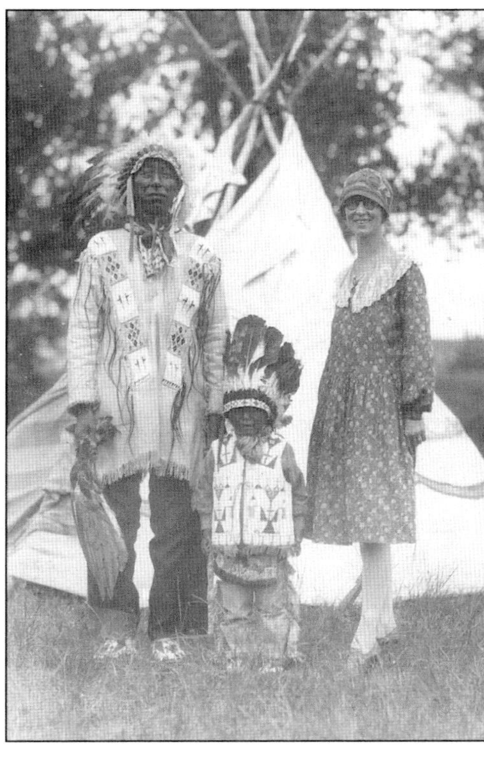

A Fourth of July celebration was held at Lib Phillip's Amusement Park (now called Lib's Park), in 1928. Activities included baseball games, swimming, and an evening dance. A special attraction was the program of dancing by Sioux Indians from the Rosebud reservation in South Dakota. Marie Herrin, Society Editor for the *Hastings Tribune*, met some of the indians, and posed for a photo with Sioux Chief Little Thunder and Andrew Little Thunder.

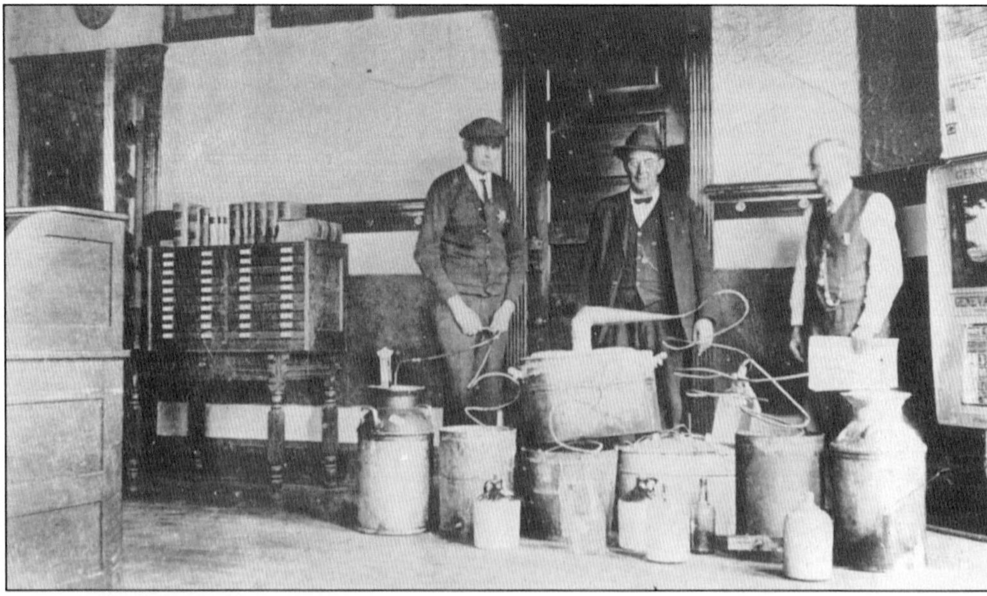

Deputy Sheriff Eric Johnson poses with a recently confiscated liquor still. The 18th Amendment to the Constitution went into effect on January 17, 1920, prohibiting the manufacture and sale of liquor. Nebraska had enacted a state prohibition three years earlier, but the amendment made liquor violations a federal offense. Hastings was no different than other towns when it came to a flood of illegal hootch.

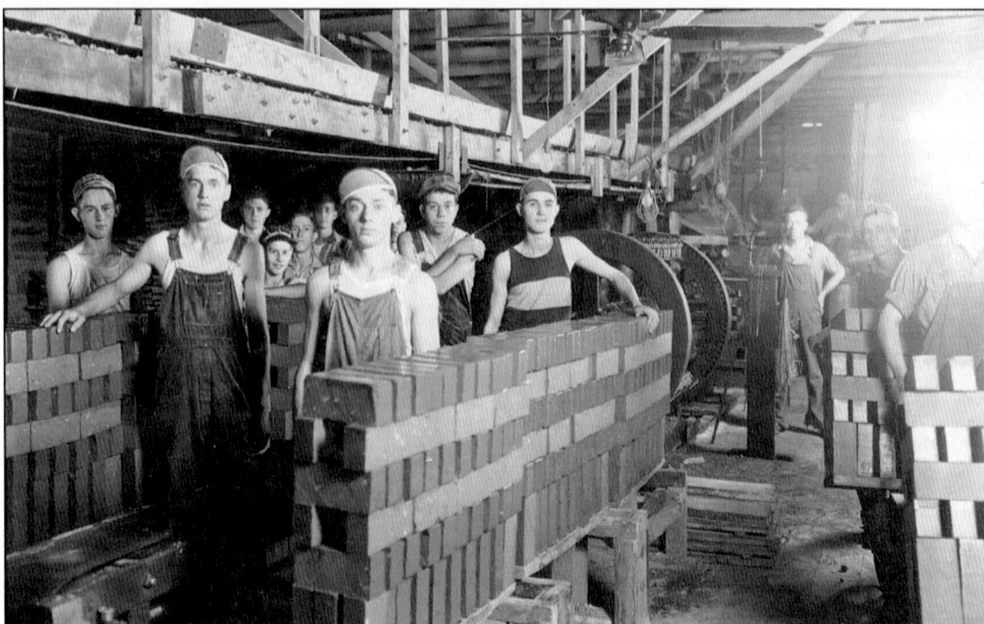

During the first three decades of the 20th century, brick making was a major industry. Over 200 men were employed by four brickyards each summer. Some of the employees of Western Brick and Supply Co. posed with green brick in July 1929. They are, from left to right: Harold Wagoner, Ed Walker, Mark Batt, Elmer Sealock, Fred Kamine, Henry Knaub, Everett Uhrich, Howard Baker, Fred Rhost, and Alex Meyer.

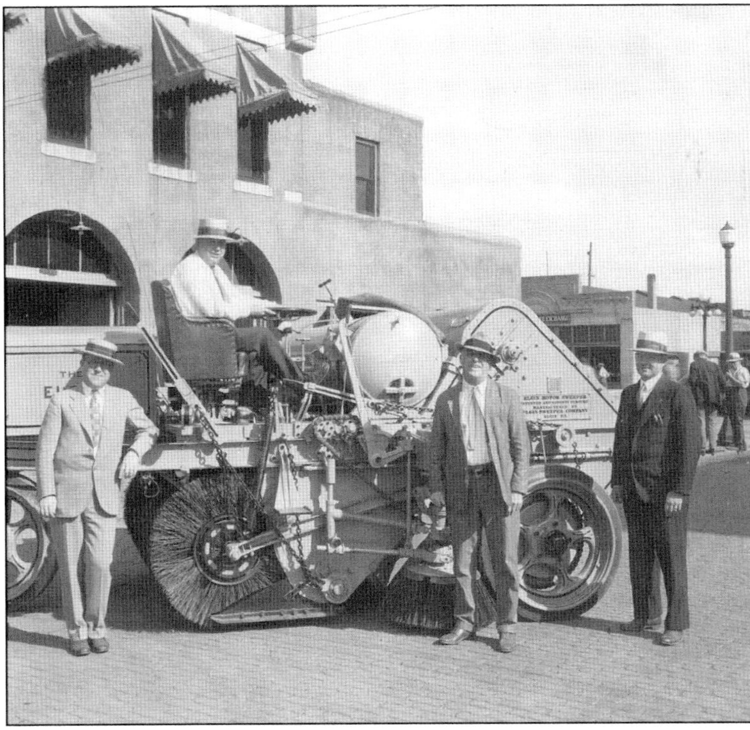

Officials pose proudly with a brand new Elgin Motor Sweeper, the city's first motorized street sweeper, in this June 1929 photograph. Streets were paved with bricks made at local brickyards, and the sweeper was needed to keep them clean. Pictured, from left to right, are: City Councilman G.H. Hunt, R. Van Guildner, William Harn, and Street Commissioner Perry T. Naylor.

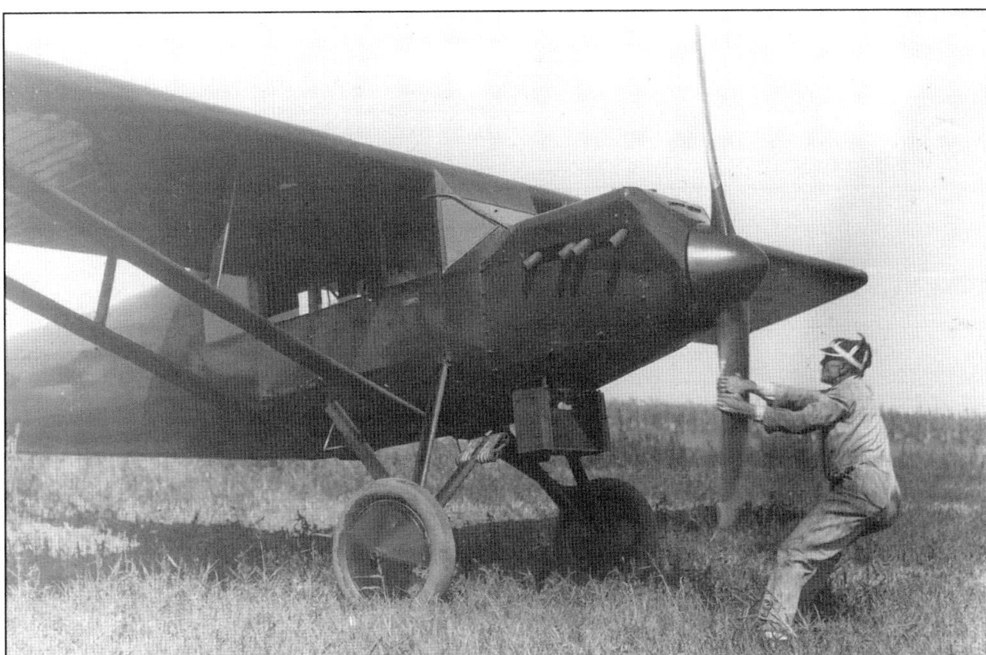

During the winter of 1927–28, aviation enthusiasts James McCreary and Clifford Currier built an airplane in McCreary's garage. The young men wanted to prove that a plane could be built inexpensively and with ordinary tools, hoping that Hastings would become a manufacturing center. The plane's name varied from "Miss Hastings" to "City of Hastings" to the "Pride of Hastings." Its first flight was on May 11, 1928, at an airfield west of town.

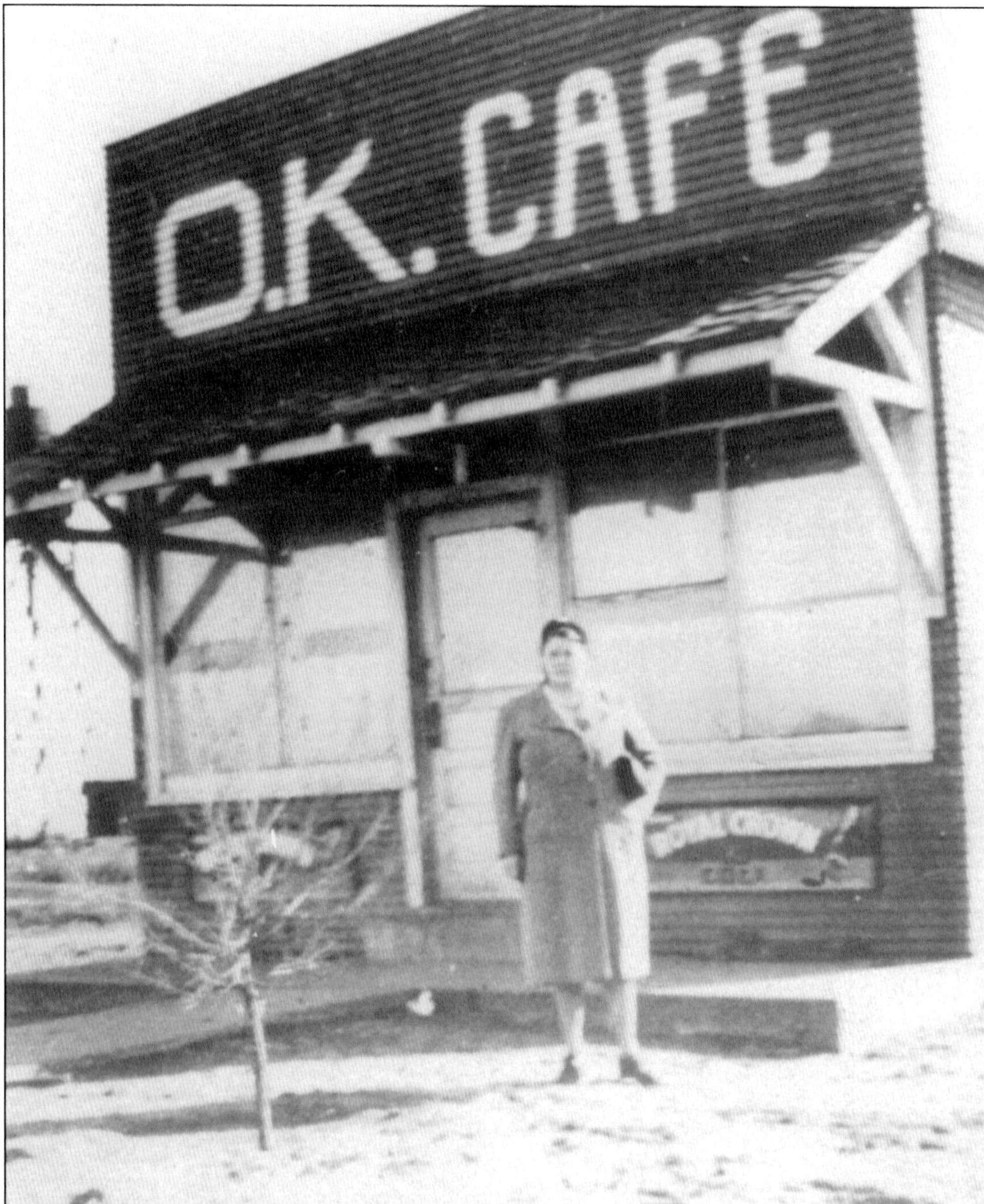


The OK Cafe is the oldest continuously operating restaurant in Hastings. It dates to the early 1920s and what was known as the "railroad cafe" (indicating its main source of business), which was located at 13th Street and East Side Boulevard. By 1927, it was called the Blue Goose Cafe, after a change in ownership. When the Union Pacific Railroad moved its yard offices to 17th Street and St. Joseph Avenue, it became necessary to move the cafe to that location. The 1930 city directory indicates that George Nemitz operated the restaurant, then named the OK Cafe. It was about the size of a single car garage, and featured one booth and four stools. Additions made over the years accommodated a growing business. In 1989, the OK moved to a vacated 10,000-square-foot car dealership on 16th Street. The cafe now has a capacity of 400, and conducts a catering service. A recently installed G-gauge model railroad consisting of 700 feet of track, two engines, and 70 cars, has become a very popular local attraction.

*Three*

# Depression and War Years 1930–1959

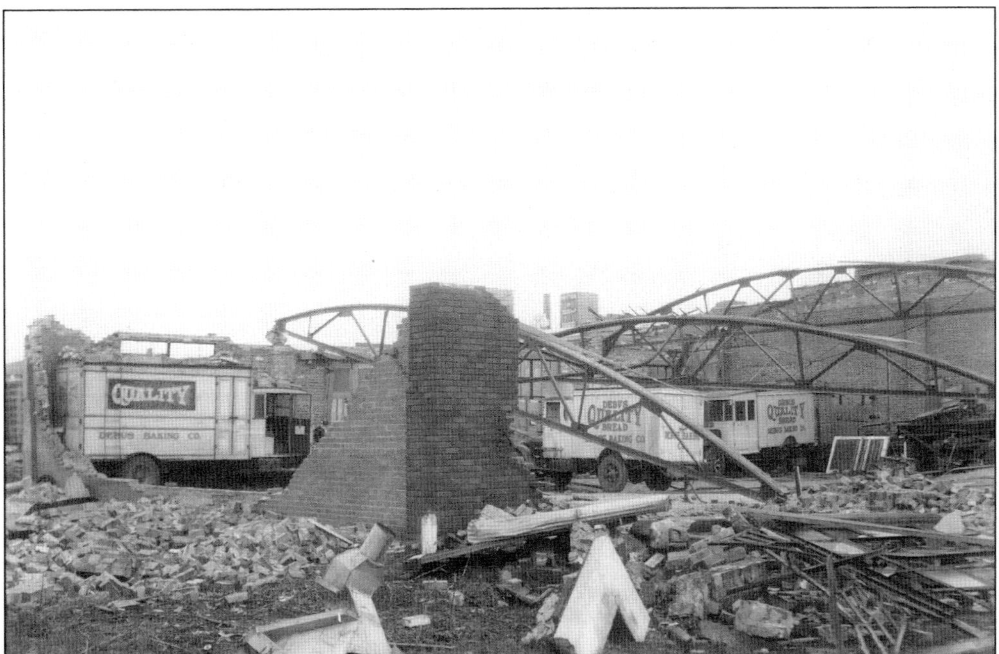


Hastings is situated in what is now termed "Tornado Alley." The dangerous storms are a concern through the spring and summer months. On May 5, 1930, a tornado traveling northward through the countryside appeared to be a practice run for another one that hit the city three days later. The tornado caused a million dollars worth of damage and killed one person. These Debus Baking Company trucks seemed to escape damage, but the building was not so lucky.

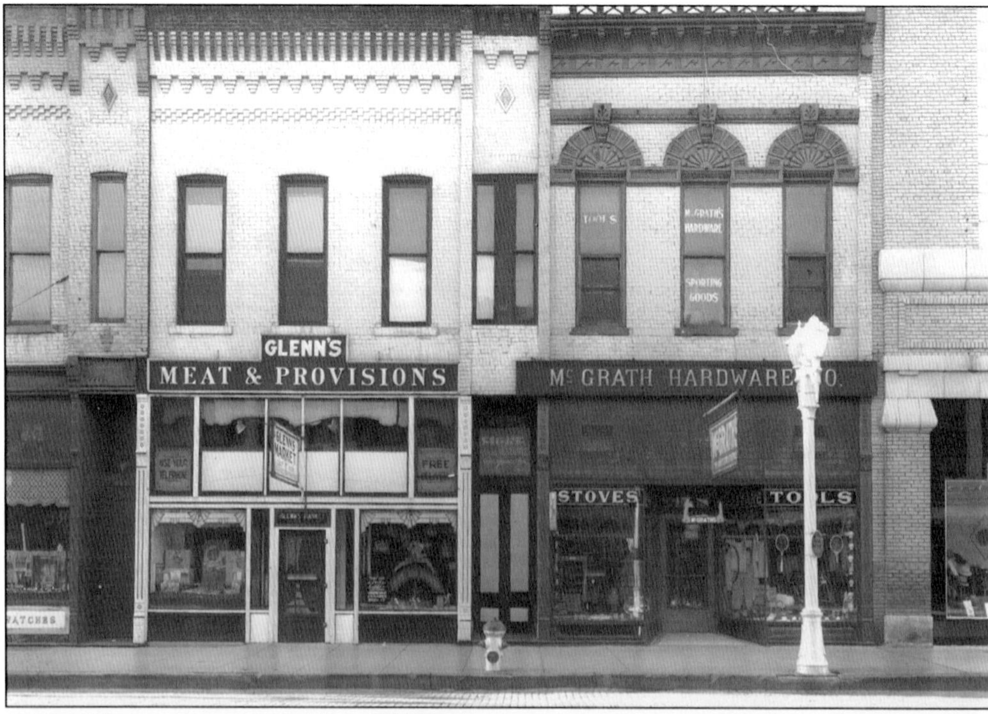


Glenn's Market, operated by Glenn W. Woolery, was a popular store for fresh meats and groceries throughout the 1930s in downtown Hastings. John H. McGrath established his longtime hardware store about 1905, offering tools, stoves, ranges, sporting goods, seeds, guns, and ammunition. By the 1920s, he added the radio to his line of products. The store was in business until 1964.

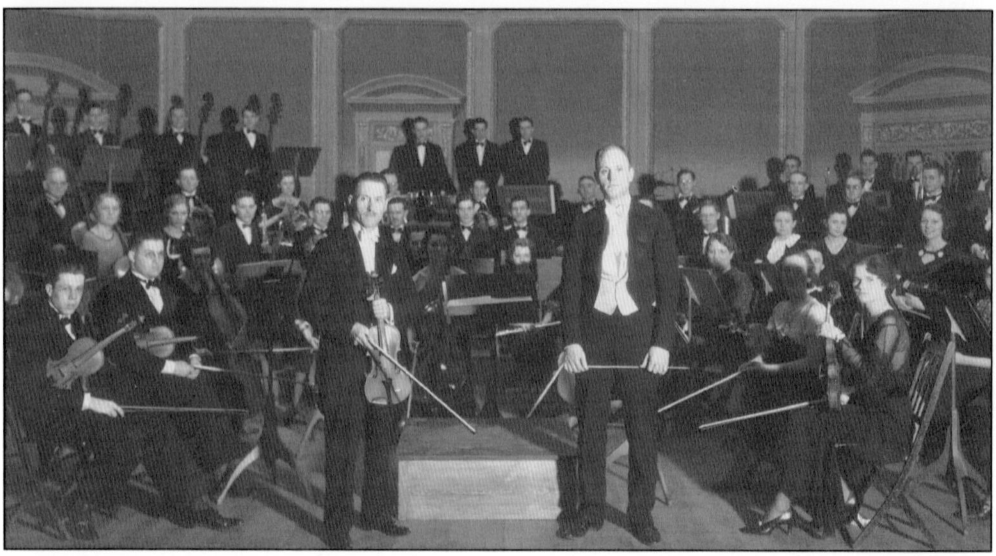

Cultural activities seemed to grow quickly during the 1920s and 1930s. Hastings College music teacher Frank Noyes converted an instrumental group into a symphony orchestra in 1925. Named the Dime Symphony, admission to the performances was only 10¢. This photo of the Hastings Civic Symphony, as it was later named, was taken in 1930. Ken Wright (left) was the first violinist, and Frank Noyes was the director.

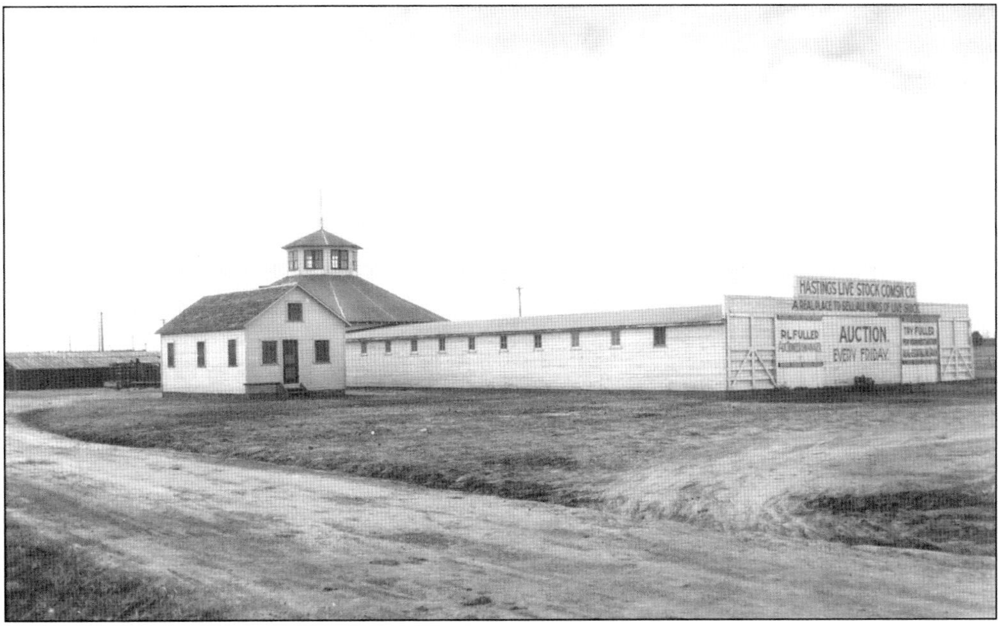


Raising livestock has been an important part of the agricultural make-up of the area. The Hastings Livestock Commission Company began operations and served as the local marketplace at 1727 West Second Street. By the time this photo was taken in 1930, auctions were scheduled for every Friday. R.L. Fuller was the manager and auctioneer.

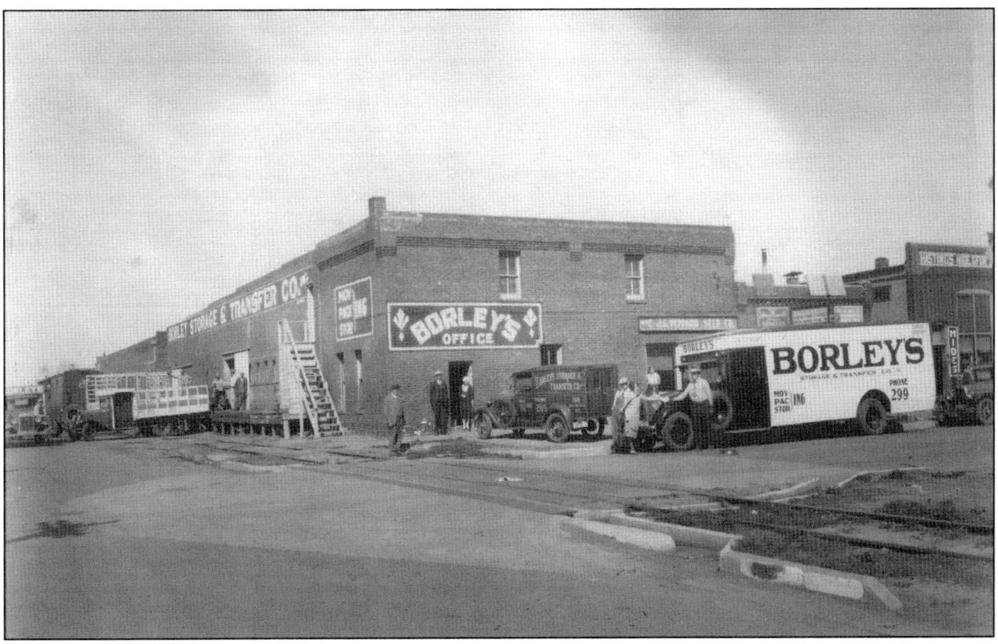


The oldest business still operating today is the Borley Storage and Transfer Company, which was established by Harry B. Borley in the 1870s. The first warehouse was purchased in 1914. Horse-drawn wagons were no longer used after a 1933 fire destroyed the stable. The company has been affiliated with the Aero Mayflower system since 1927, providing service nationwide. The business still operates from this building on South Lincoln Avenue.

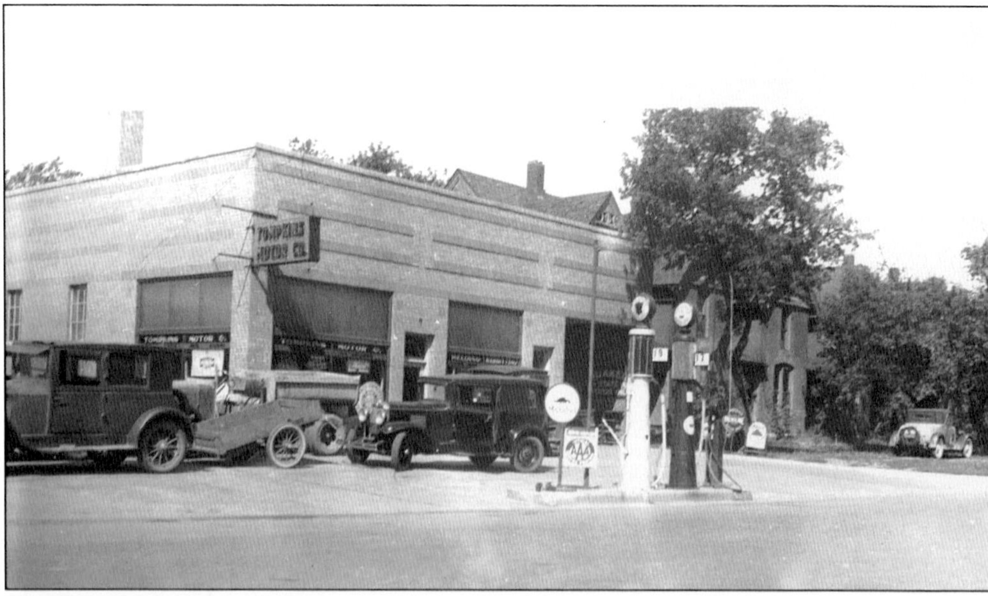

The Tompkins Motor Company was located at 207 North Lexington Avenue in 1930. In addition to selling gasoline, Charles N. Tompkin's business met the need for more extensive automotive mechanical work, which included: machine work, welding, cylinder boring, babbitting, and shaft grinding. Other members of the Tompkins family founded Hastings Battery and Electric Co., which is still operating.

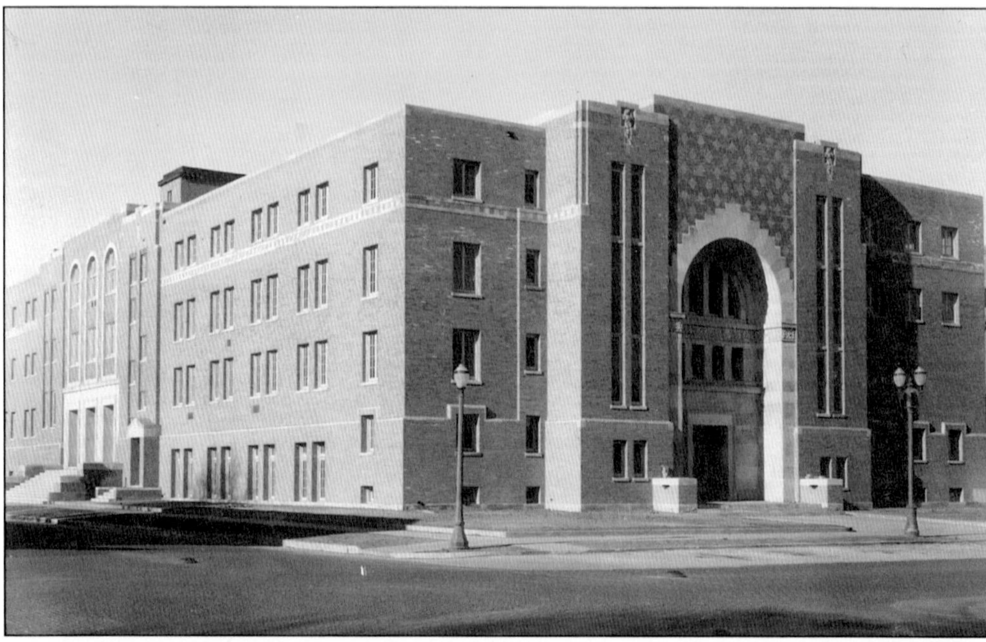

On September 28, 1919, the Shrine announced plans to build a new Masonic Temple at Sixth and Hastings, which replaced the old facility on Second Street. It was not until 1928, however, that bids were let for the new $30,000 building, and the cornerstone was laid that September. The new temple opened two years later, with 1,300 masons present for the ceremonies. The building is located across the street from the city auditorium.

Firemen building a training tower on the southwest corner of First and Burlington take time out for a photograph in July 1931. After completion, the tower was five stories high. There was no roof, only an I-beam from which life ropes and other equipment was attached during training. The *Tribune* reported that, "it was braced so high winds should strike it, a sway of as much as four feet at the top would still leave it free from snapping."

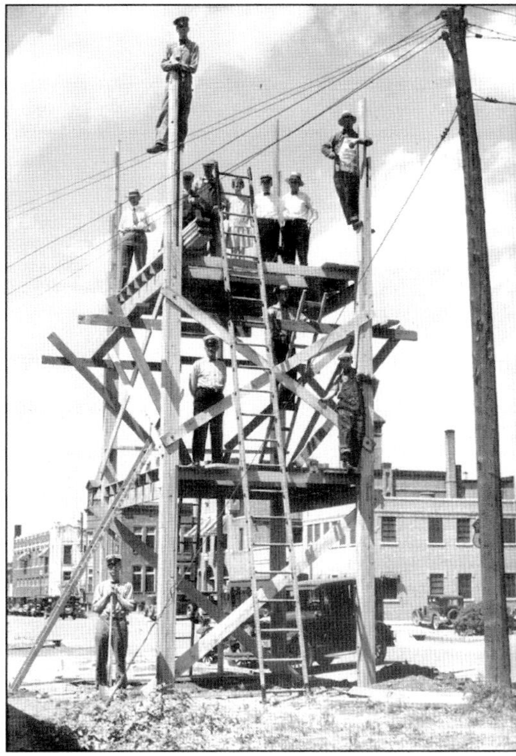

A daring bank robbery during the Depression provided some excitement for the city in 1931. In the early morning of February 25, three men broke into the Hastings National Bank and took 14 employees hostage as they came to work. Leaving with over $27,000, the robbers were soon involved in a gun battle with police at their rented house on East Sixth Street. Some officers were taken hostage, and using them as a shield, the bank robbers were able to escape. They were later caught and imprisoned.

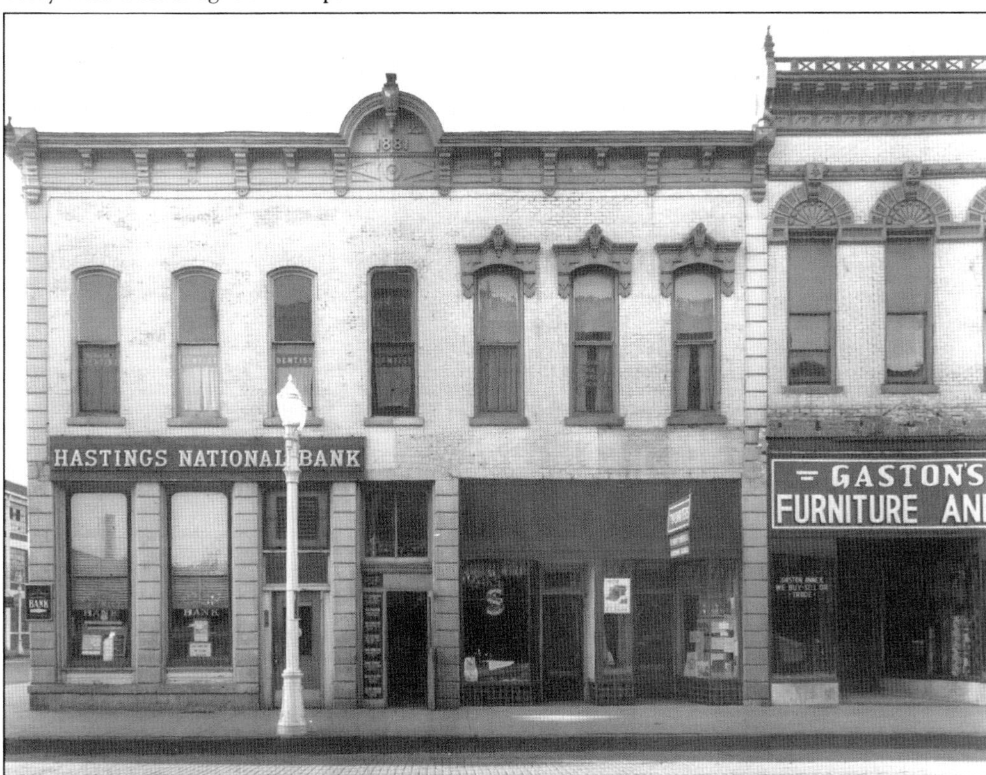

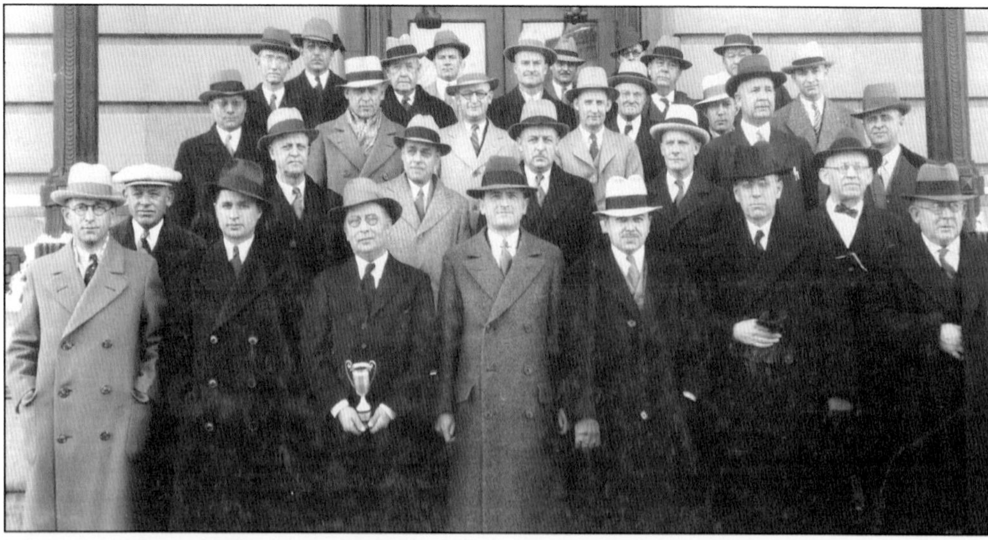

Many community leaders were members of the Hastings Kiwanis Club, as well as the Lion's, Rotary, Sertoma, Jaycees, and Optimist Clubs. Kiwanis members in 1932, from left to right, were: (front row) Charles Uerling, Harry Schultz (in cap), Ben Sherman, Anton Topp, Floyd Reed, Roscoe Hewett, Dr. E.E. McDade, Dr. E.J. Latta, Col. Hansell; (second row) Judge L.H. Blackledge, E.G. Lawson, E.J. Whitney, Dean F.R. Lee, Dr. E.B. Hamel, W.G. Pauley; (third row) F.E. Weyer, L.L. Cady, O.A. Riley, F.L. Youngblood, Harry Havery, Robert Kennedy, William Dutton Jr.; (fourth row) Dr. E.A. Thomas, Herman Schroeder, Judge J.W. James, Edwin Stratton, J.T. Cottingham, John Lawler, Howard Turpit, C.E. Staley, and R.R. Damerell.

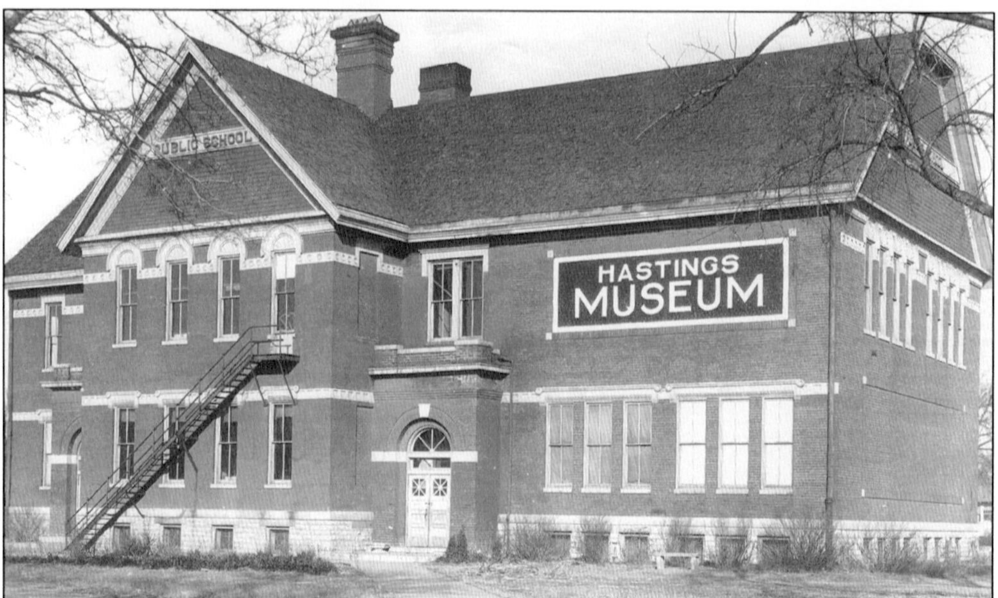


The Hastings Museum was founded in 1926, occupying the old Hawthorne School. The collections assembled by Professor Walter J. Kent and A.M. Brooking, with the help of many others, outgrew the first building in only a few years. This is the second museum, which was located in the old Morton School on West Fifth Street, from 1932 until the present museum opened in 1939.

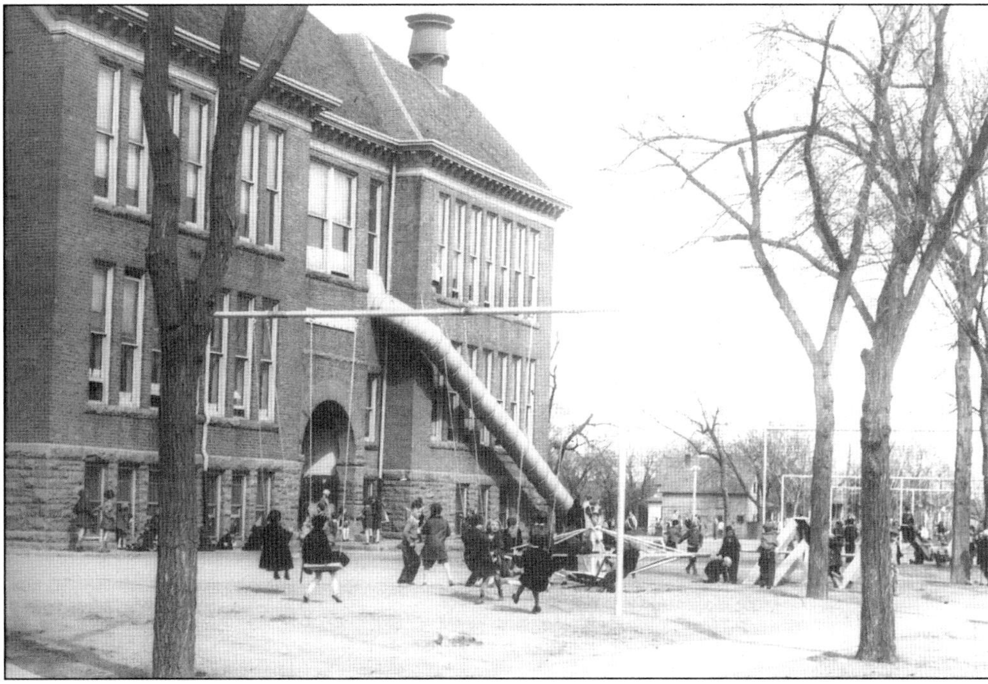

The children outside seem to be enjoying those precious few minutes called recess in this March 1935 photograph. Alcott School was built in 1891, and was located at 325 East Third Street, west of the current school. It was equipped with the tube-style fire escape as were most schools of the day.

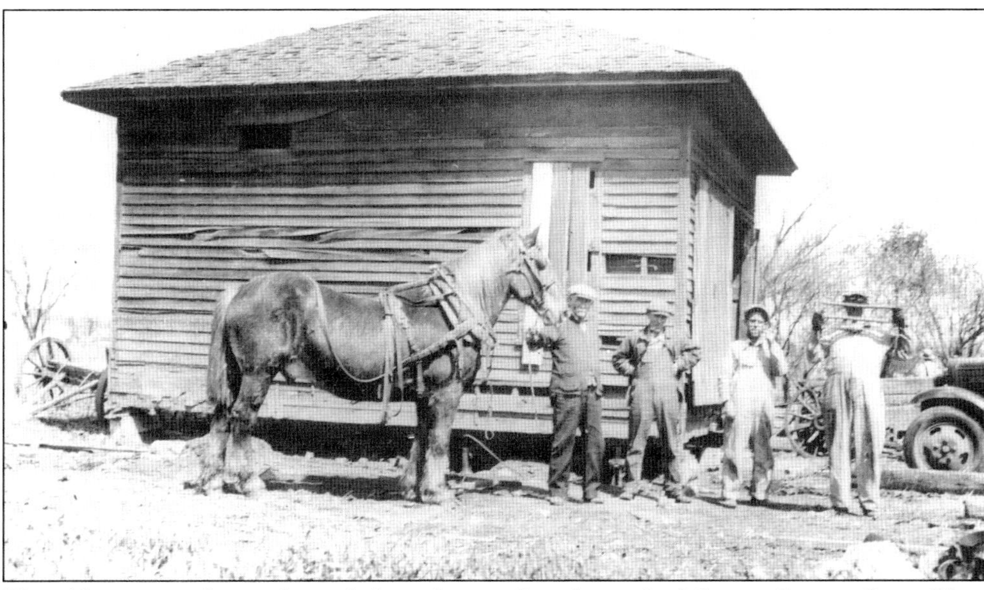

The old county jail once housed the infamous "manburner" of Custer County, Print Olive, during his trial in Hastings. The old jail had been moved several times, serving as a shed for its owners. It was being moved to D Street and Elm Avenue when this photo was taken. The stand-alone jail was located on the northeast corner of Third and Hastings until the new courthouse was built in 1890.

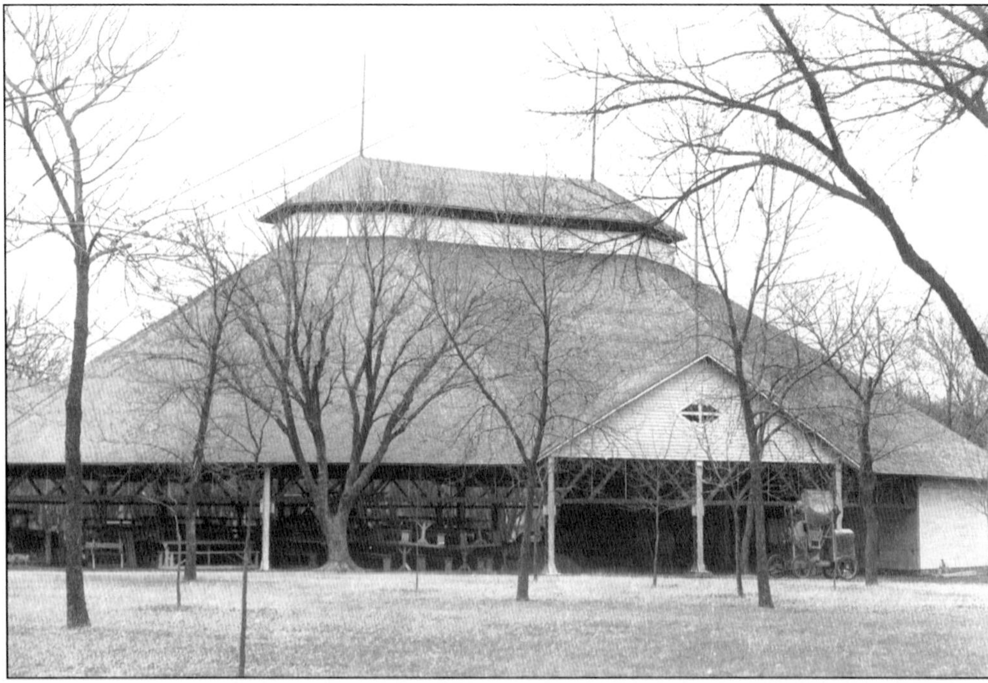

Twenty-four acres of land on West Third Street was a gift from Mr. and Mrs. Dewitt Palmer and Mr. and Mrs. Daniel C. Crane to the city during the Christmas of 1886. Originally known as Palmer Park (the Palmers contributed the larger piece of property), it was named Prospect Park by 1915. The park was home to thousands of travelers and attendees of the Chatauqua programs, which started here in 1905. The large steel reinforced pavilion (today a Hastings landmark), was built in 1907. It can accommodate 3,500 people.

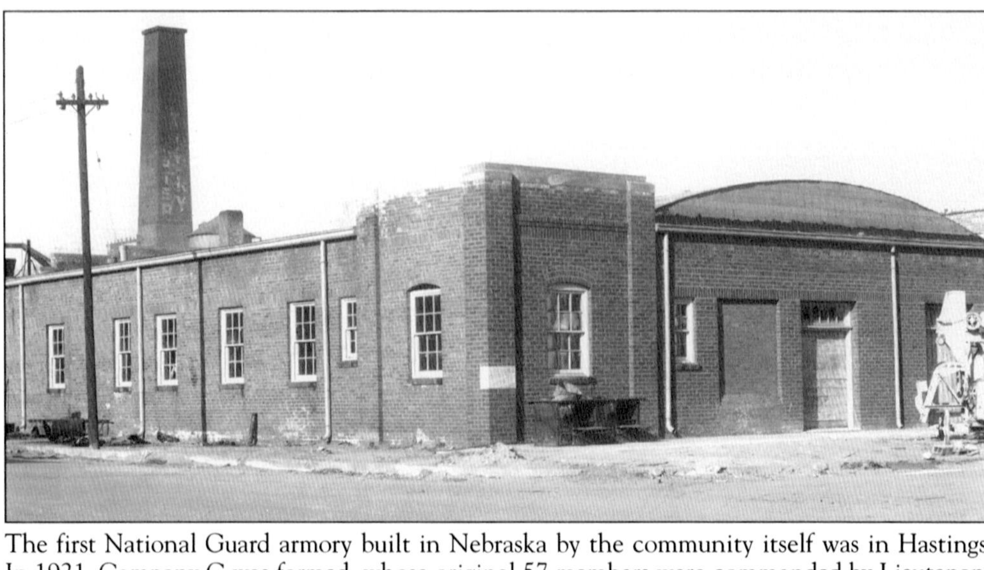

The first National Guard armory built in Nebraska by the community itself was in Hastings. In 1921, Company G was formed, whose original 57 members were commanded by Lieutenant Col. W.A. McDaniel. All of Company G's equipment as well as that of the 130th Ambulance Company was destroyed in a 1934 fire that heavily damaged the armory at First and Lexington. It was soon rebuilt without the upper floor, but it retained its outside walls.

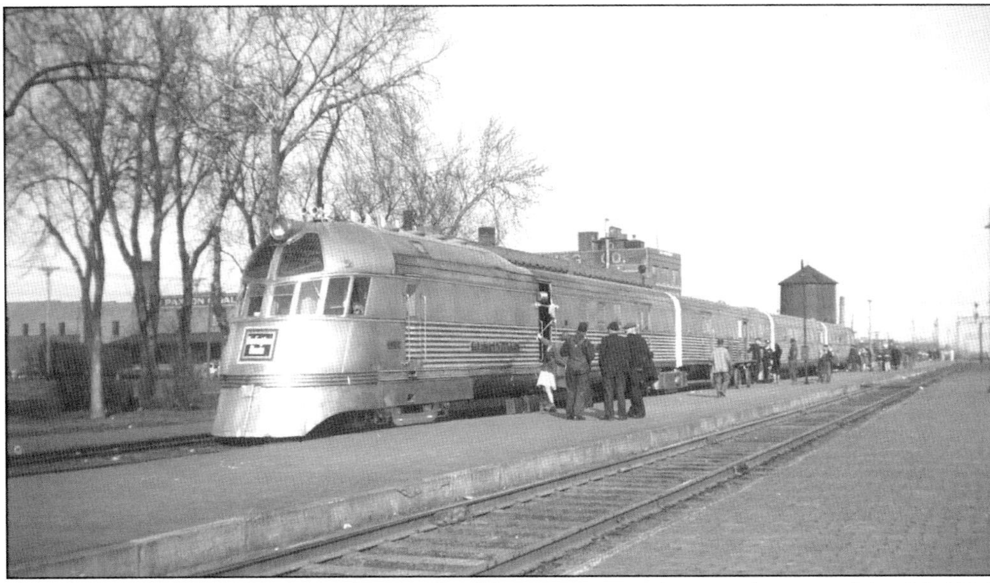

Anxious for free entertainment, the people of Hastings enjoyed a special treat on May 26, 1934, when the silver Denver Zephyr streaked through town on its record-setting run from Denver to Chicago. The train averaged a speed of 77-miles-per-hour, and made the trip in 13 hours. Two weeks later it stopped here to allow people to climb aboard and tour the modern train. For years after, the Zephyr made a regular three minute stop at 10:30 p.m.

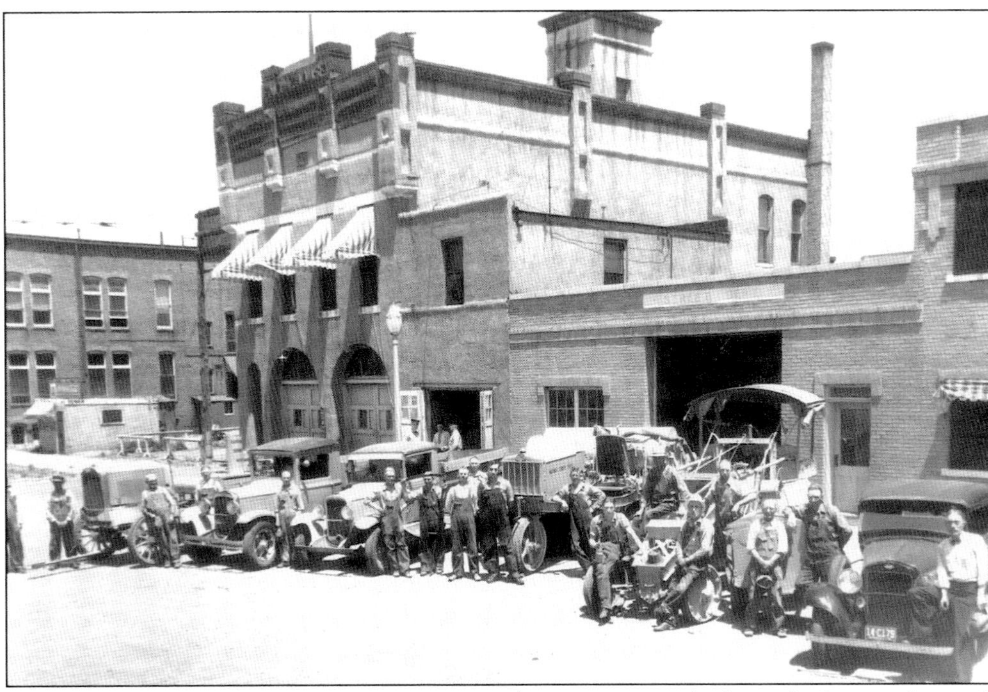

In the 1920s, the city street department occupied a new garage, which was built onto the south end of the fire station in the 100 block of North Burlington. In 1930, the new police station once again added to the south end of the structure, which then stretched all the way to First Street. Street employees displayed their equipment for this 1934 photograph.

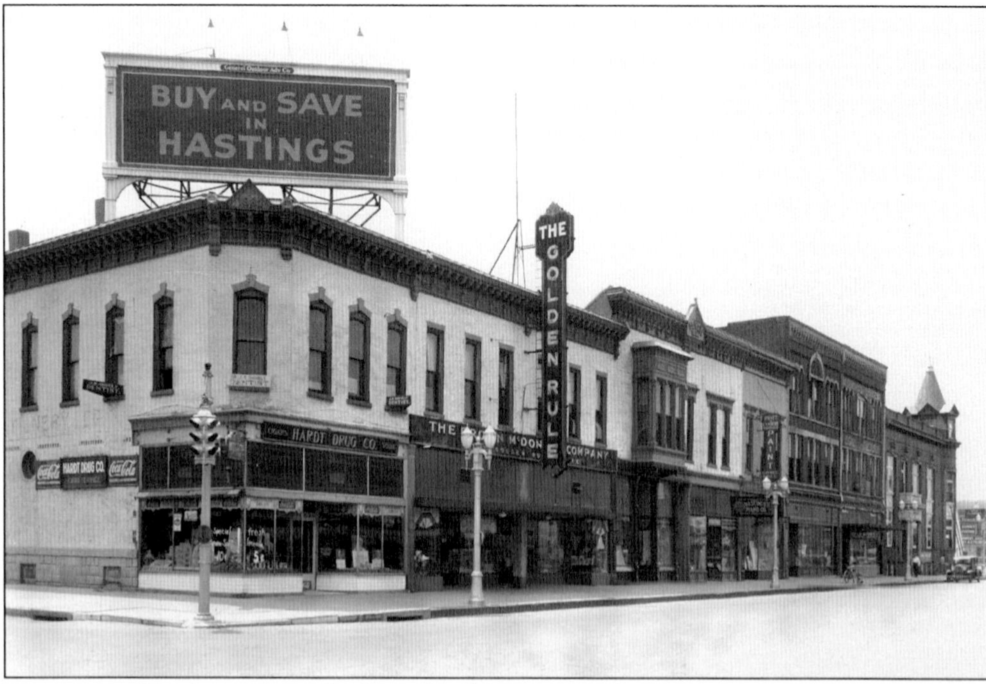


Patrons in coffee shops often talk about the old days, and what was in this or that building. This is the south side of Second Street, between Burlington and Lincoln Avenues as it appeared in 1938. The Hardt Drug Store, which advertised fresh lemonade for 5¢ in its front window, is now home to Big Dally's Deli. The Goldenrule Clothing store was opened in 1930, and became the J.M. McDonald Company in 1948.

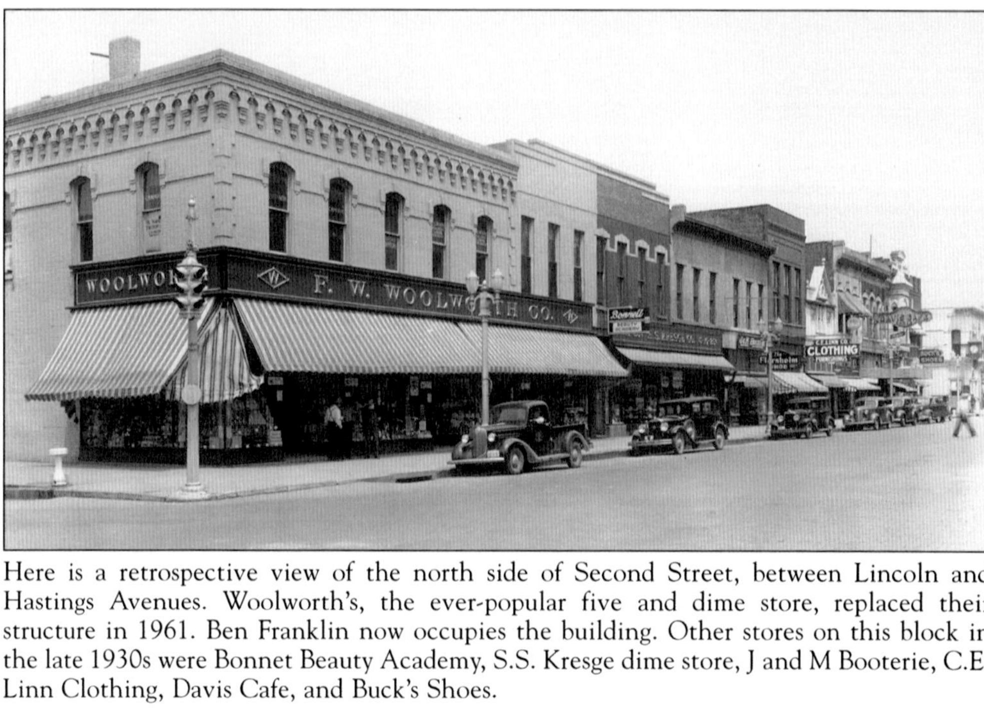


Here is a retrospective view of the north side of Second Street, between Lincoln and Hastings Avenues. Woolworth's, the ever-popular five and dime store, replaced their structure in 1961. Ben Franklin now occupies the building. Other stores on this block in the late 1930s were Bonnet Beauty Academy, S.S. Kresge dime store, J and M Booterie, C.E. Linn Clothing, Davis Cafe, and Buck's Shoes.

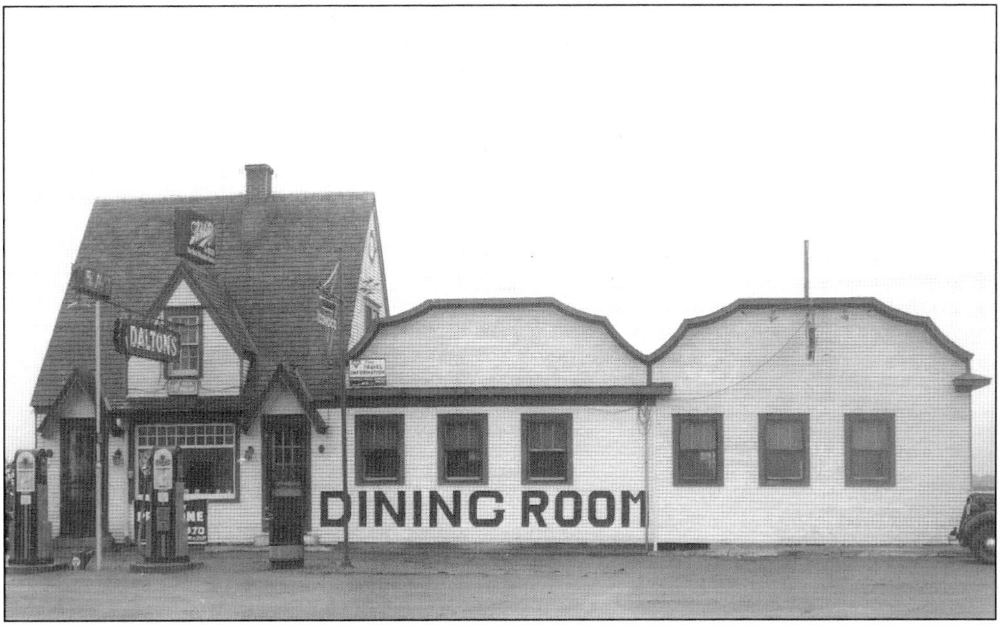


This is Dalton's Cafe and Service as it appeared on December 22, 1937. The station and cafe, located on State Highway Six, was an extremely popular stopping place for motorists in the days before Interstate 80 made the highway a secondary route. Dalton's later built a larger café, which is now called Andy's Cafe. The gasoline station is no longer there.

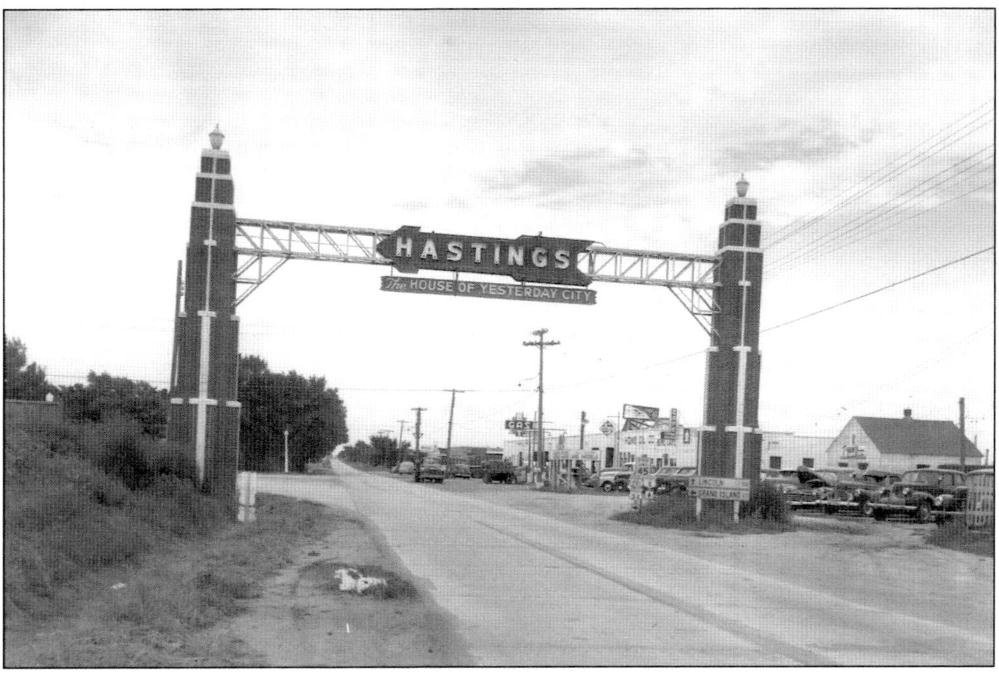


One of the works projects during the 1930s was the construction of two "gateway" signs. One was located at South Street and Highway Six on the east side of town, and another (pictured) just west of Burlington Avenue on Highway Six.The addition of the narrow sign helped to guide tourists to the "House of Yesterday" museum.

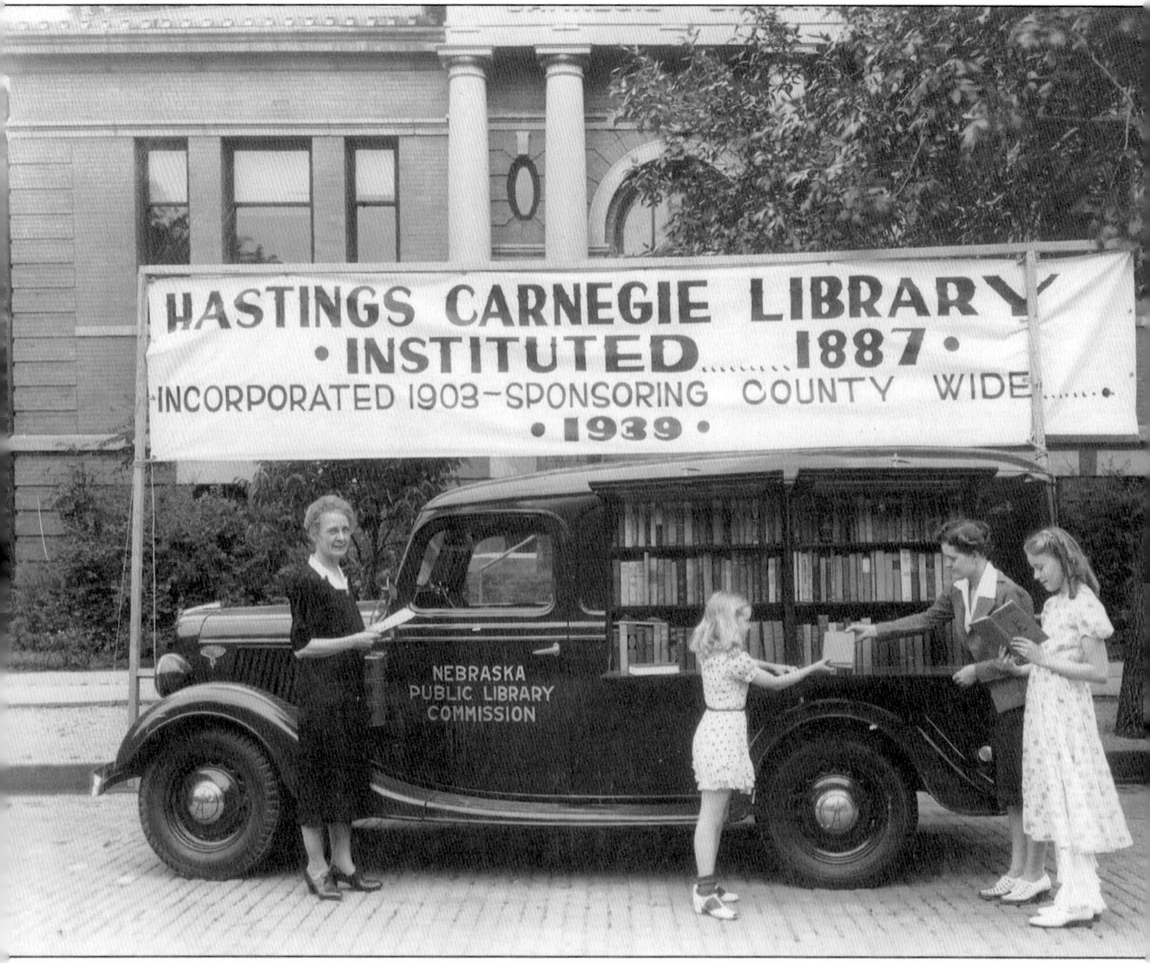


The public library can trace its beginning to the second floor of a downtown store in 1887. The Hastings Carnegie Library was the first in the state to offer services to the whole county. Ellen D. Smith (left), shown here in 1939, was responsible for initiating the bookmobile service. This specially built Ford truck visited the villages and rural schools in Adams County. Mrs. Smith was head librarian from 1936 until 1957.

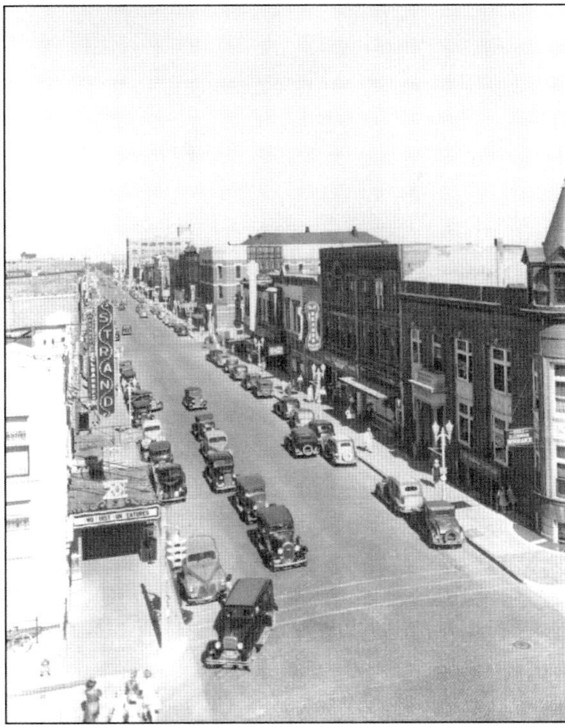


A photographer positioned on the roof of the *Tribune* building took this picture of Second Street looking east on a peaceful day in 1940. Little more than a year later, America was plunged into a world war. With the influx of construction and military personnel from the naval ammunition depot project, Hastings became a metropolis almost overnight.

After entering the war against Japan and Germany, the country had to tighten its belt and conserve so supplies could reach our soldiers and sailors. The rationing program began in 1942, when schoolteachers were utilized to register householders and consumers. Registration was held for food ration stamps between May 4th and 7th, and in November for gasoline. The ration board operated from the city auditorium.

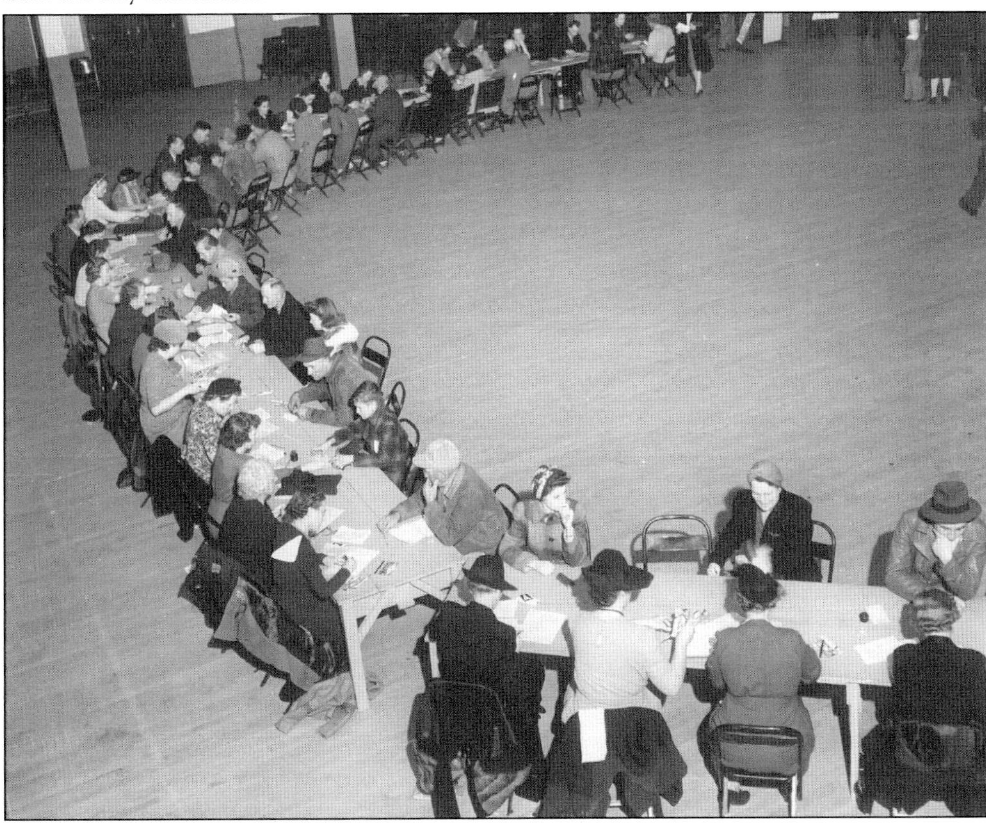

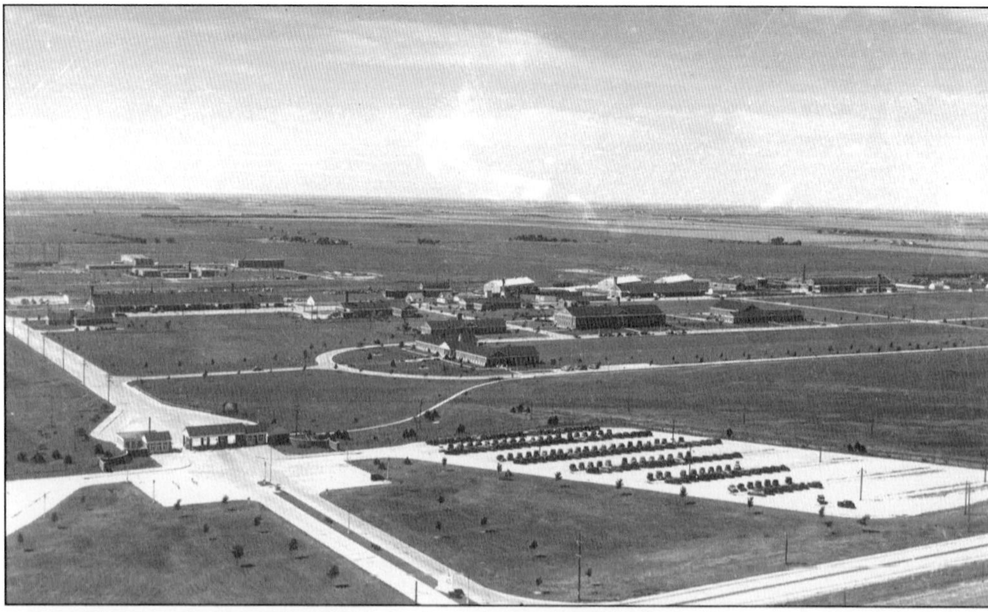

Six months after the December 1941 attack on the Pearl Harbor Naval Base, the Navy Department announced that a $45 million ammunition depot would be built southeast of Hastings. The facility, which started production in 1943, occupied over 49,000 acres in Adams and neighboring Clay Counties. More than 1,900 sailors, marines, and coastguardsmen, and 6,600 civilians were employed there. Only the administrative buildings are shown in this photo.

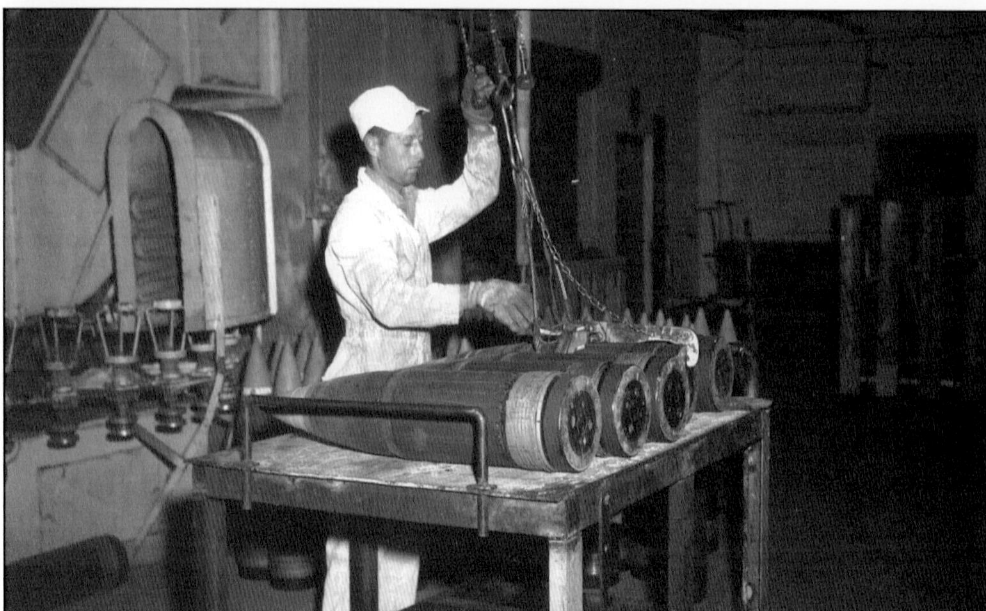

Wages for a line worker at the Naval Ammunition Depot was 74¢ per hour, for a 60-hour workweek. NAD Hastings was the largest of four inland plants, producing 40% of the Navy's needs. In 1964, over 10,000 acres were transferred to the Department of Agriculture for a meat animal research center. The administration buildings and their accompanying 640 acres became the Central Nebraska Technical College in 1966.

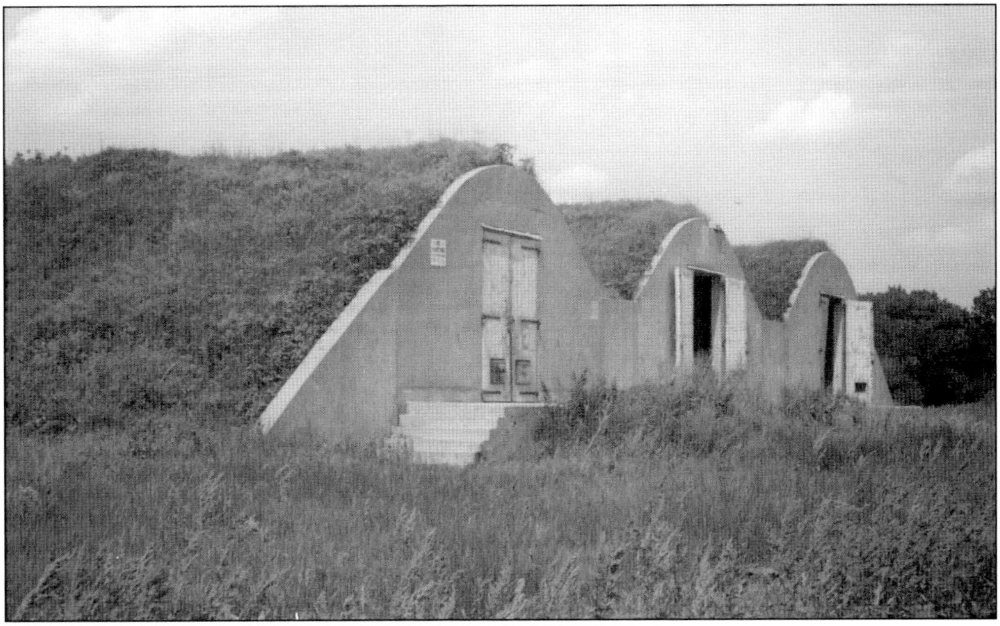

Hundreds of storage bunkers dot the ammunition depot land, which held bombs, mines, rockets, depth charges, torpedoes, and 40-mm to 16-inch shells. The bunkers, varying in size, were constructed of reinforced concrete, and covered with earth and vegetation. Some featured concrete blast shields, which were located in front of the doors, to minimize damage from an accidental explosion.

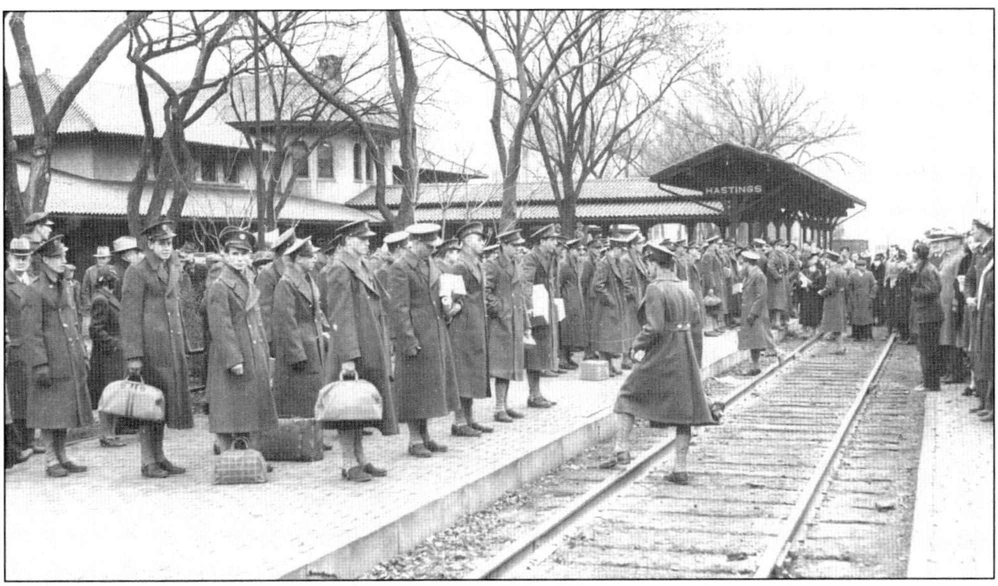


The railroads had also suffered during the Depression, but World War II provided a boom in business. The Burlington as well as the Union Pacific Railroad was used to transport munitions from the NAD to the West Coast. Troop trains carried military personnel across the country on a regular basis. Like their counterparts in World War I, troops are shown waiting for the next arrival at the Burlington depot. The Dutton-Lainson Co., its current owner, recently restored the 1902 depot.

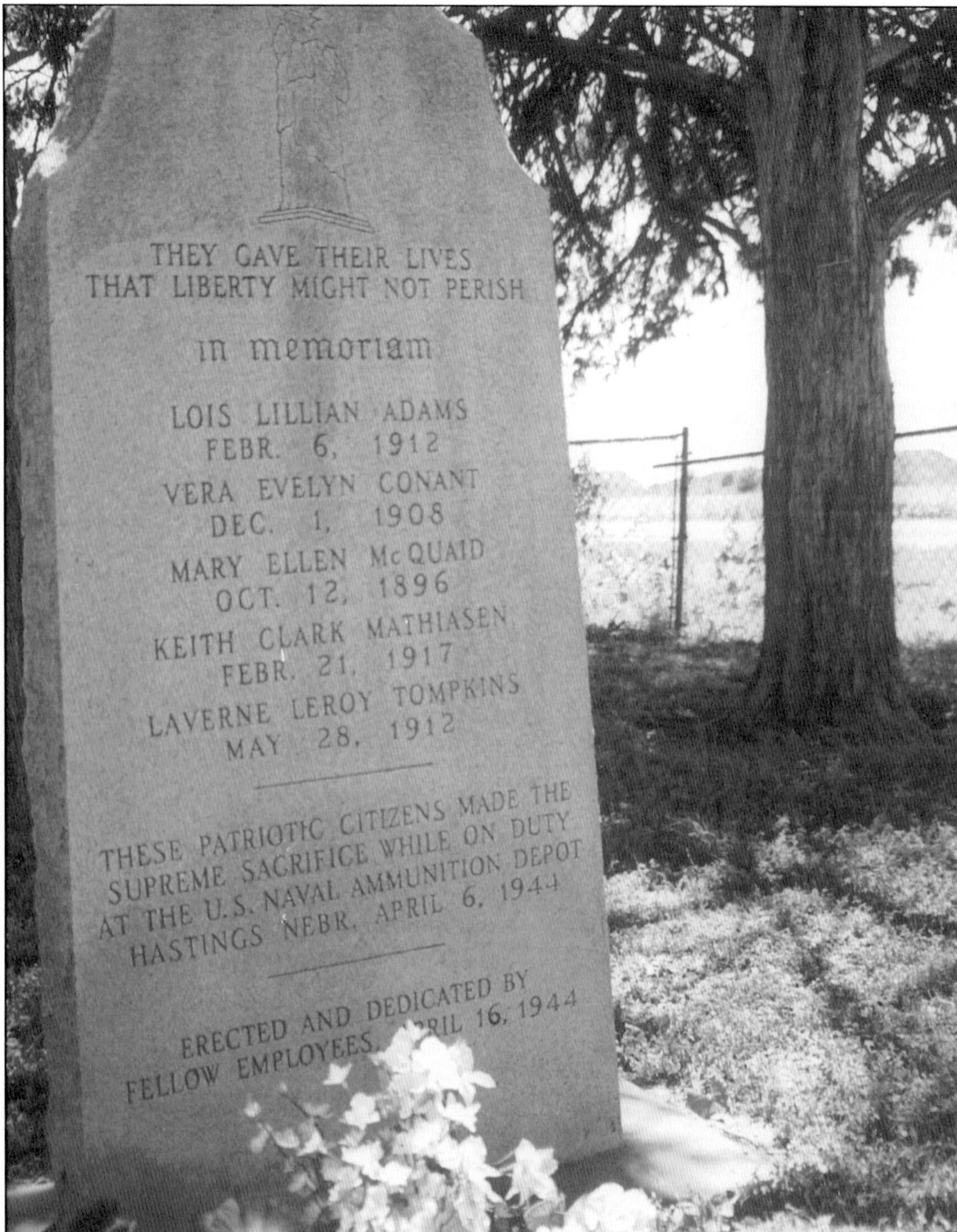


Many safety precautions were in place to protect workers at the Naval Ammunition Depot, but it was inherently dangerous work. During World War II, there were four accidental explosions, which killed 21 and injured 142 civilian and military personnel. In April 1944, an explosion in the bomb and mine loading area claimed eight lives. Three bodies were identified, and the ashes of the other five were buried in the small cemetery south of Inland, on the NAD. Fellow employees erected a memorial for them which read in part, "These patriotic citizens made the supreme sacrifice while on duty at the U.S. Naval Ammunition Depot Hastings Nebr. April 6, 1944. They gave their lives that liberty might not perish." Munitions storage bunkers can be seen in the background.

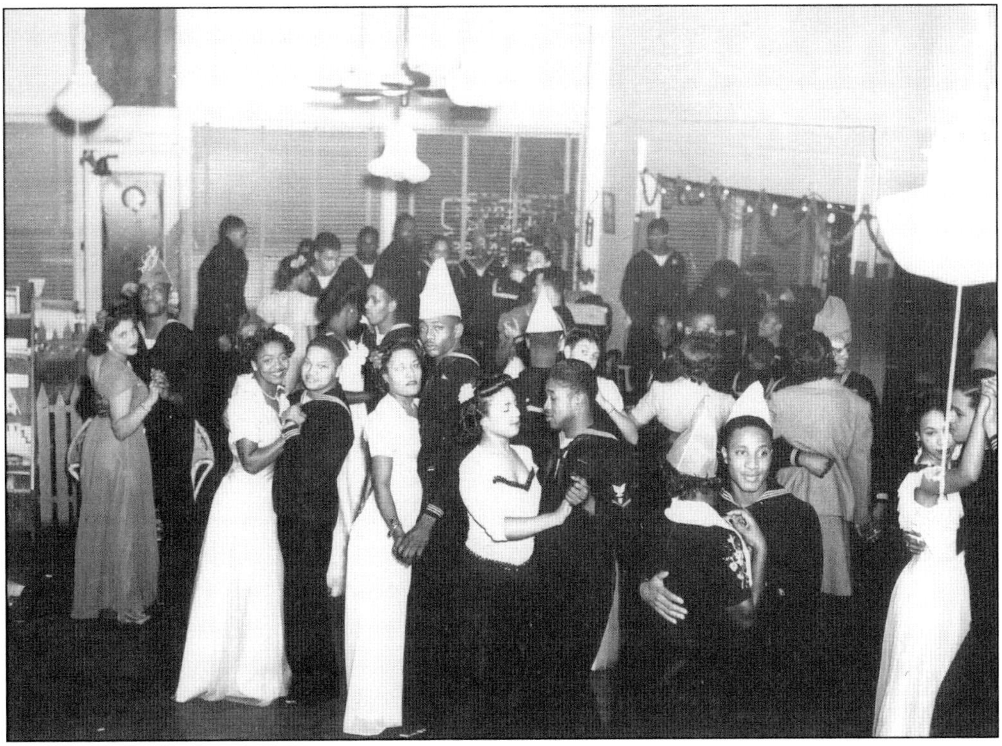

A servicemen's center was established two doors east of the Rivoli Theatre and was later moved to the old YWCA building at 509 West Second Street. In August 1943, Lanham Act funds were received for operation of the center. A Colored Servicemen's Center was then opened at 624 West First Street in downtown Hastings, with 300 people in attendance.

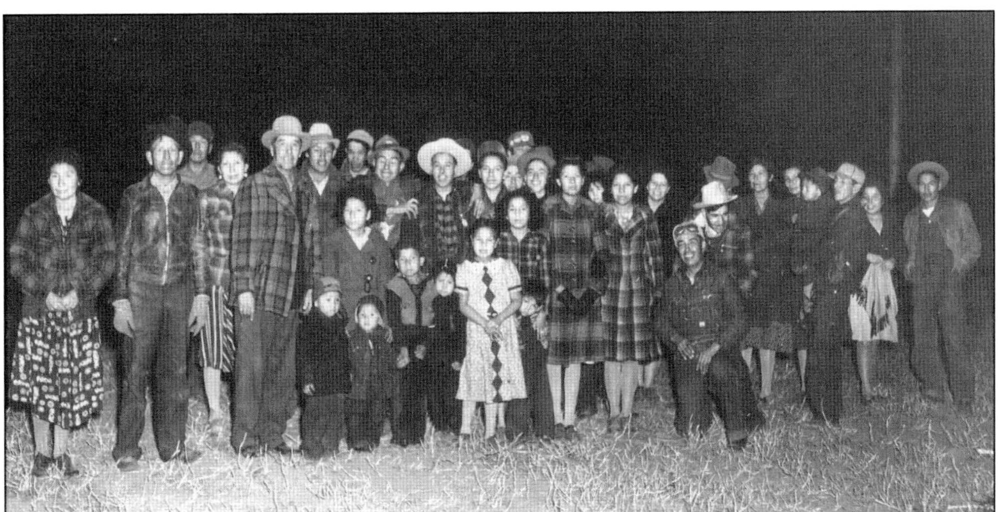

The NAD was a massive construction project, which required a large number of workers. Employees in Hastings businesses were asked to work four-hour night shifts on the site, as there was a serious shortage of construction workers. In addition, help was brought in from outside the area, which included 50 Chippewa Indians, and several hundred Sioux from the South Dakota reservations. Part of the Sioux contingent and their families posed for this night-time photo.

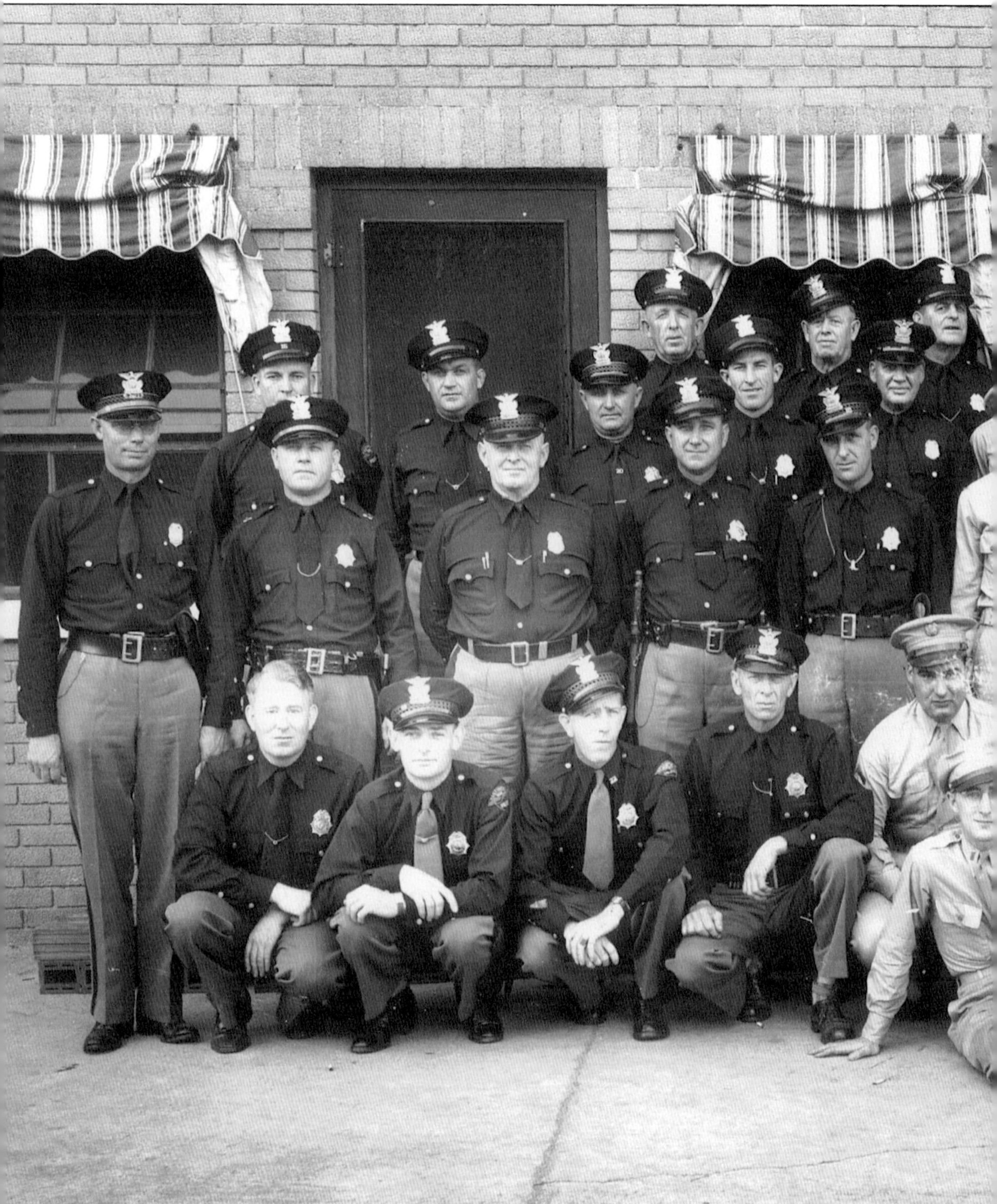

During the war years, Hastings' population had increased by over 7,000. To accommodate the influx of people, the Navy constructed housing at Spencer Park, which consisted of 875 single units and 24 two-story buildings. A 20-acre trailer court called "Pleasant Hill," on the county fairgrounds at 14th Street, was also established. Pleasant Hill and Spencer Park were not always

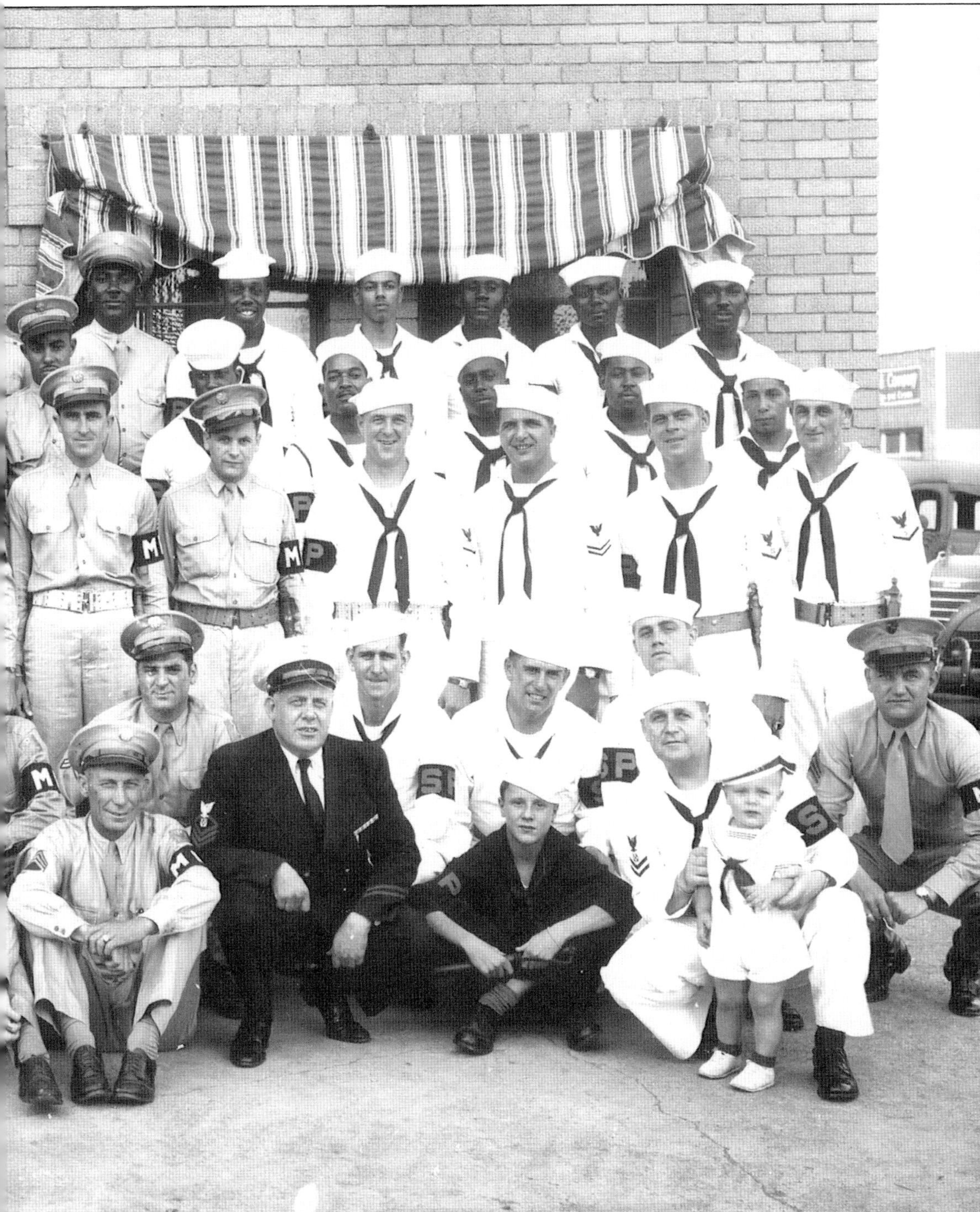

pleasant, requiring military police units to augment the city police. Military police and shore patrol personnel from the Navy, Coast Guard, Marines, and Army (from the Harvard Army Air Corps Base) posed with Hastings policemen in front of the Burlington Avenue station house in 1944.

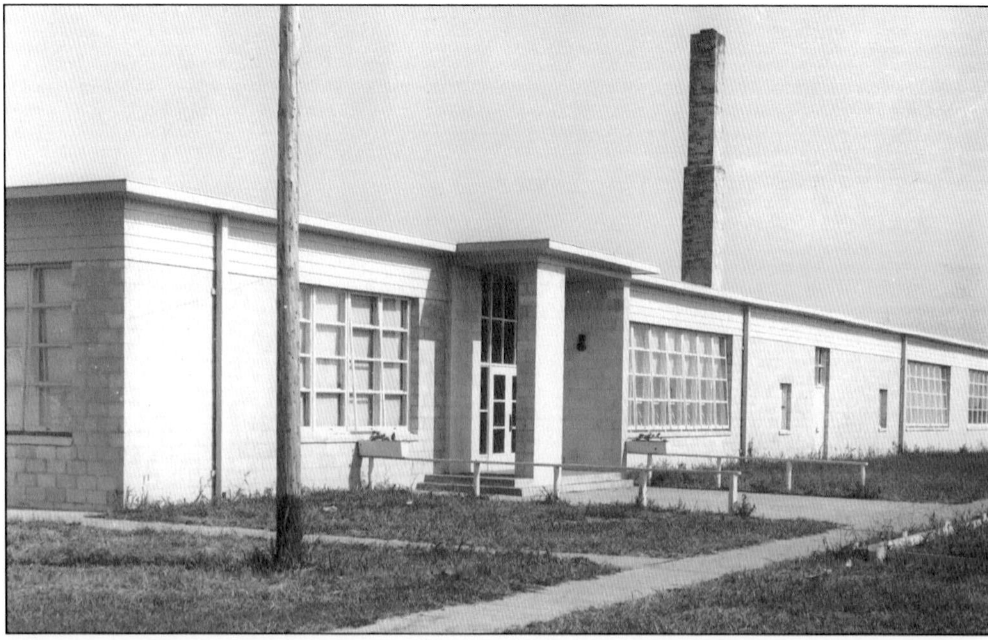

The 10-room Spencer Park School was built by the Navy in 1944, at Fifth Avenue and C Street. Principal Viola Elliott started the first hot lunch program in the city there. The school featured a special classroom equipped for handicapped children. During the war, enrollment was up to 600 students. The school closed in the early 1970s and has since been torn down.

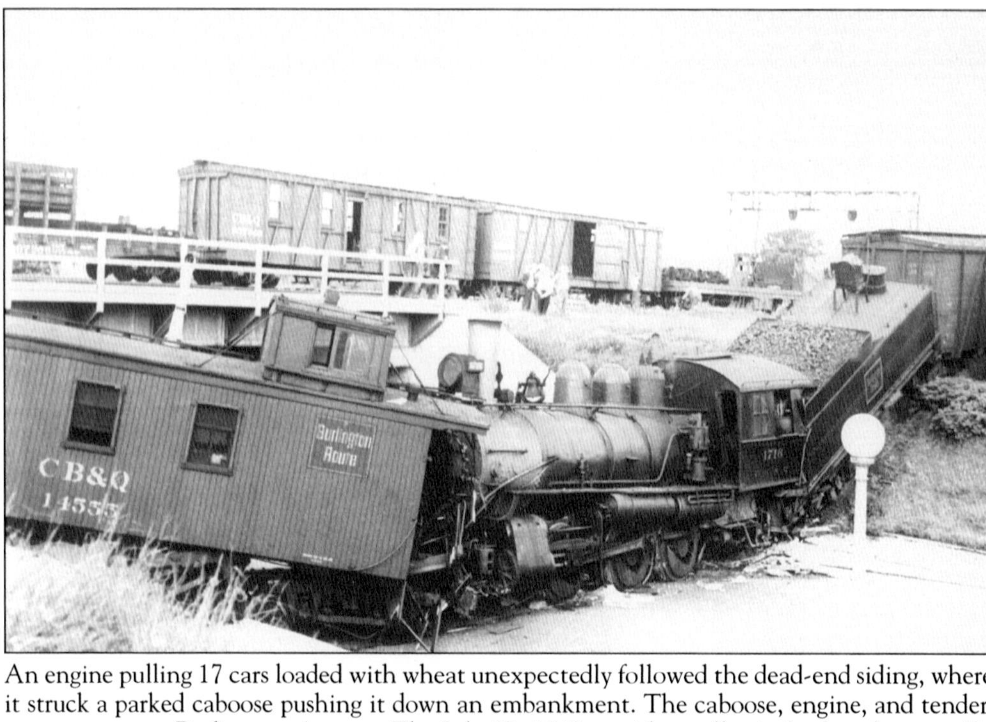


An engine pulling 17 cars loaded with wheat unexpectedly followed the dead-end siding, where it struck a parked caboose pushing it down an embankment. The caboose, engine, and tender, came to rest on Burlington Avenue. The July 27, 1943, accident effectively shut down traffic until the train was removed with a large crane.

Probably the most famous athlete from Hastings was Johnny (Cotney) Hopp. He played major league baseball from 1939 until 1956, for the St. Louis Cardinals, Boston Braves, Pittsburgh Pirates, and the New York Yankees. Hopp "strikes" a pose in his Boston Braves uniform in 1946.

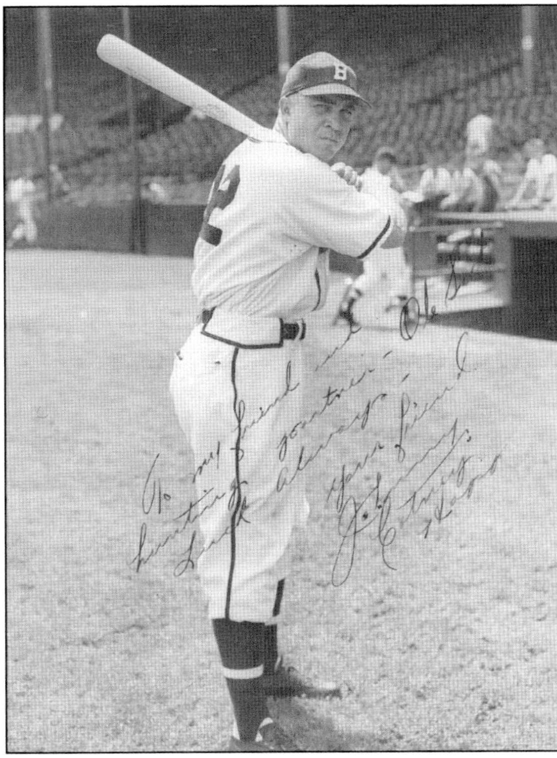

Nebraska has its share of bad weather and storms, including tornadoes and blinding blizzards. The winter of 1948–49 was the worst the city had seen. On the night of November 18, 1948, a massive blizzard completely paralyzed the city. The awnings of several stores, including Montgomery Ward's, sagged or broke under the weight of the snow that completely buried cars.

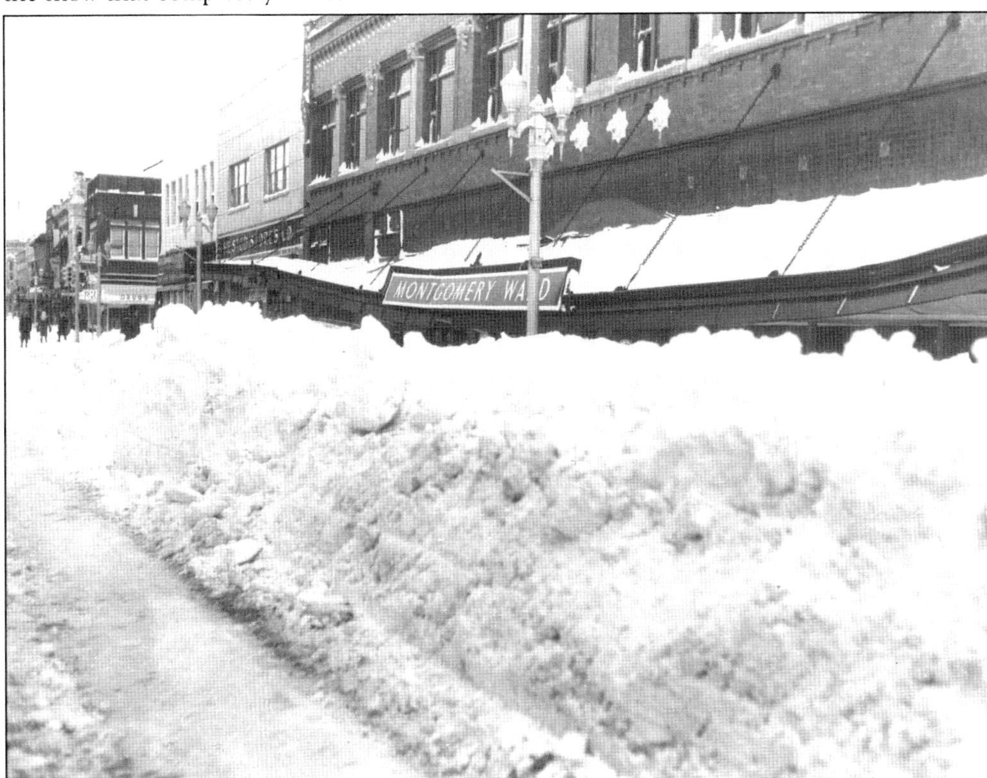

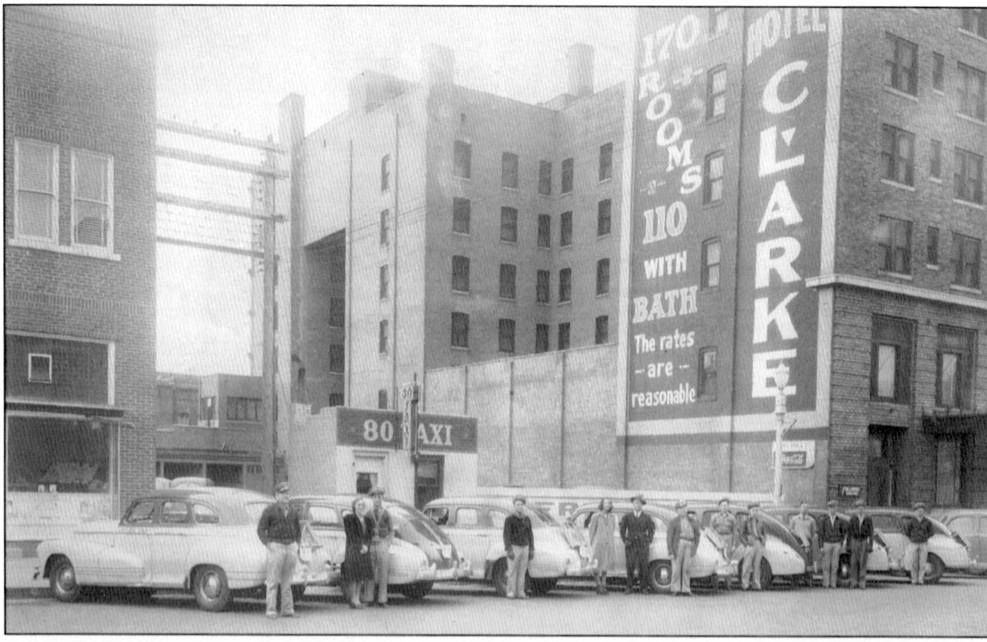


Harry B. Borley operated a hack service in 1879, before changing to freight hauling. In the late 1940s, Hastings had two cab companies, 80 Taxi and the Yellow Cab Company. Cabs and employees of the 80 Taxi Line pose in front of their office near the Clarke Hotel. They are, from left to right: Ben Brown, Lillian and Edgar Johnson, Morris Fuller, Betty Fuller, Homer Fuller (owner), Dean Cropley, Louis Linderman, David Powers, and Lloyd Linderman.

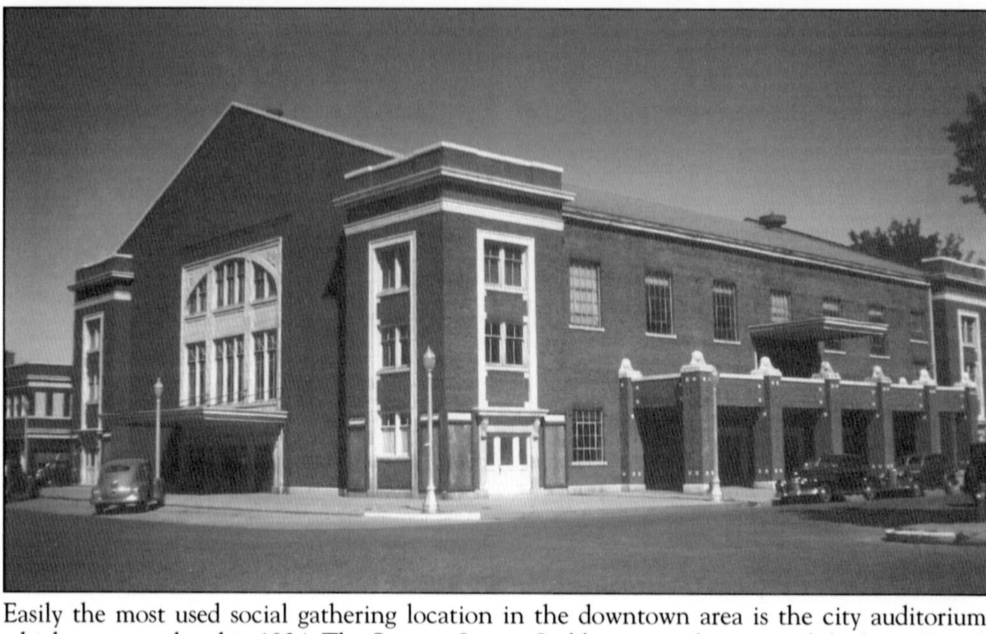

Easily the most used social gathering location in the downtown area is the city auditorium, which was completed in 1924. The Stanner Livery Stable previously occupied the lot at Fourth Street and Hastings Avenue. Activities have been as varied as the times and included a movie theatre, college and high school commencements, Shrine and Odd Fellows conventions, vaudeville shows, political rallies, circus, trade shows, and DARE graduations.

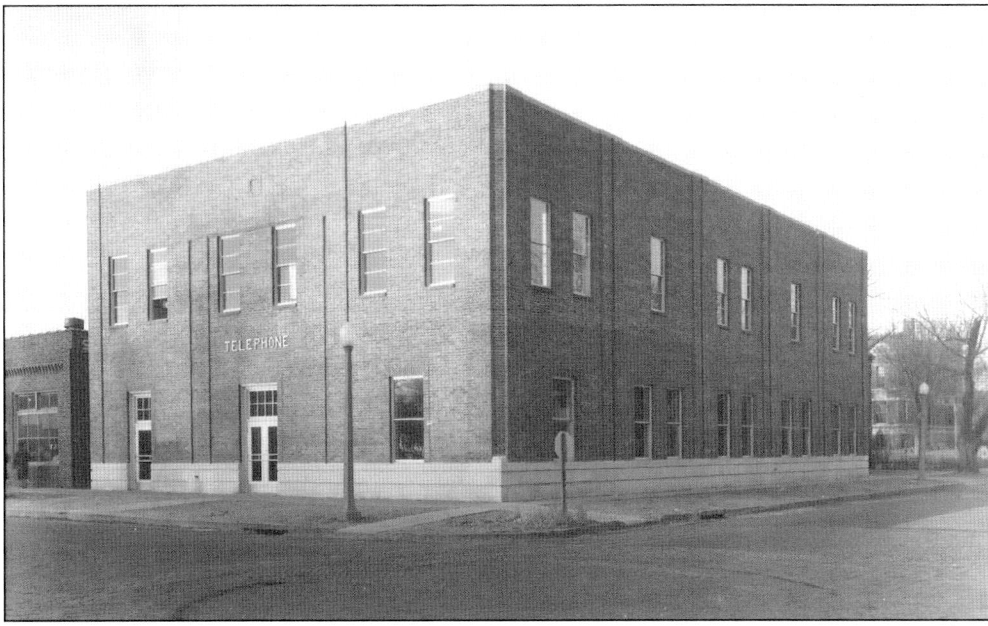


The American Bell Company started the first telephone service in town in 1881. There were 1,500 subscribers by 1903, and the following year the Hastings Independent Telephone Company was established. This 1950 building was constructed by The Lincoln Telephone and Telegraph Co., which absorbed both services in 1914. Today, Alltel Communications provides telephone service.

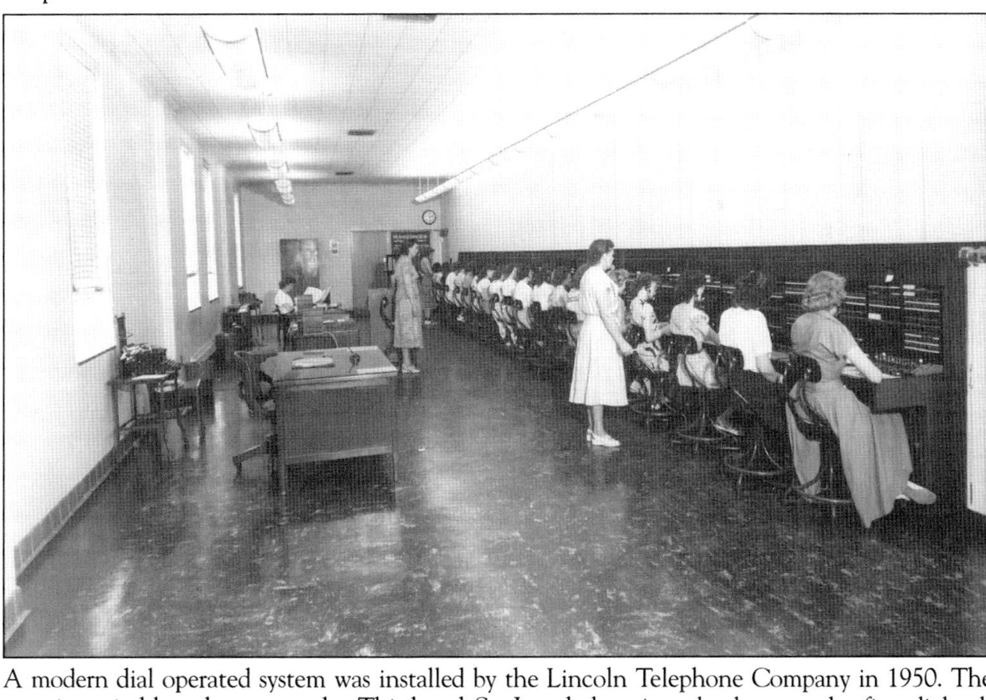

A modern dial operated system was installed by the Lincoln Telephone Company in 1950. The upstairs switchboard room at the Third and St. Joseph location also became the first dial toll center in Nebraska. Long distance operators could call straight through to distant phones for the first time.

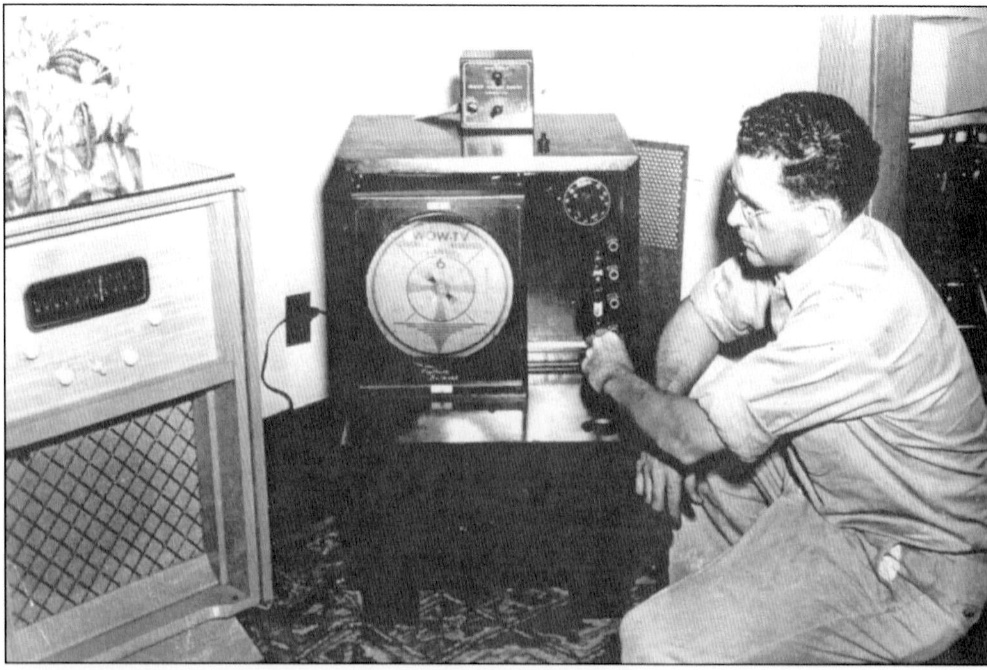


In 1949, the first television set in Hastings was purchased by radio technician Roger Hill. He is shown adjusting the new set. The first television signals did not appear until September 1950, when microwaves relayed programming from the East Coast. KHOL-TV in Axtell, Nebraska, was the first to provide reception in this area.

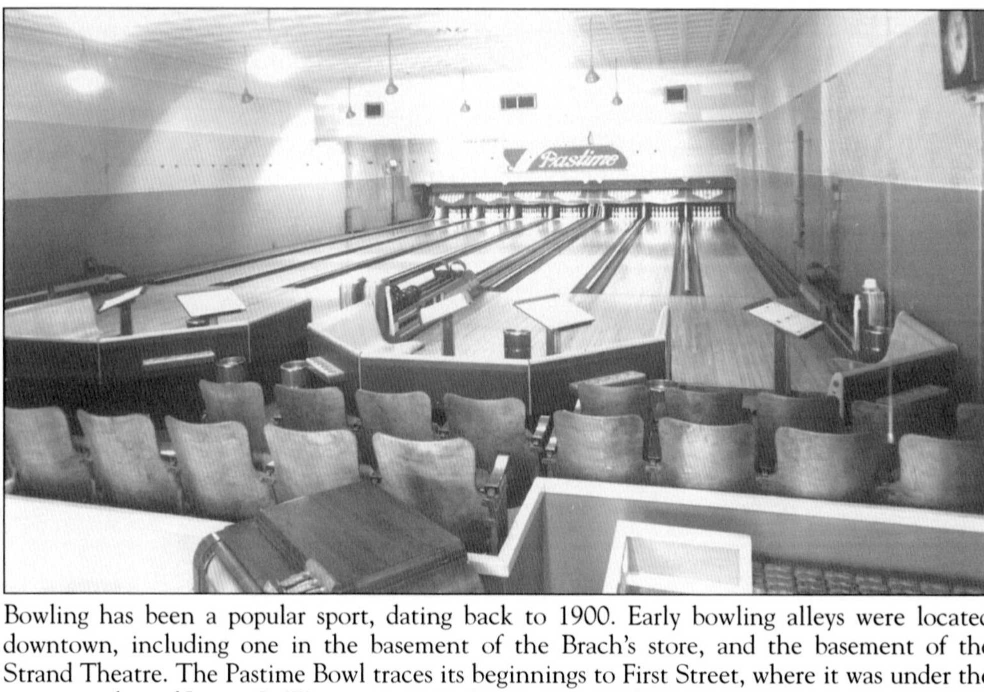


Bowling has been a popular sport, dating back to 1900. Early bowling alleys were located downtown, including one in the basement of the Brach's store, and the basement of the Strand Theatre. The Pastime Bowl traces its beginnings to First Street, where it was under the proprietorship of James C. Watson in 1944. Henry Grasmick soon took over, and his Pastime is shown here in the early 1950s

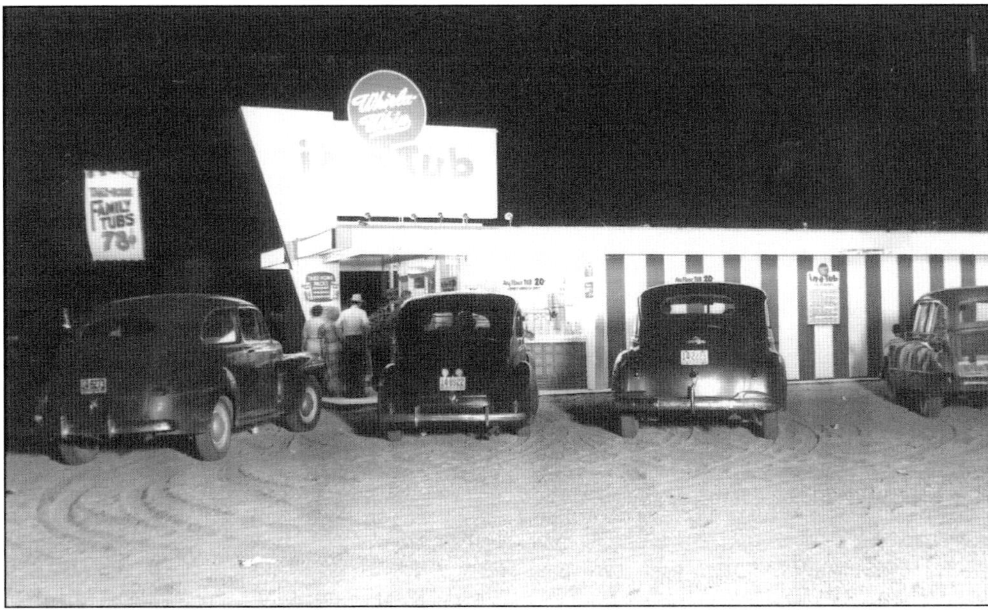


The Whirla-Whip at 1008 South Burlington Avenue (current location of Godfather's Pizza) was a favorite stop for food and ice cream treats. Transforming from window to car-hop service in the 1960s, the drive-in was known for being the south turn-around point for car enthusiasts who enjoyed cruising Burlington Avenue during the summer evenings.

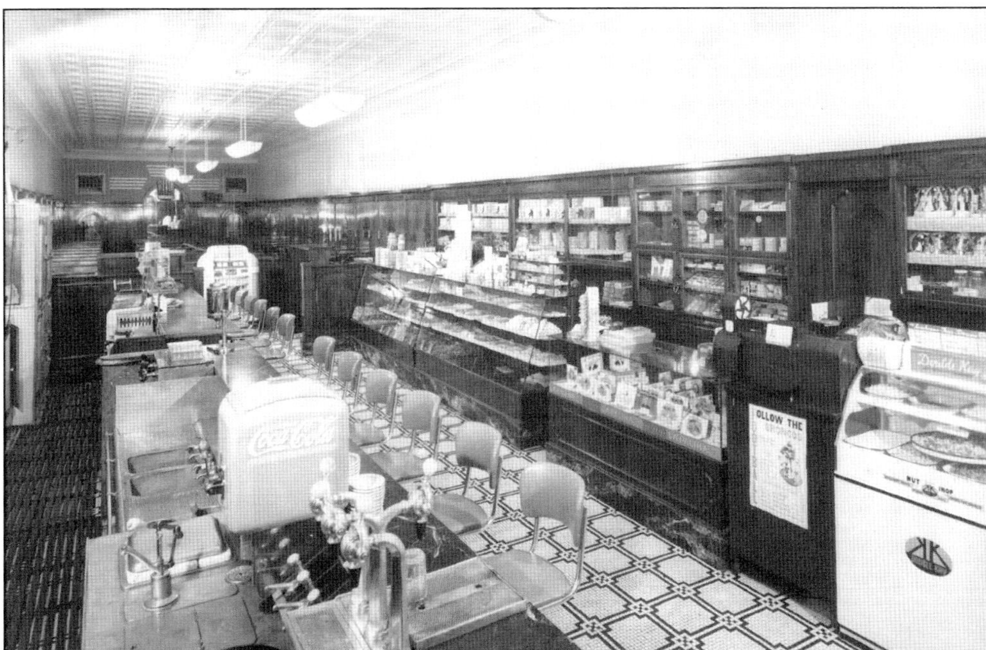


The Queen City Confectionery and Cafe, located at 608 West Second Street, was a social center for years. Downtown shoppers could rest and enjoy meals, sodas, cherry cokes, and sundaes. A fire on September 23, 1926, caused around $40,000 damage to the diner, which was rebuilt and re-opened a few months later. The landmark business closed its doors for the last time in 1955.

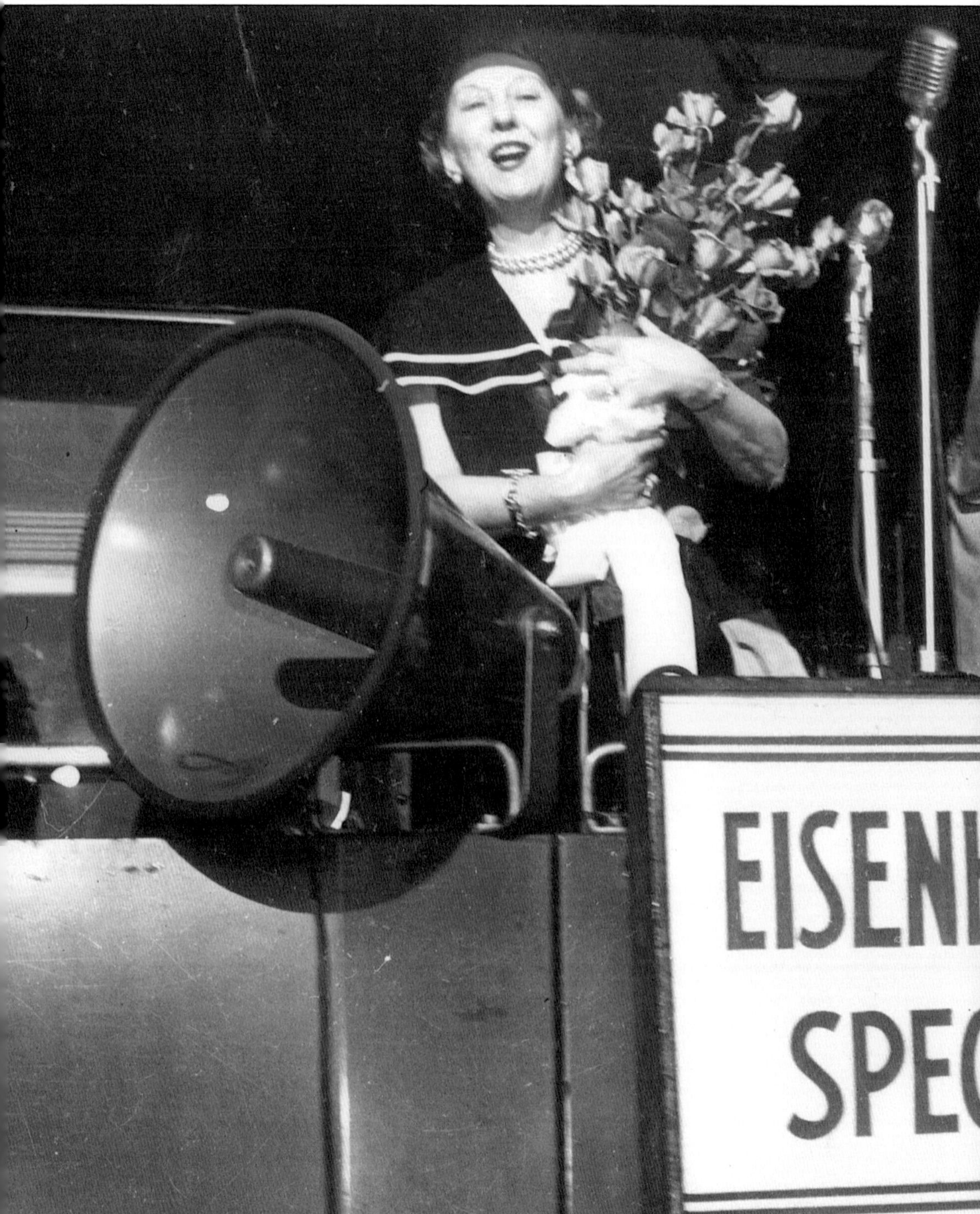


General Dwight D. Eisenhower and wife Mamie stopped at the Burlington Railroad station on July 3, 1952, during his presidential campaign. Past state senator and Hastings businessman, Fred A. Seaton, who served as a campaign staff member, is standing to the right of Eisenhower. Several other presidential visitors have stopped by over the years, such as President Benjamin

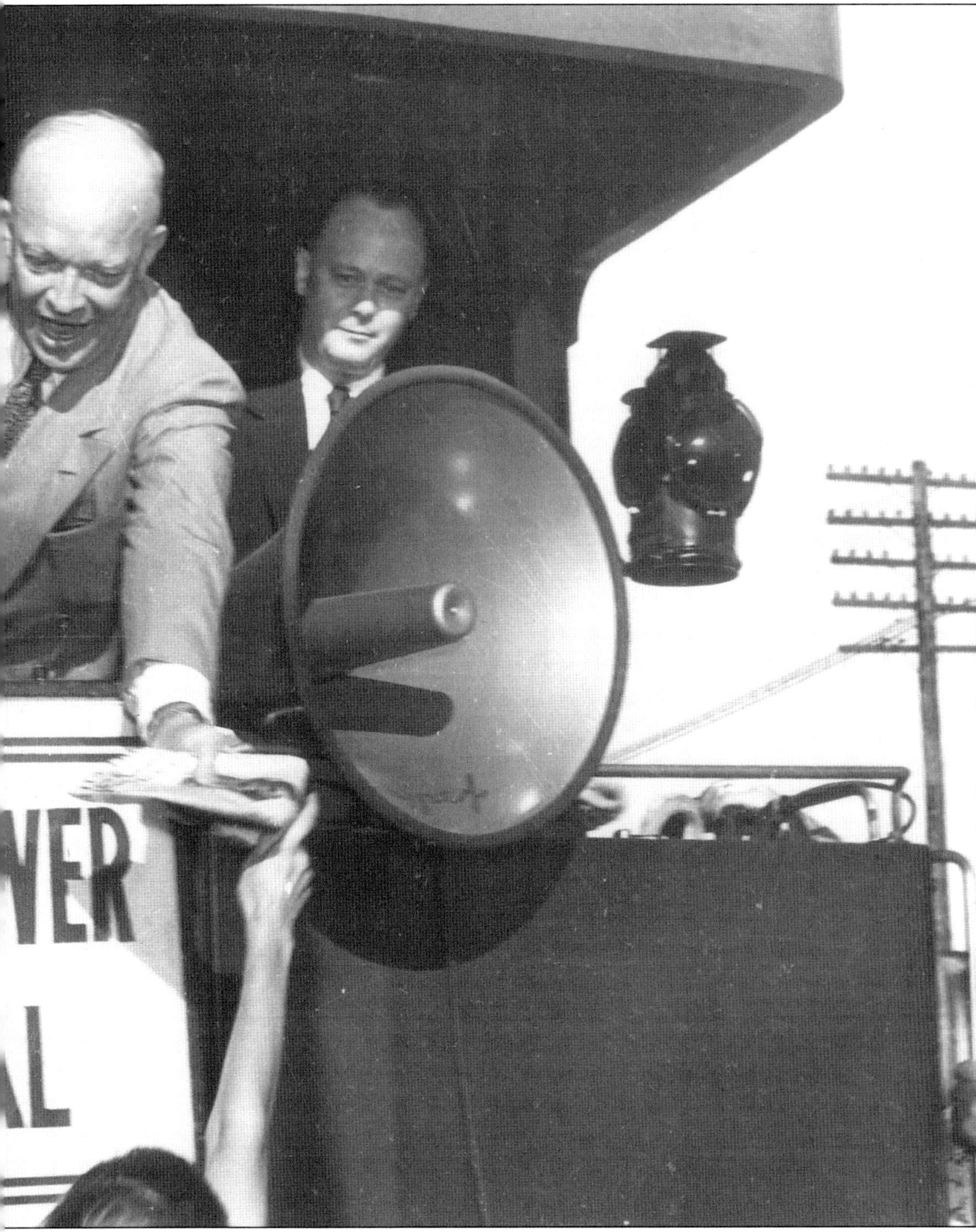

Harrison in 1891, Governor William McKinley in 1893 (he became president in 1897), vice presidential candidate Theodore Roosevelt in 1900, and as President in 1903, President William Howard Taft in 1911, Senator Harry S. Truman in 1943, Senator John F. Kennedy in 1959 (he became president in 1961), and President Ronald W. Reagan in 1988.

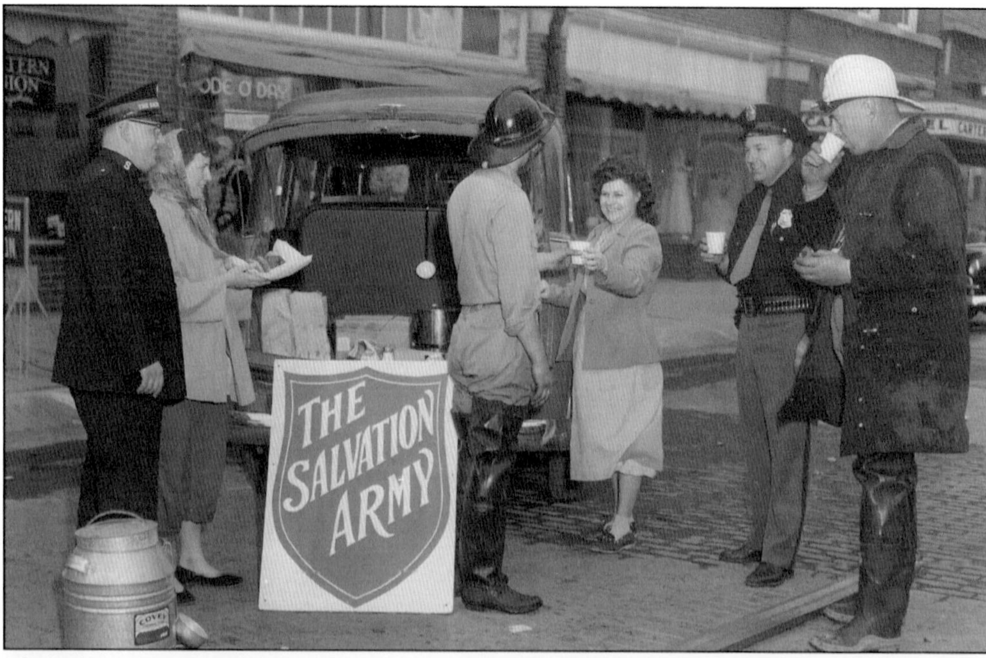


The Salvation Army and the American Red Cross have been valuable relief agencies for many years, particularly through the Depression. During the 1930s, they supplied local residents and transients with necessary food, blankets, and clothing. Transients could sleep in the old city jail overnight and were given a bologna sandwich when they left. The Salvation Army was on the scene of the Coast-to-Coast store fire in 1953, to supply firemen and policemen with coffee and rolls.

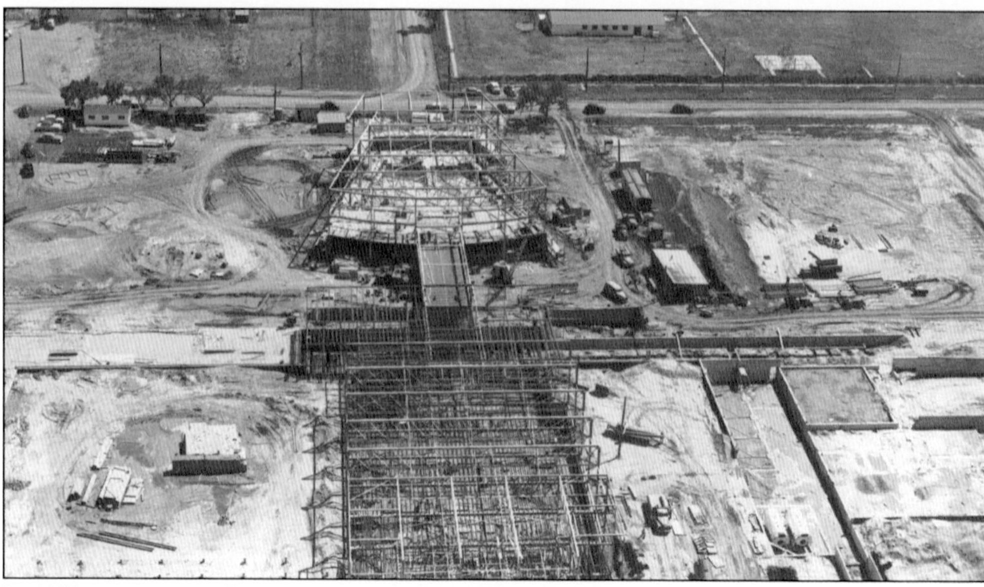

In 1953, construction began on a new senior high school building on the old county fairgrounds property at 14th and Burlington Avenue. Bonds had been approved by voters the previous year, which amounted to $1,790,000. Shown under construction, the new school was dedicated on September 28, 1955, with the U.S. Commissioner of Education, Samuel M. Brownell officiating.

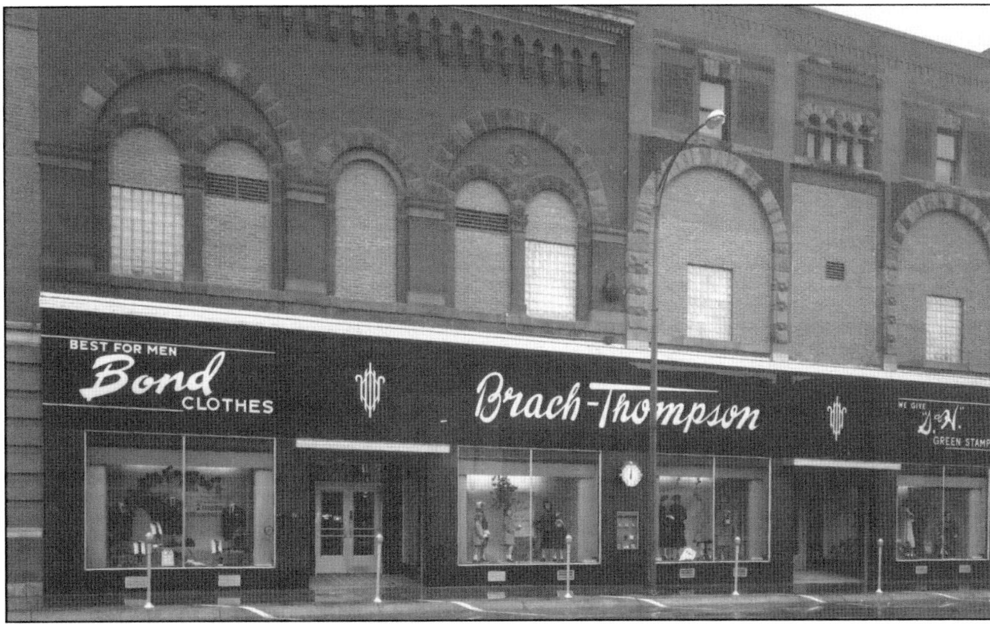


Wolbach's department store was established in 1875. A year later when William Brach joined the firm, it became known as Wolbach and Brach's. Brach became company president in 1907, and by 1953, Burton Thompson was the owner. The ever-popular store even featured a beauty shop. Brach-Thompson's changed hands again in the 1960s, when it was sold to George Schweser, who owned a Nebraska-based department store chain.

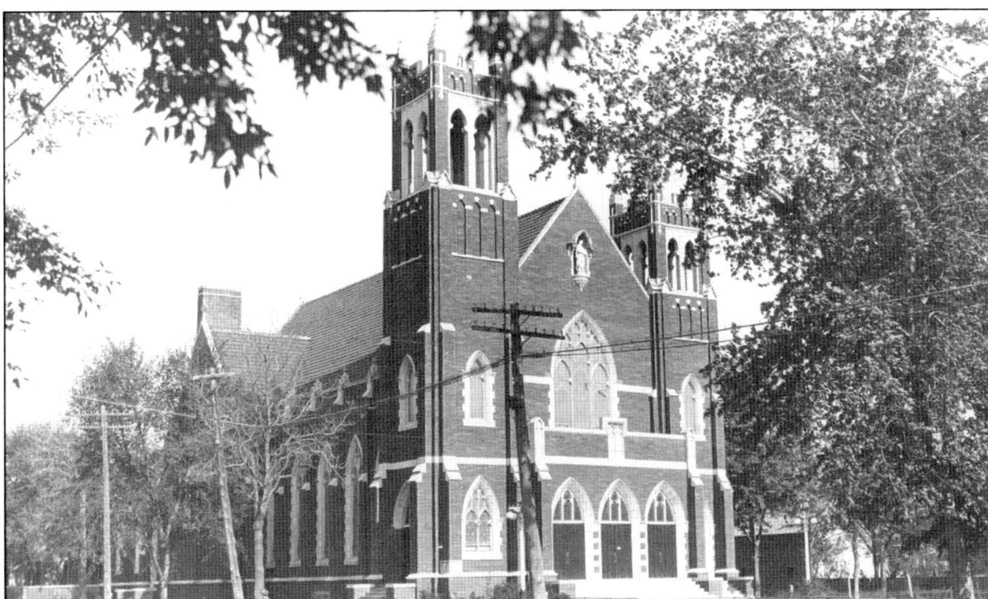

The St. Cecilia's parish in Hastings dates back to 1878. Their first church cost $1,800 to build and was located near Second Street and Minnesota Avenue. The cornerstone for a new church was laid on the southeast corner of Seventh Street and Kansas Avenue, with dedication taking place in December 1912. The block from Kansas to Colorado Avenue now contains the church, a rectory, convent and chapel for nuns, and school gymnasium.

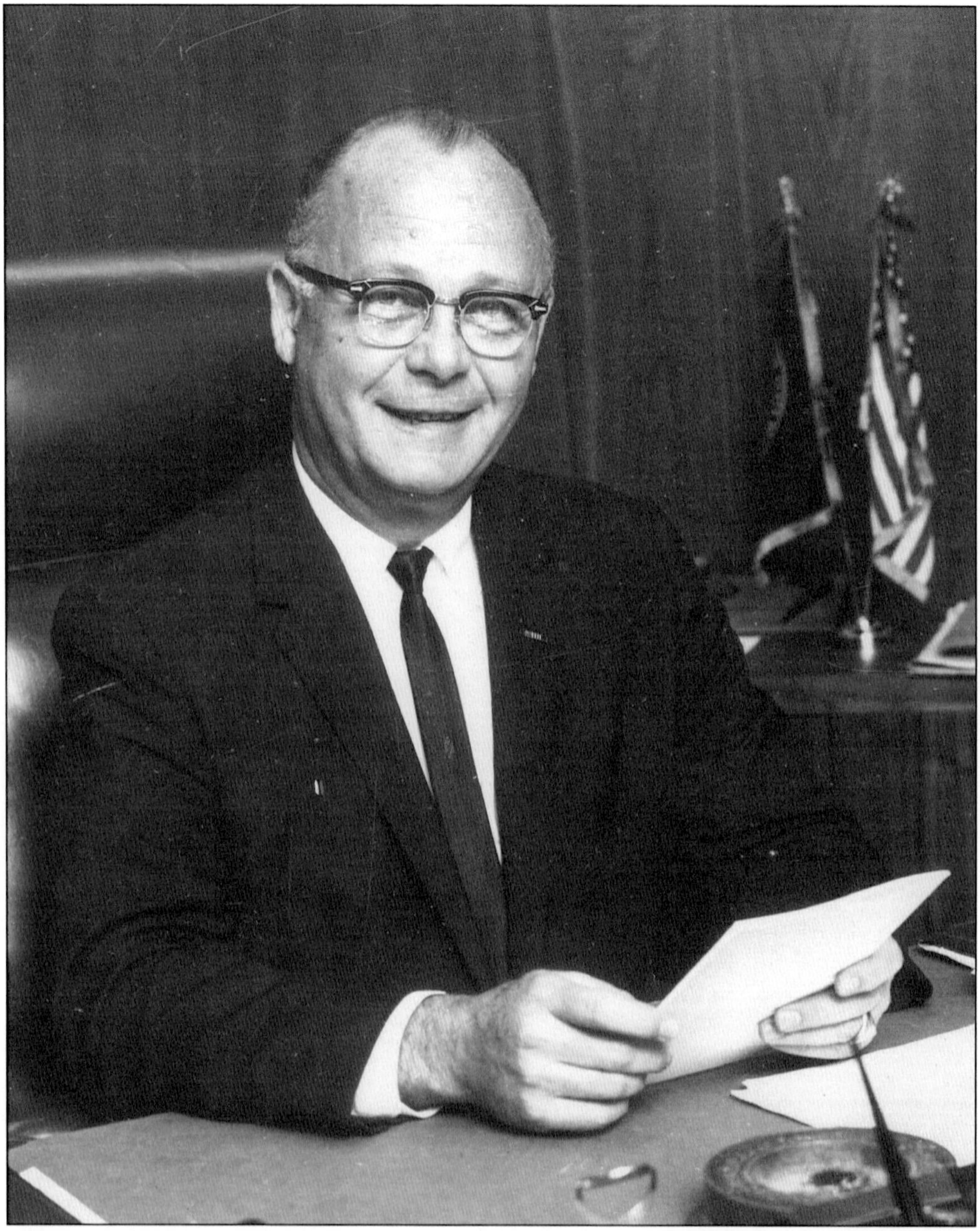

Fred A. Seaton began learning the newspaper business while attending high school and college in Manhattan, Kansas. The Seatons purchased the *Hastings Tribune* in 1937. Fred demanded high quality work from his employees, which helped to significantly increase circulation. The Seatons added to their enterprises by acquiring newspapers in Alliance, Nebraska; Winfield and Coffeyville, Kansas; Sheridan, Wyoming; and Lead, South Dakota. They also owned radio stations in Manhattan and Coffeyville, Kansas, as well as Hastings. The Seaton Group also owned KHAS-TV in Hastings. Fred Seaton was also a successful politician, having been elected to the state legislature in 1945 and 1947. In 1951, he was appointed to fill a vacancy for a U.S. Senator from Nebraska. He was appointed Assistant Secretary of Defense by President Eisenhower, and later served at the White House and as Secretary of the Interior.

*Four*

# A Future of Progress 1960–2001

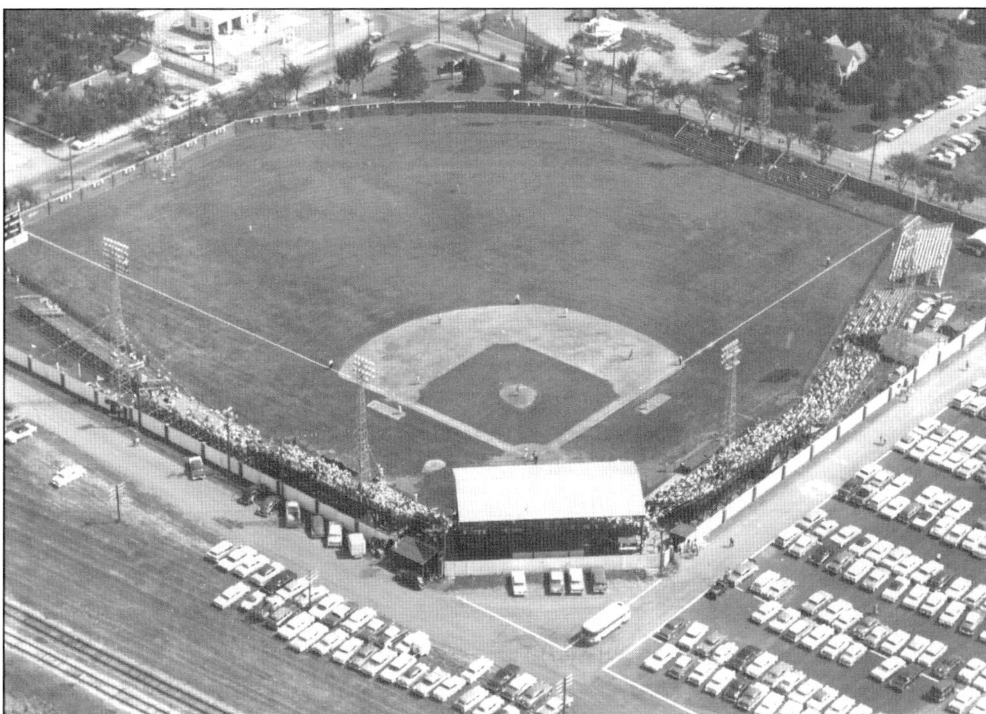

Pershing Field at South Street and Elm Avenue was dedicated on October 7, 1941, exactly two months before the Japanese attack on Hawaii. In 1948, it was renamed Duncan Field, in honor of Don Duncan who had passed away. Duncan had been very active in youth baseball. The field is home to the American Legion Junior Baseball team, who hosted the Little World Series tournaments in 1959, '60, '61, and '69.

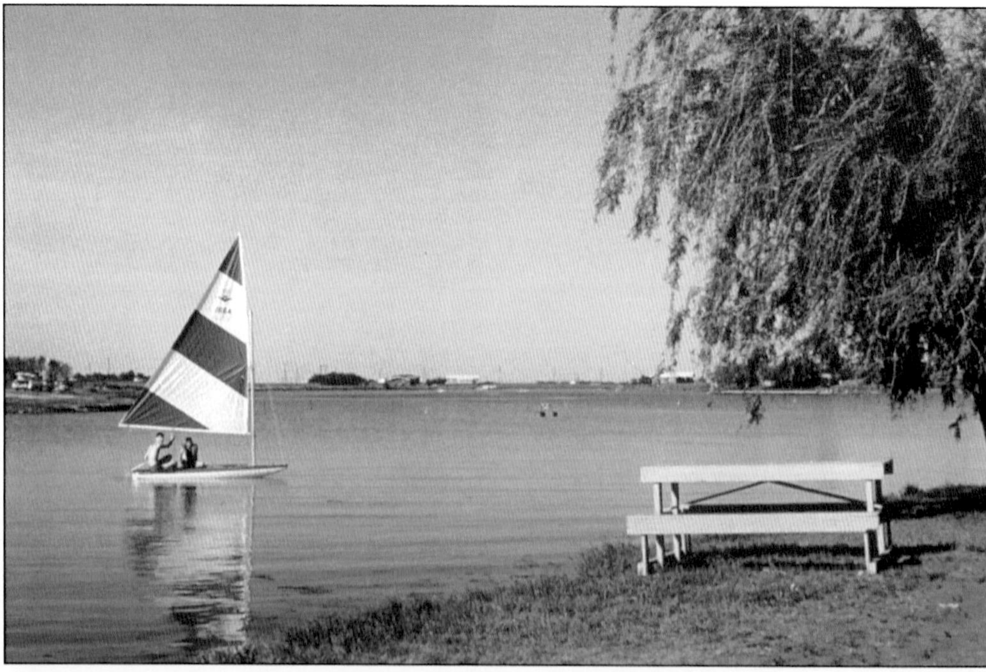

The concept for a lake originated during a city council meeting in 1955, when Mayor C. Wendell Foote spoke about new recreational facilities for the city. Land at the northwest edge of town was purchased from Frank Rodine, and Hastings Lake became the largest park in the city system at 60 acres. Water is supplied by the overflow from steam powered generators at the utility plant. Oliver Wendell, Ben Sherman, and the Nielsen brothers gave easements for development of a residential area around the east end of the lake.

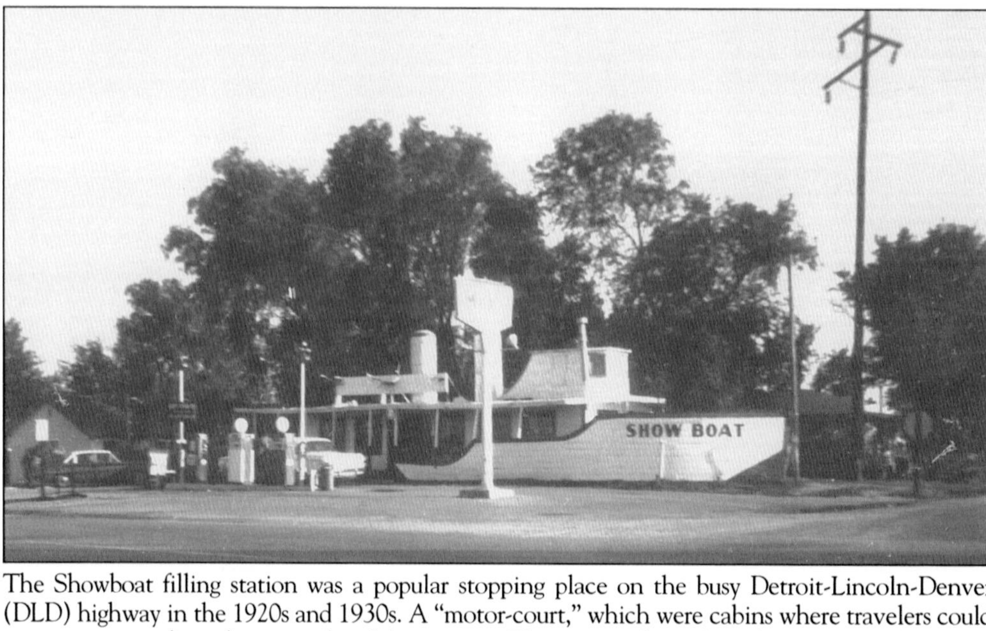


The Showboat filling station was a popular stopping place on the busy Detroit-Lincoln-Denver (DLD) highway in the 1920s and 1930s. A "motor-court," which were cabins where travelers could stay, was situated on the east side of the station. The unique, boat shaped structure—which was located on the southeast corner of Highway Six and Showboat Road—has since been demolished.

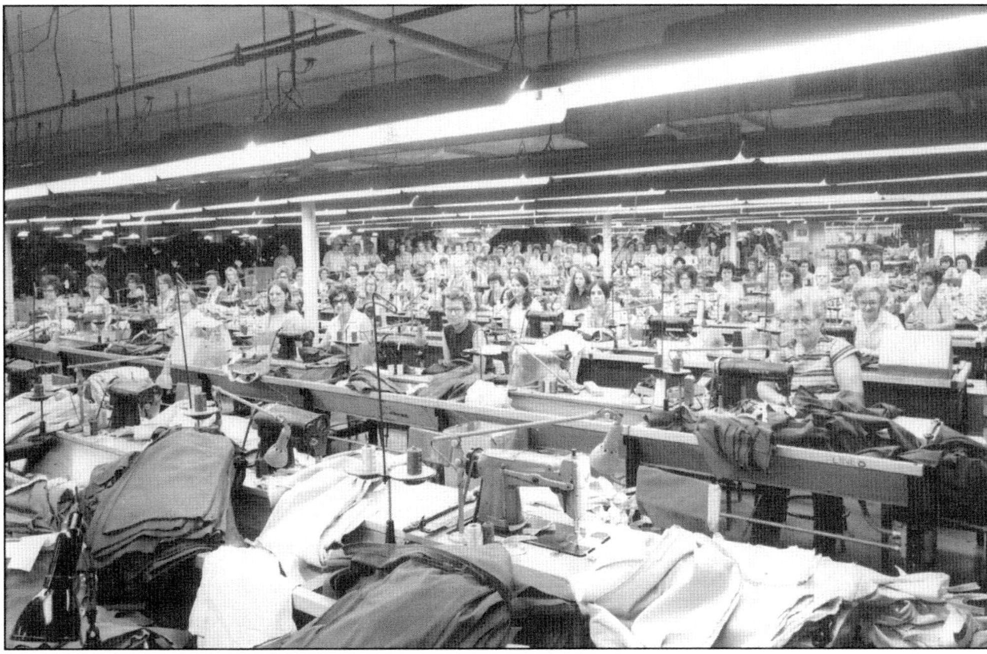

The 130 employees of the Mode O'Day plant stop their work while a photographer snaps a picture. The company, a division of Gamble-Skogmo, Inc., manufactured women's dresses, blouses, uniforms, lingerie, and sportswear. Mode O'Day was located on East South Street near Duncan Field.

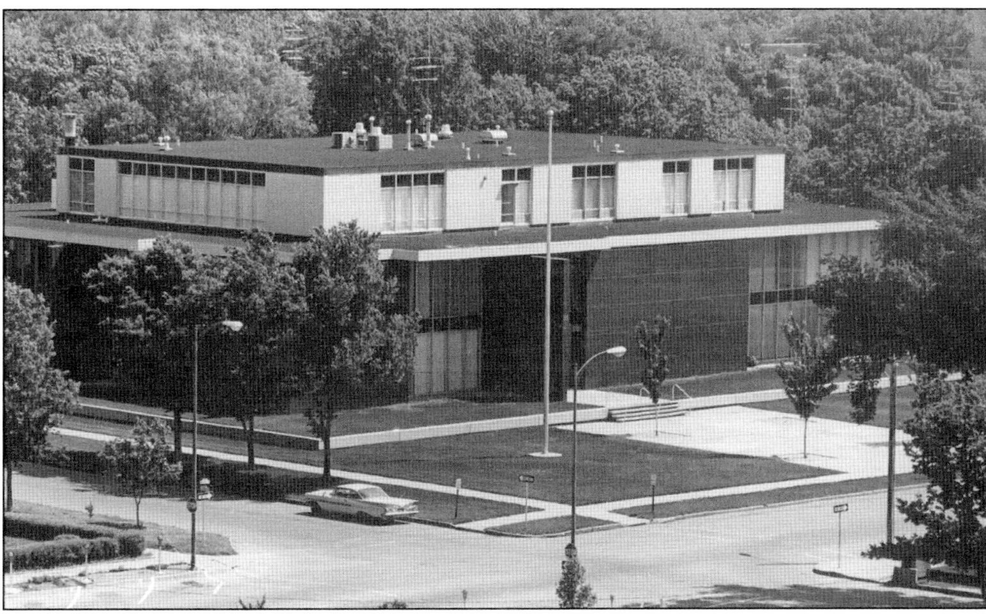

Open house for the county's new courthouse was held in August 1964. The 64,000-square-foot building is made of marble, granite, aluminum, and carrara glass. The exterior features 800 slabs of red granite from South Dakota. A popular feature of the new courthouse was a small pool and fountain, which was inhabited by a variety of small fish. Located on the main floor, it was removed during a major remodeling project in 2000.

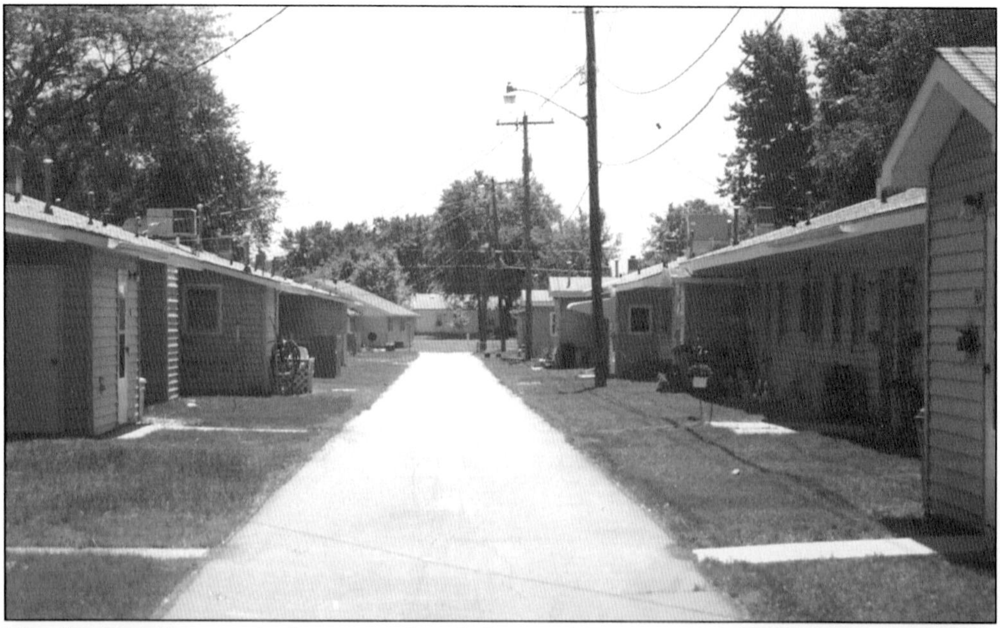

The Hastings Housing Authority purchased the naval housing area called Spencer Park from the government in 1954. The Good Samaritan Society became interested, bought the property, and remodeled the units for the elderly. Good Samaritan Village is now the largest retirement community in the state, with over 900 residents and 375 employees.

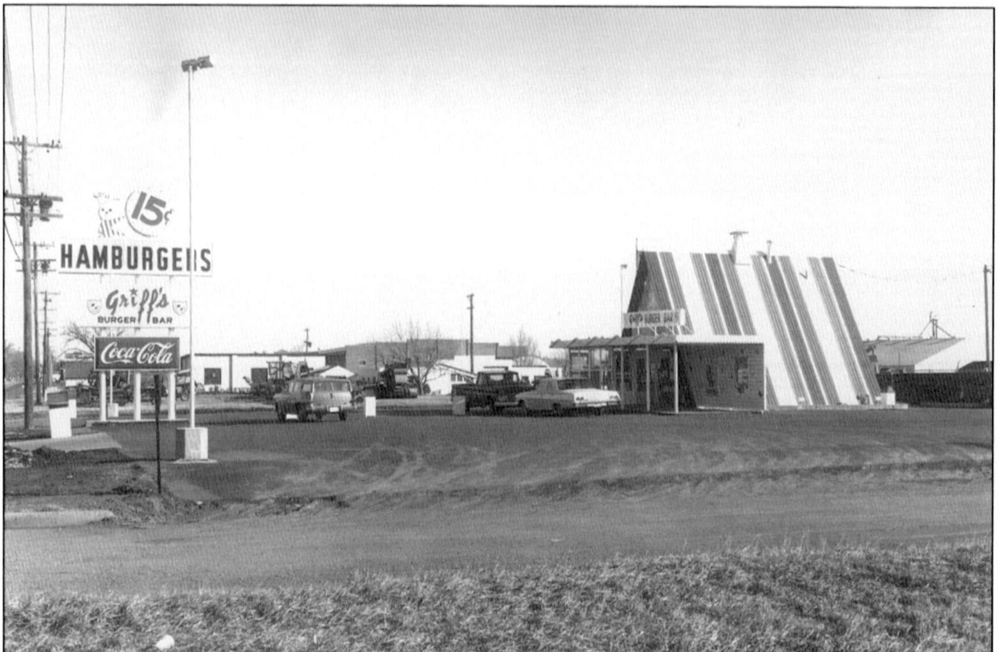


By the 1950s and '60s, eating out became more popular, partly due to booming fast food, hamburger stands, and drive-ins. Customers could walk up to, or inside to get their orders, or be served in their car. Popular Hastings drive-ins included: A&W, Dandy's 15¢ Hamburgers, Whirla-Whip, and Griff's Burger Bar, which was located at 2017 West Second Street.

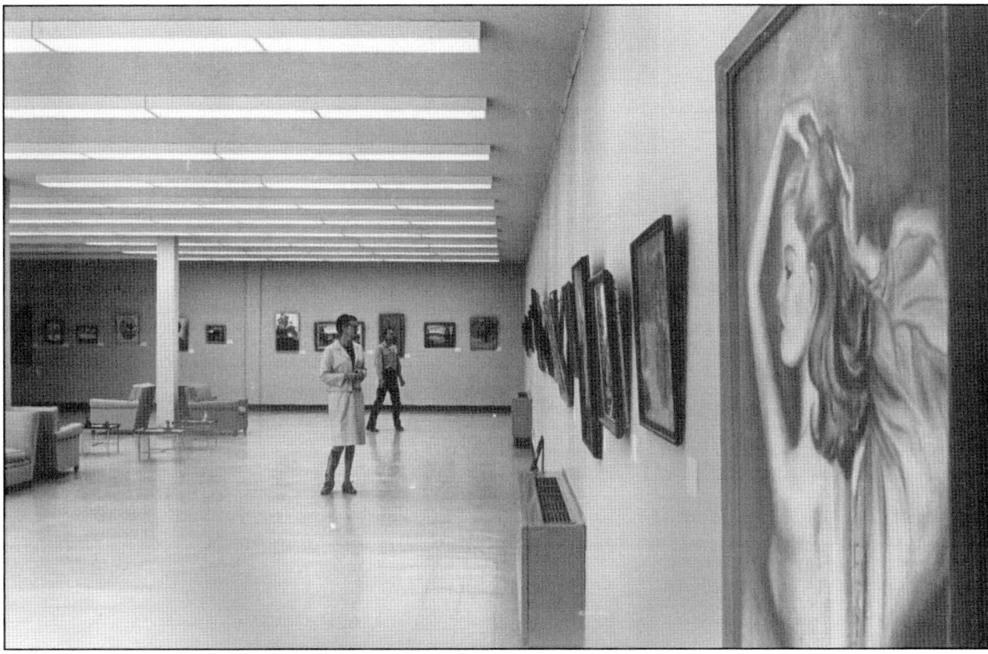

Mrs. George Classen, Mrs. J.M. Davis, and Mrs. Blanche Garratt organized an art exhibit at the House of Yesterday, in 1961. The purpose of the exhibit was to ascertain the amount of local art activity in Hastings. The response was so overwhelming that space became a problem. As a result, the Hastings Art Club was formed that fall. The city library was one of several locations that the club used for displays.

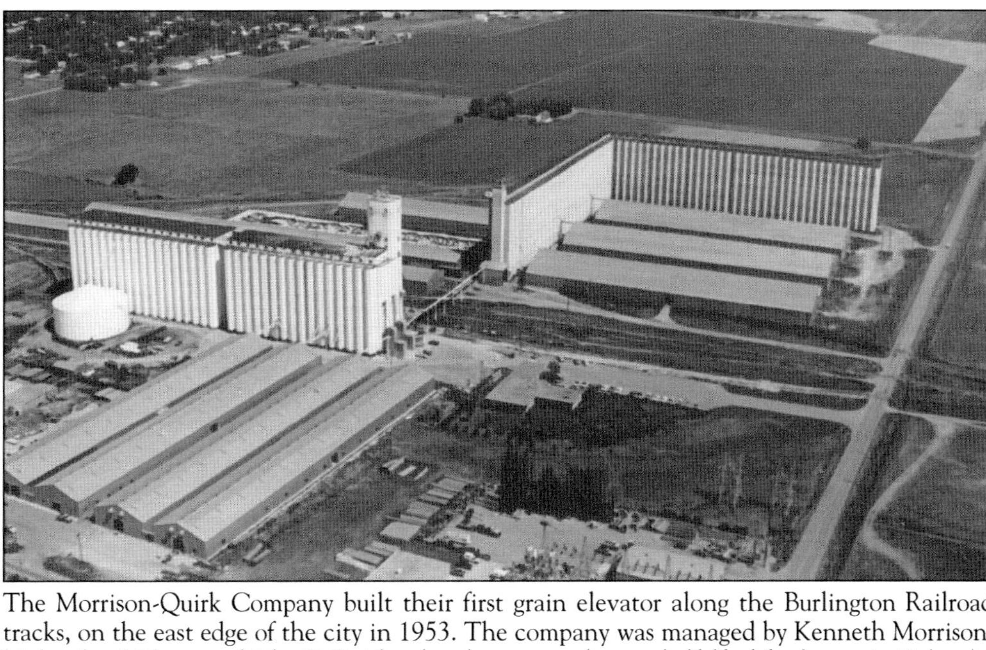

The Morrison-Quirk Company built their first grain elevator along the Burlington Railroad tracks, on the east edge of the city in 1953. The company was managed by Kenneth Morrison, his brother Milton, and John P. Quirk, who also operated several alfalfa dehydrators in Nebraska and Iowa. Cattle feeding and farming were also part of their enterprises. The expanded elevator complex shown had a 23-million bushel capacity.

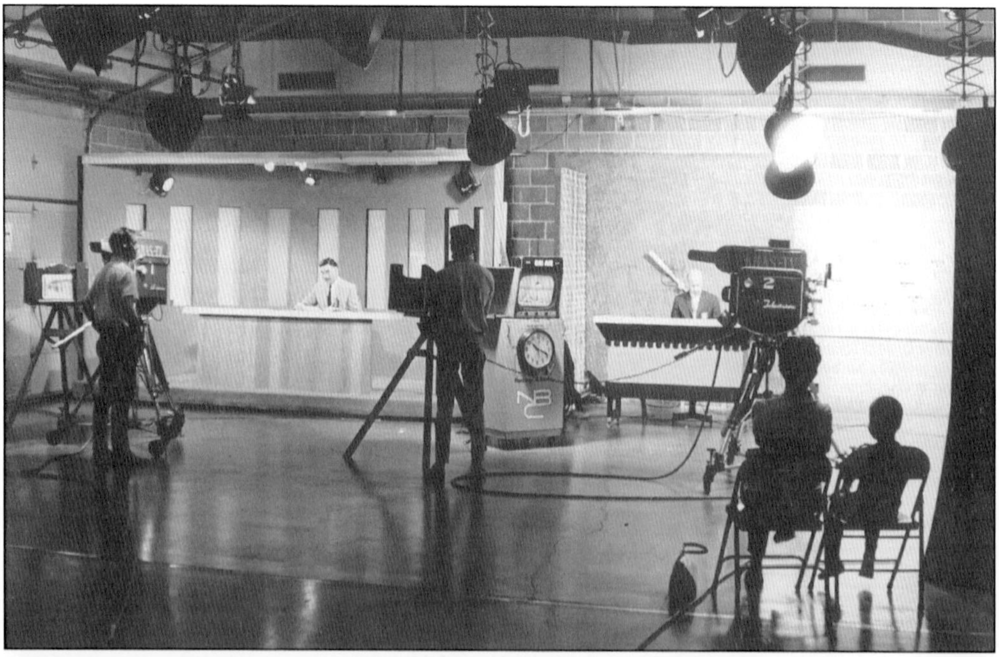

On January 1, 1956, KHAS-TV, Channel 5, went on the air. The NBC affiliate was owned by the Nebraska Television Corporation with Fred Seaton (president), Duane Watts (vice president and general manager), Lloyd Kissinger (secretary), and Fred Irons (treasurer). News anchor Lloyd Thomas (left) and sportscaster Dave Hill are shown giving the 10:00 news.

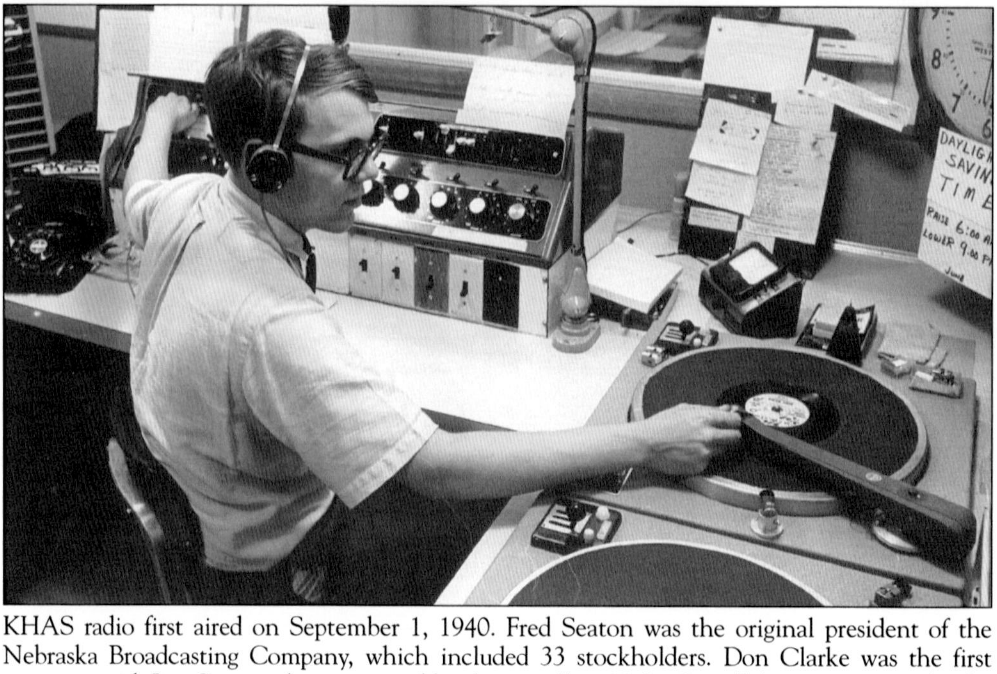

KHAS radio first aired on September 1, 1940. Fred Seaton was the original president of the Nebraska Broadcasting Company, which included 33 stockholders. Don Clarke was the first treasurer, with Jim Conway (secretary and legal counsel) and John Powell (station manager). The station was located in the *Tribune* building until recently relocating to the KICS radio building. On May 25, 2001, a new radio station, KLIQ, "The Breeze," began broadcasting from Hastings.

One of the most identifiable landmarks in the city is the Fisher Rainbow Fountain, which is located in front of the utilities building. The fountain was built for an electrical exposition at the 1932 county fair, and named for reigning mayor Jacob Fisher. It continues to delight all who watch its night-time streams of colored water (or is it Kool-Aid?). A variety of built-in colored floodlights provide the many beautiful hues.

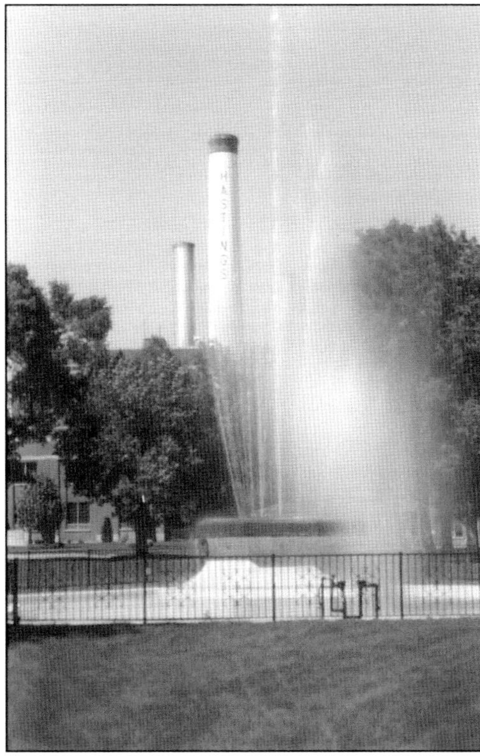

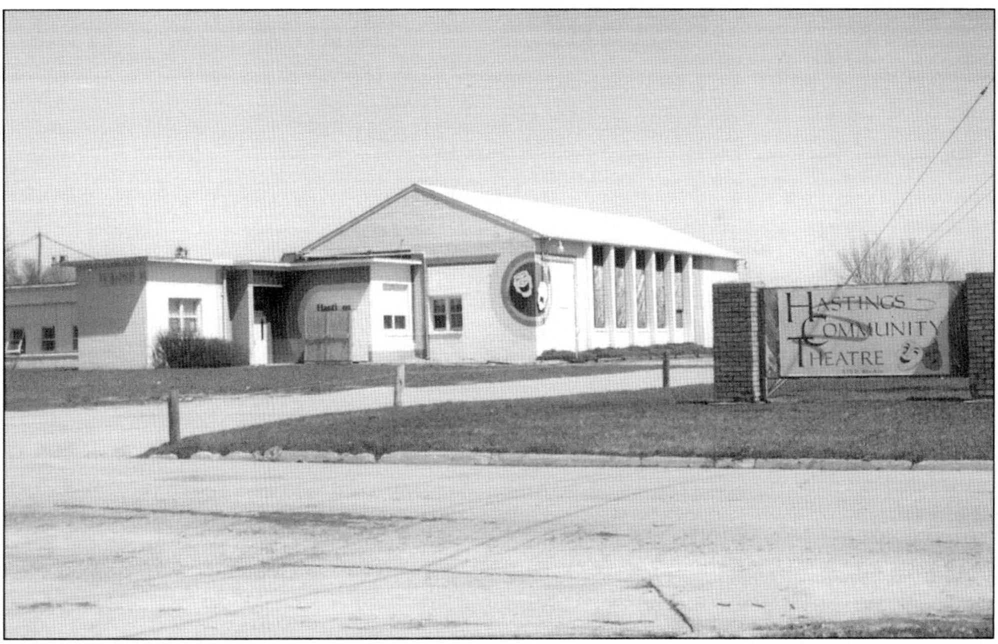


The Hastings Little Theatre was organized in 1927, and featured "Rollo's Wild Oat" for the March 23 opener. A. Lawrence Mortensen, a high school speech teacher, organized the company, which operated until 1938. In 1959, Milton E. Hoffman and others established the Hastings Community Theatre. They performed at several different locations until Good Samaritan Village donated a building rent-free in 1979. The HCT is in their 42nd year of fine productions.

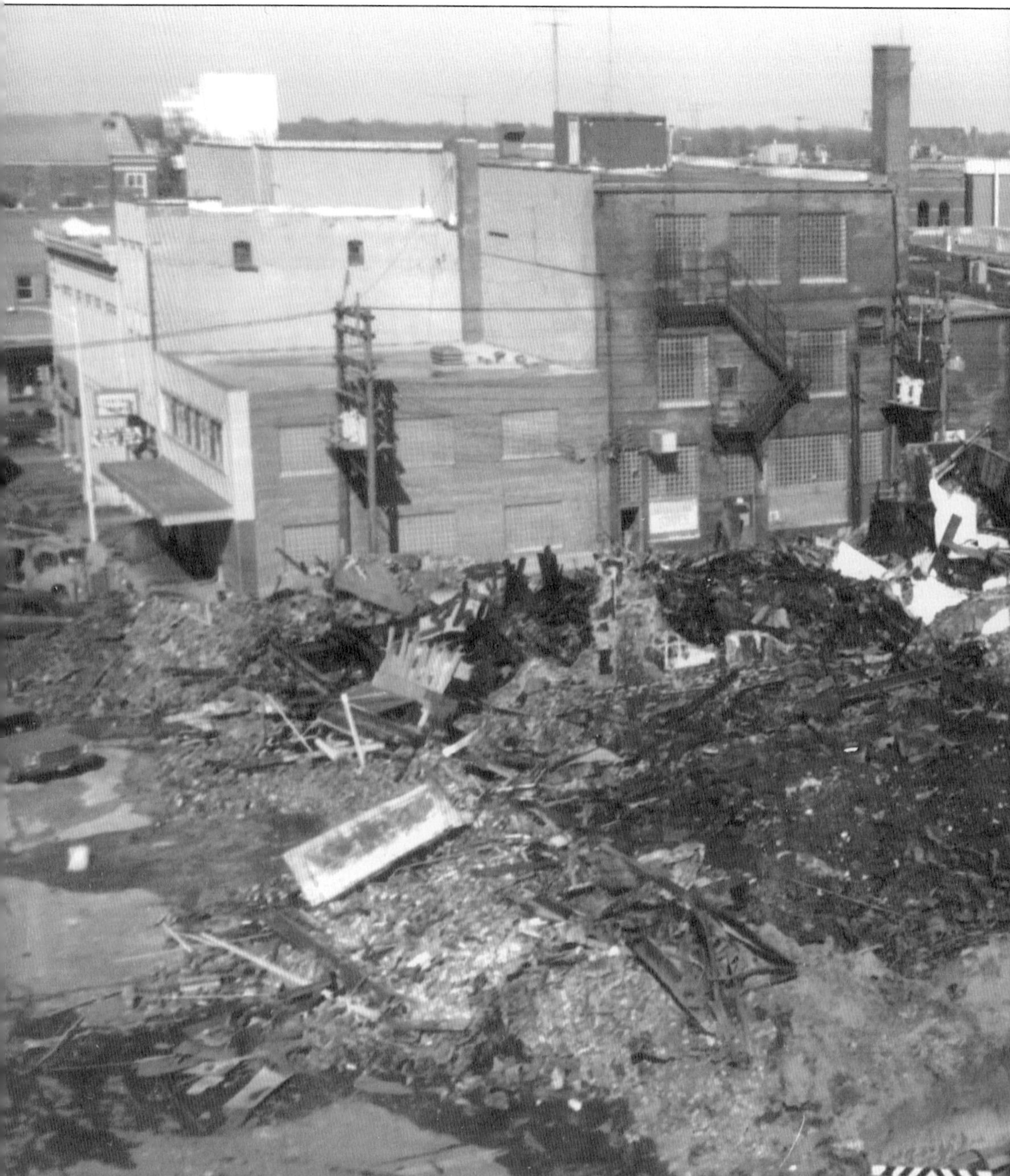

In the early morning hours of February 10, 1979, police patrol officers converged on First Street and Hastings Avenue. A loud boom and orange flash over the downtown area brought the officers to the scene. What they saw resembled a war torn European city during World War II. An explosion and resultant fire, caused by a leaking gas main, destroyed three businesses—Wickerland, Victory Barber Shop, and Ben Sherman's Clothing. The blast shattered windows, ejecting merchandise onto the sidewalks over a four-square-block area. Firefighters soon arrived on the scene from their station, which was two blocks away. The fire was under control within

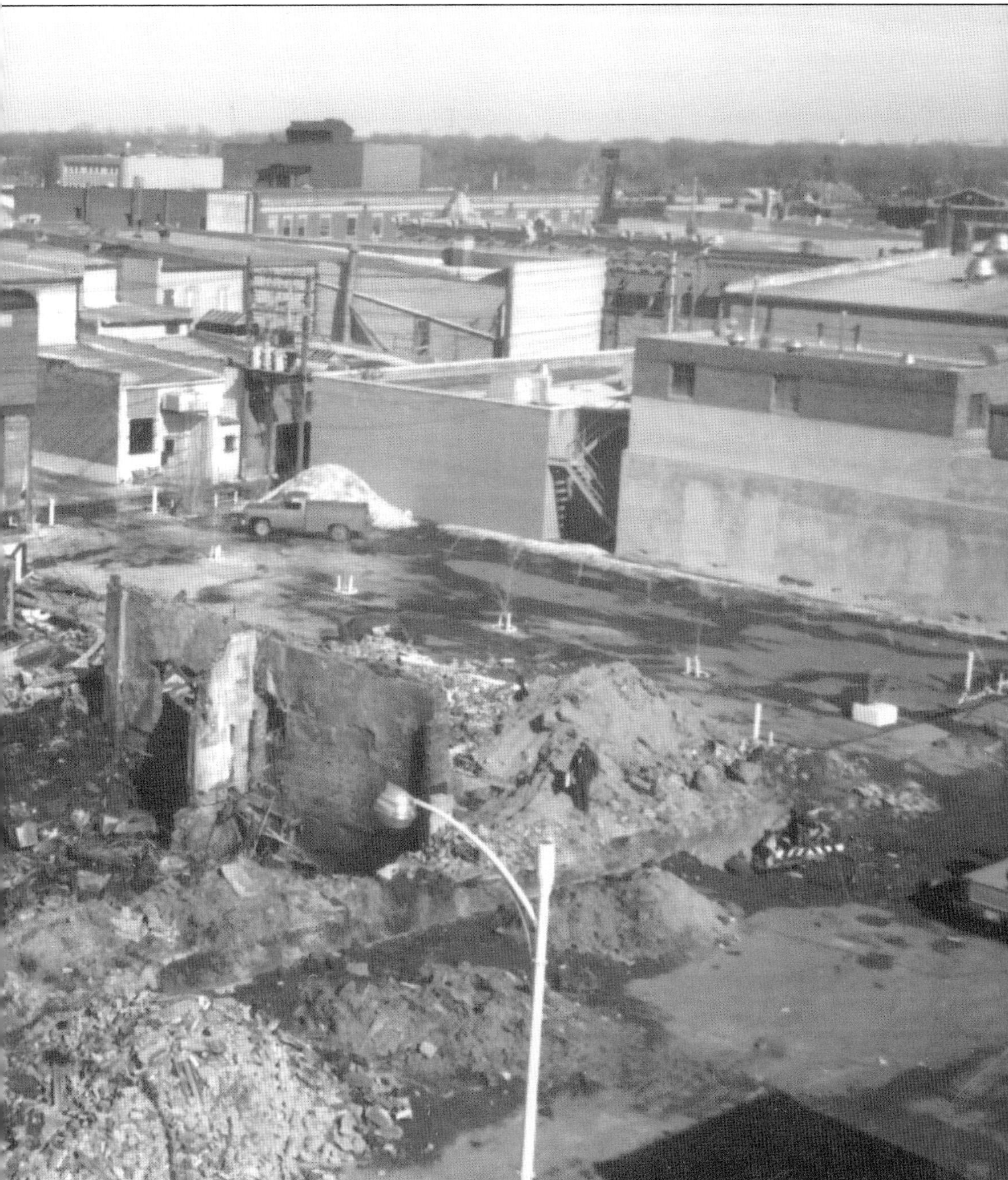

three hours, but required the assistance of over 100 firemen from several area departments. A section of the downtown was cordoned off due to additional reports of leaking gas lines, as well as security concerns for affected businesses. Governor Charles Thone visited the scene the following day and declared it a disaster area. Sixty-five members of the Nebraska National Guard were called in to provide perimeter security, relieving local law enforcement officers. This photo was taken after considerable clean up had taken place.

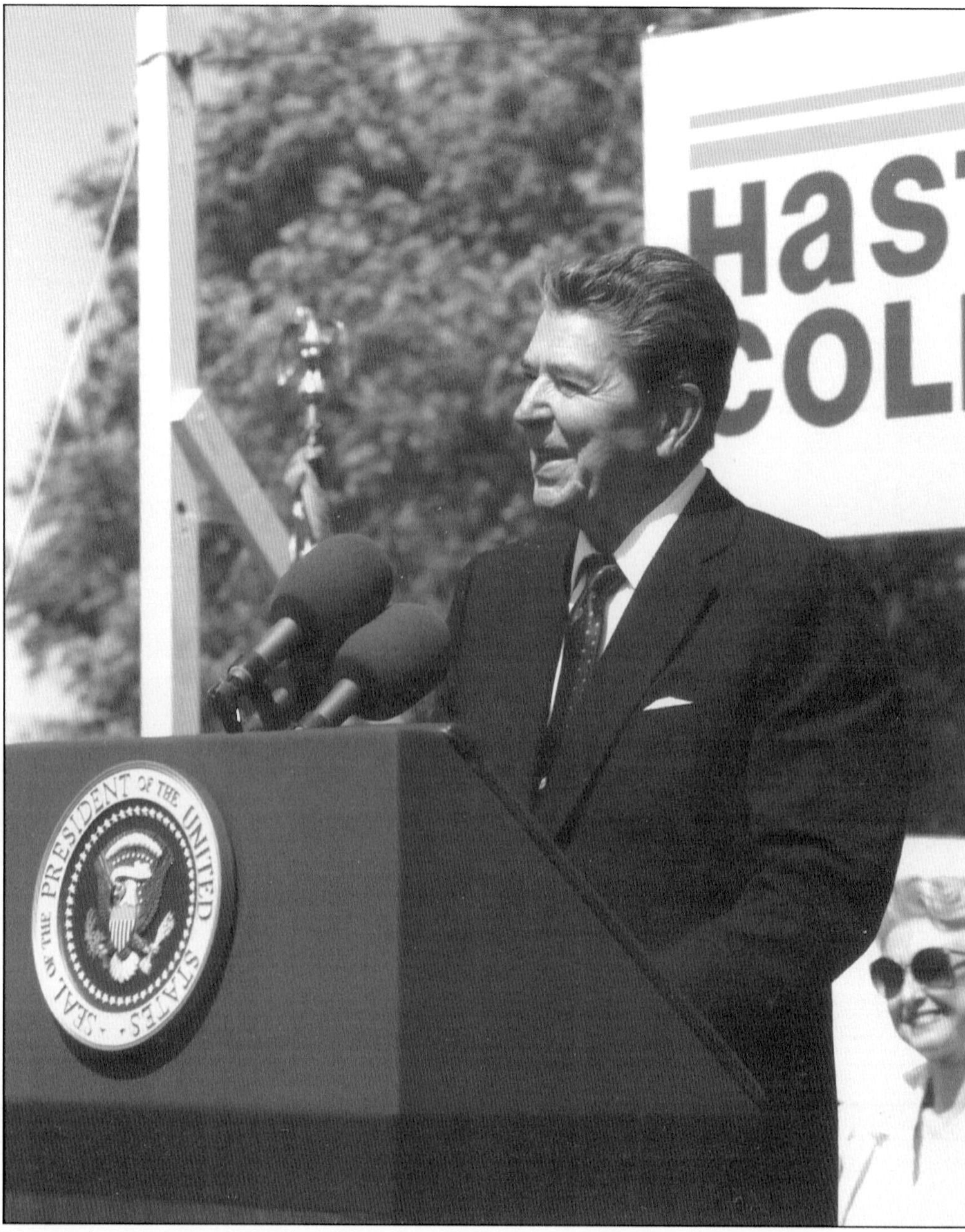


Hastings' most recent presidential visit took place on September 6, 1988, for the dedication of the C. J. and Marie Gray Center for the Communication Arts, at Hastings College. President Ronald Wilson Reagan dedicated the new building and was the first voice heard on the new radio station, "And now it's my pleasure to be the first person to say, radio station KFKX is on the air!" College officials presented the President with an honorary doctorate of communications, in recognition of his past work in radio, television and film, and his notoriety as the "Great Communicator." Upon receiving the doctorate, Reagan lightened the moment by saying, "I always suspected the first degree they gave me was honorary." Speeches were given by Governor Kay Orr, Robert Gray, and local dignitaries, College President, Dr. Thomas Reeves, Dr. Dwayne Strasheim, and Mayor Hal Smith.

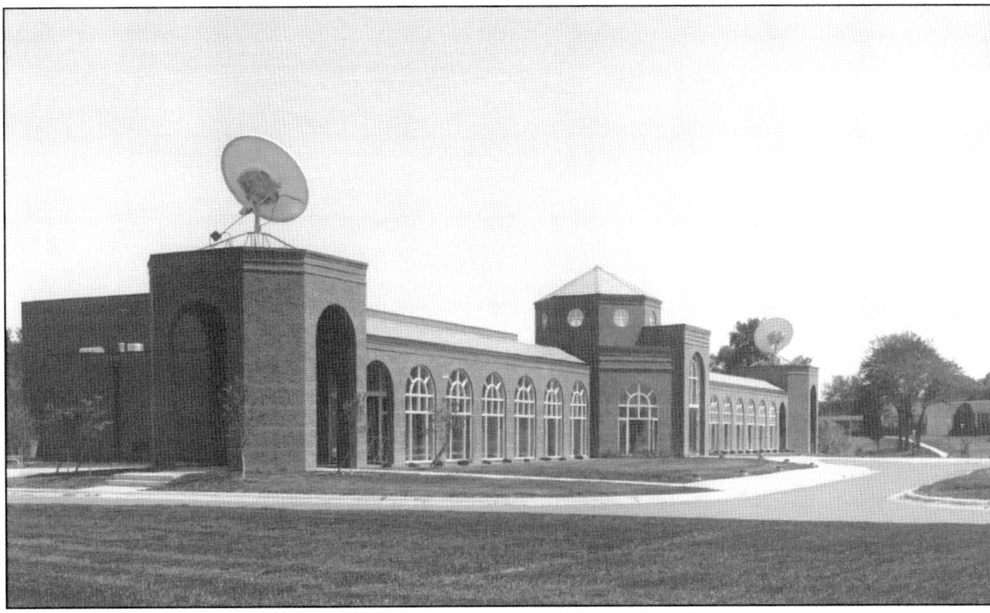

Ground was broken for the C.J. and Marie Gray Center for the Communication Arts, on May 18, 1986, at the Hastings College Campus. The honorable Charles Z. Wick, director of the United States Information Agency officiated. The Gray Center opened for classes in the fall of 1987, and was dedicated by President Reagan the following year.

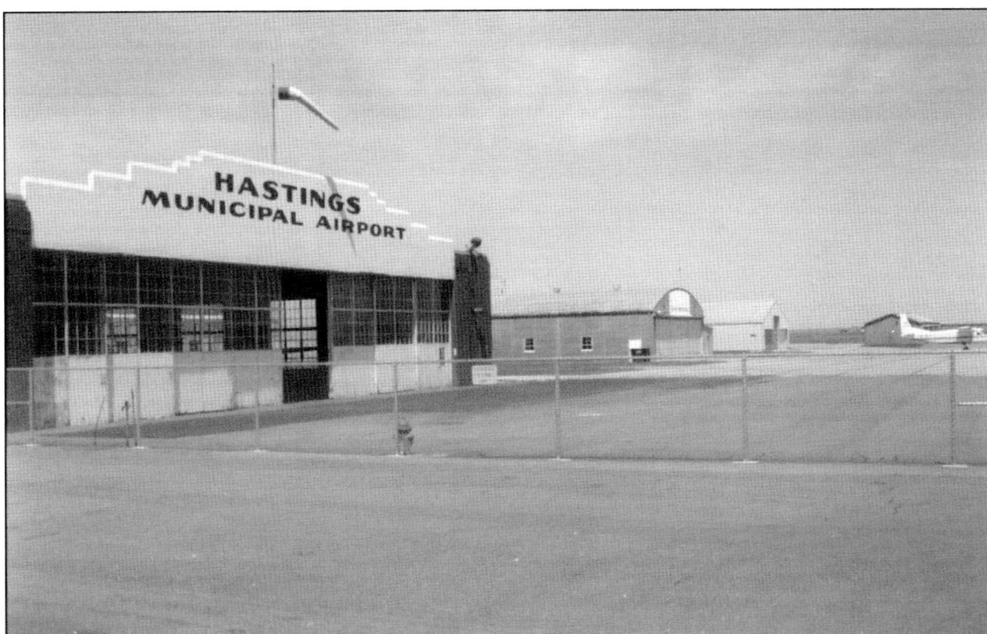


After a bond issue was approved for a local airfield, the city council purchased 160 acres of the Shattuck farm property northwest of 12th and Marian Road for the site. The Great Plains Aircraft Company was formed in 1930, by Dr. E.C. Foote, Frank Cushing, Carl Matthiesen, Dr. G.H. Hansen, William Dutton, Herman Stein, and H.J. Dunn. The company built this brick hangar and hired two pilots. In 1932, the company dissolved, selling its assets to the city.

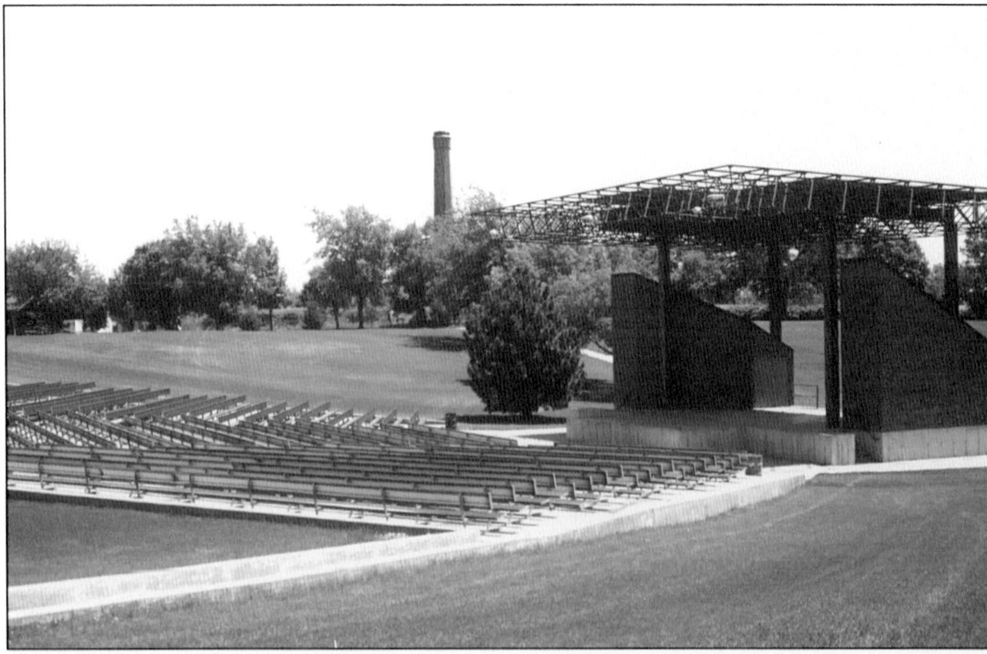

The old Western Brick and Supply Co. grounds on East D Street became a new city park in 1982. Home to the Cottonwood Prairie Festival, the park features a walking trail, basketball court, grills, picnic tables, and playground. City-sponsored concerts as well as other activities are held at the park's amphitheater. The hilly terrain is popular for winter sledding. The old kilns and a smokestack still occupy part of the grounds.

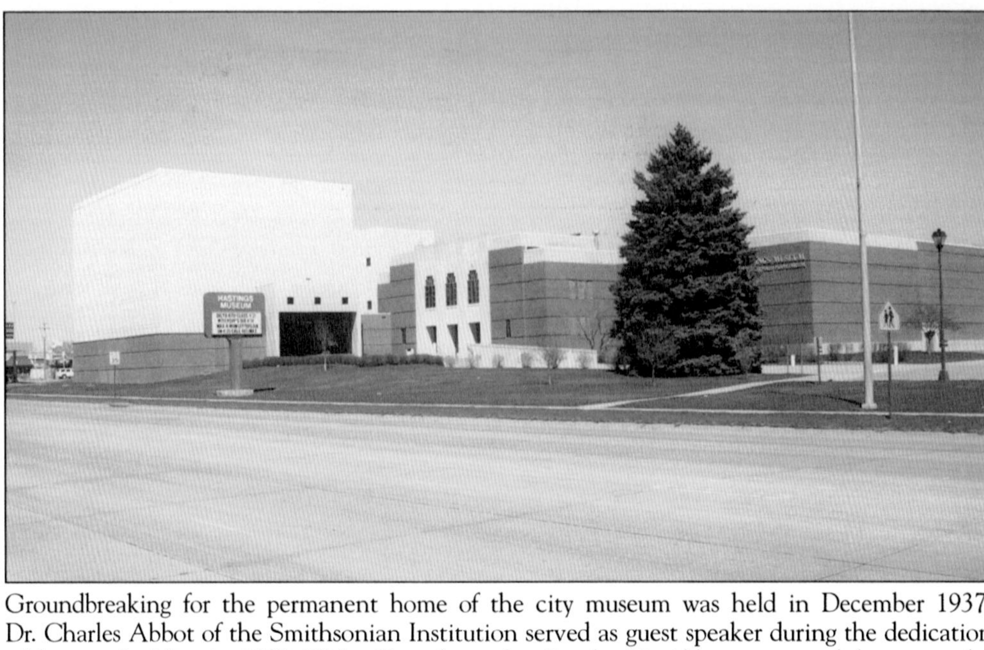


Groundbreaking for the permanent home of the city museum was held in December 1937. Dr. Charles Abbot of the Smithsonian Institution served as guest speaker during the dedication of the new building in 1939. Wife of board member Stanley H. Abbott suggested the name, the House of Yesterday, which was used for many years. Today, the Hastings Museum of Natural and Cultural History features the first Lied IMAX theatre in Nebraska, which was added in 1994.

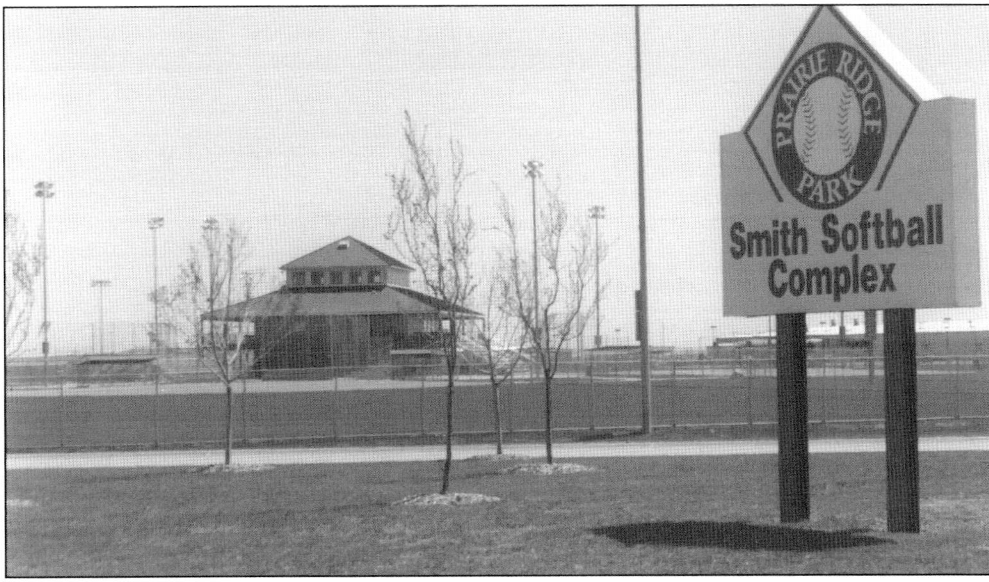


The Bill Smith Softball Complex, located in the 60-acre Prairie Ridge Park on the north edge of Hastings, began operating in 1995. The Nebraska Softball Association officiates at championship tournaments. The city uses the seven-field complex for city league games and maintains the facility. A three-level building contains offices, locker rooms, and a public lounge. The third level serves as an observation floor for scorekeepers, media, and announcers.

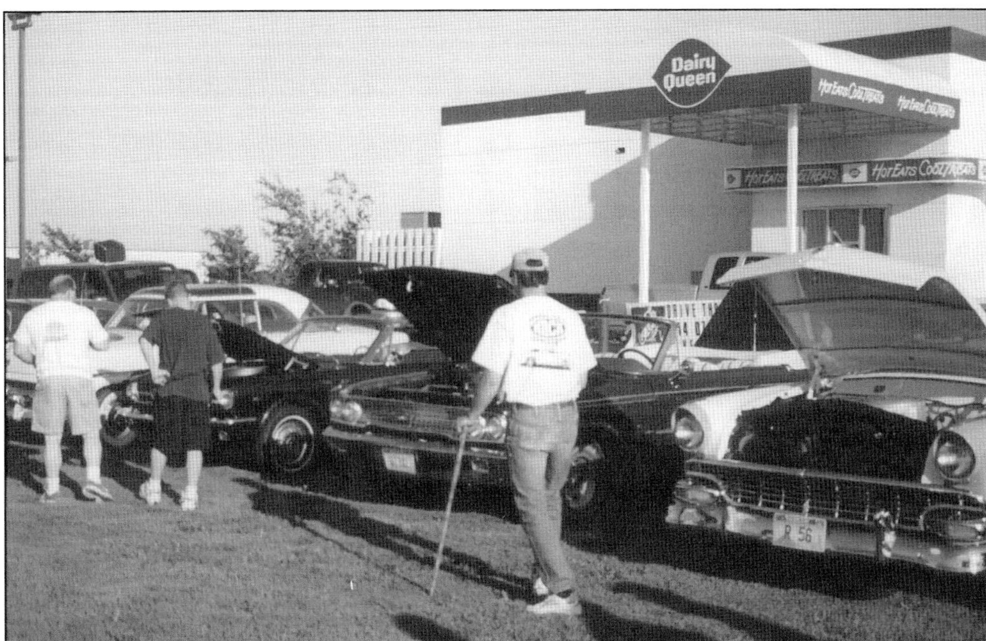


Hastings has experienced a strong northward growth over the last 15 years. In addition to housing, three churches, three car dealerships, four motels, two major discount stores, one bank, two gas stations, three restaurants, a manufacturing plant, and other businesses have been built north of the Highway 281 overpass. Spectators enjoy looking over the classic and antique cars at one of those new businesses, Dairy Queen, who sponsors cruise nights through the summer months.

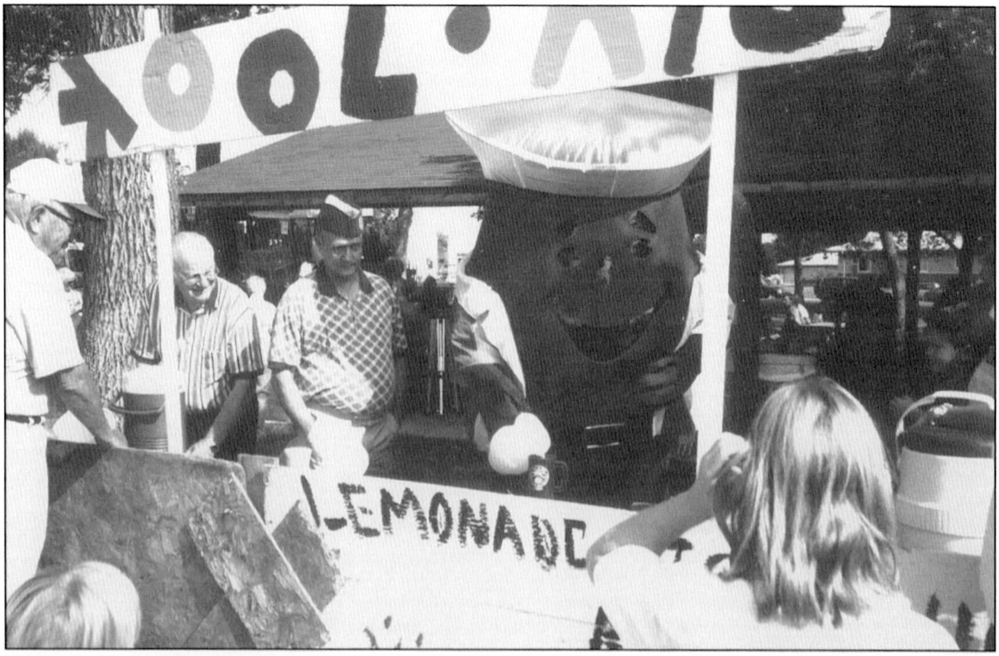


Kool-Aid Man pours the first cup of the popular soft drink to kick off the inaugural "Kool-Aid Days," in August 1998. The annual celebration honors the sweet drink, which was invented here. The highly successful event drew 5,000 visitors, who consumed 450 gallons of Kool-Aid. A 56-foot-long Kool-Aid stand was built, which was touted as the world's largest. Games, music, and dancing rounded out the event which children and adults alike enjoyed.

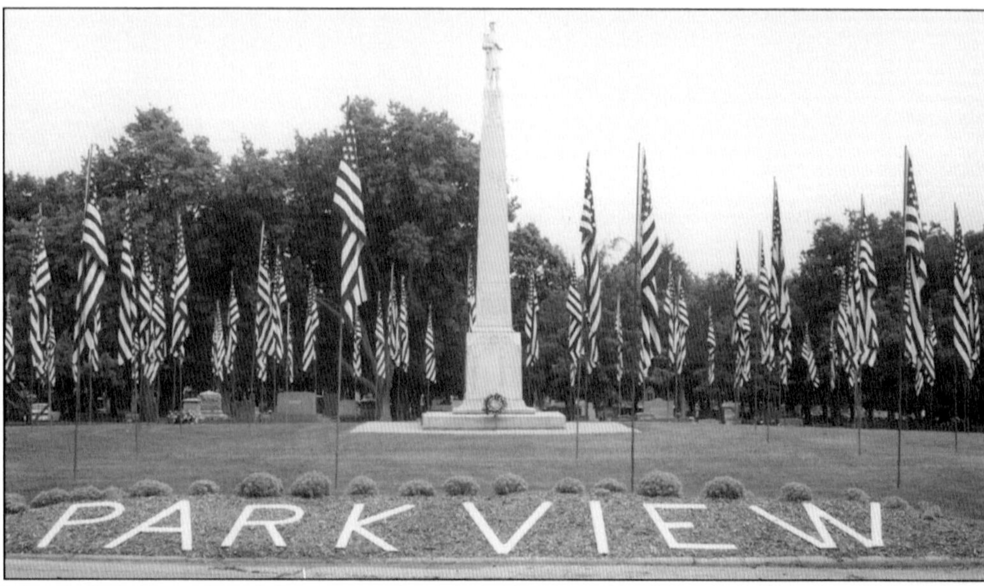


The Parkview Cemetery Association was formed in 1886. The North Elm Avenue cemetery is home to the G.A.R. memorial, which was previously located at the old courthouse. Each Memorial Day, military services are performed by the local Veterans of Foreign Wars, American Legion, and Disabled American Veterans clubs in remembrance of those who gave their lives in defense of the United States.

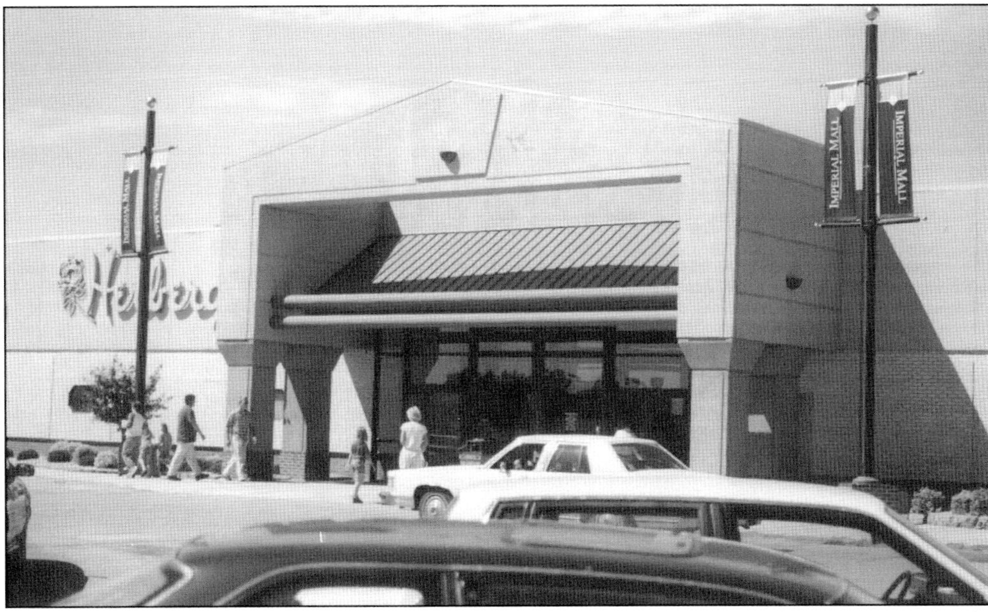


Construction began in 1968 on a new shopping complex at 12th and Marian Road. The Imperial Mall officially opened in August 1970, boasting 266,000 square feet of space, and parking for 2,000 cars. Walgreen Drug, McDonald's Clothing, and Woolworth's were among the first stores established in the mall. It has undergone re-modeling through the years and continues to serve as a popular social as well as shopping experience.

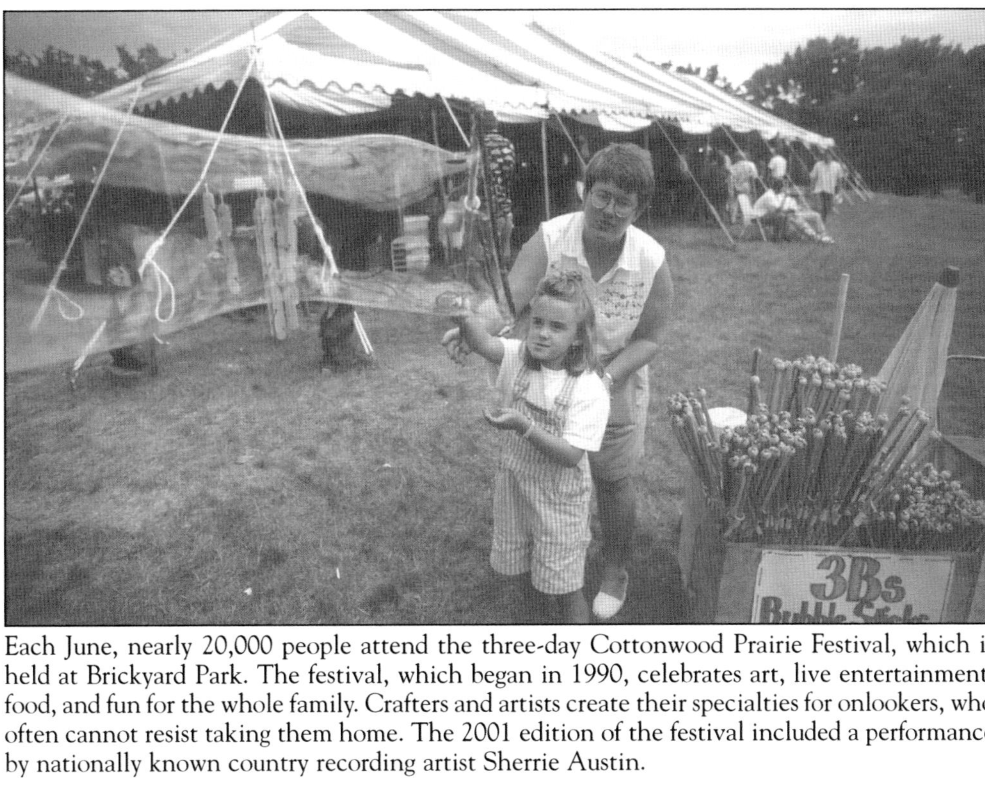


Each June, nearly 20,000 people attend the three-day Cottonwood Prairie Festival, which is held at Brickyard Park. The festival, which began in 1990, celebrates art, live entertainment, food, and fun for the whole family. Crafters and artists create their specialties for onlookers, who often cannot resist taking them home. The 2001 edition of the festival included a performance by nationally known country recording artist Sherrie Austin.

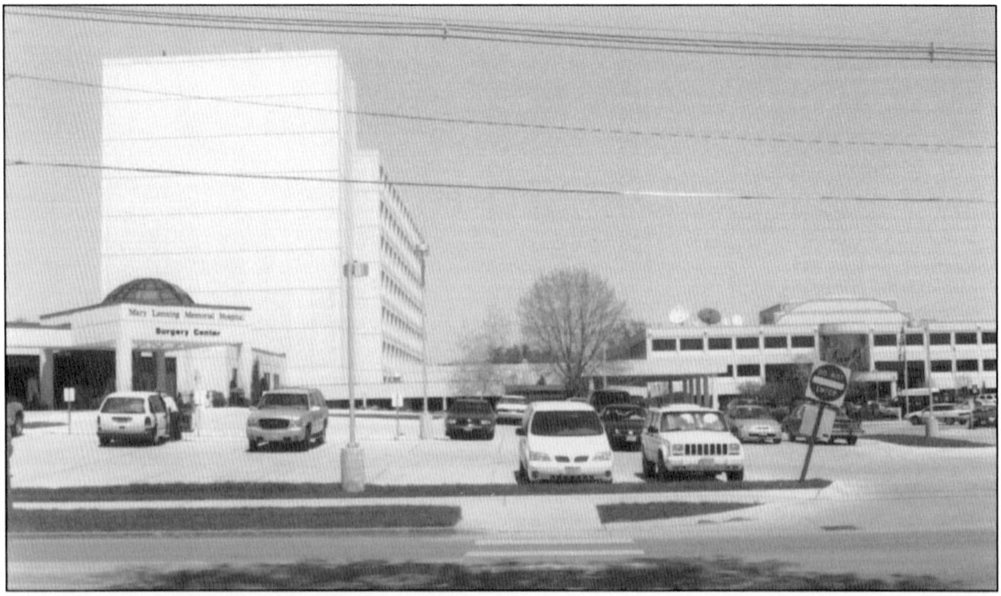

Mary Lanning Memorial Hospital has served the Hastings and surrounding area since 1915, and has continually expanded its facilities and services. The new seven-floor building replaced the old hospital in 1970. The Medical Services Building (right) contains the Creighton University School of Nursing (MLMH campus), the school of radiology, a rehab and wellness center, and other specialized services and doctor's offices. In 2001, the most recent addition was the new surgery center (left).

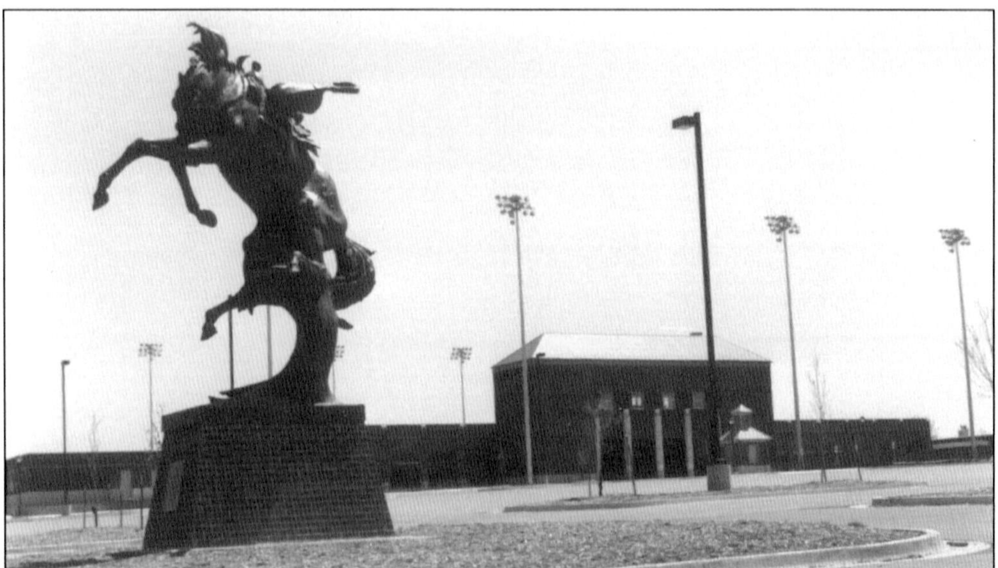

The Osborne Legacy Project "is a bold step to enhance the facilities and programs at Hastings College," stated college president Richard Hoover in 1997. The first phase shown here is the new 3,000-seat A. H. Jones Stadium for football, soccer, and track. The Osborne Family Sports Complex is named after the 22 Osborne family members who have attended Hastings College, including Dr. Tom Osborne. Osborne, now a U.S. Congressman, was the popular and successful coach of the Nebraska Cornhusker football team.

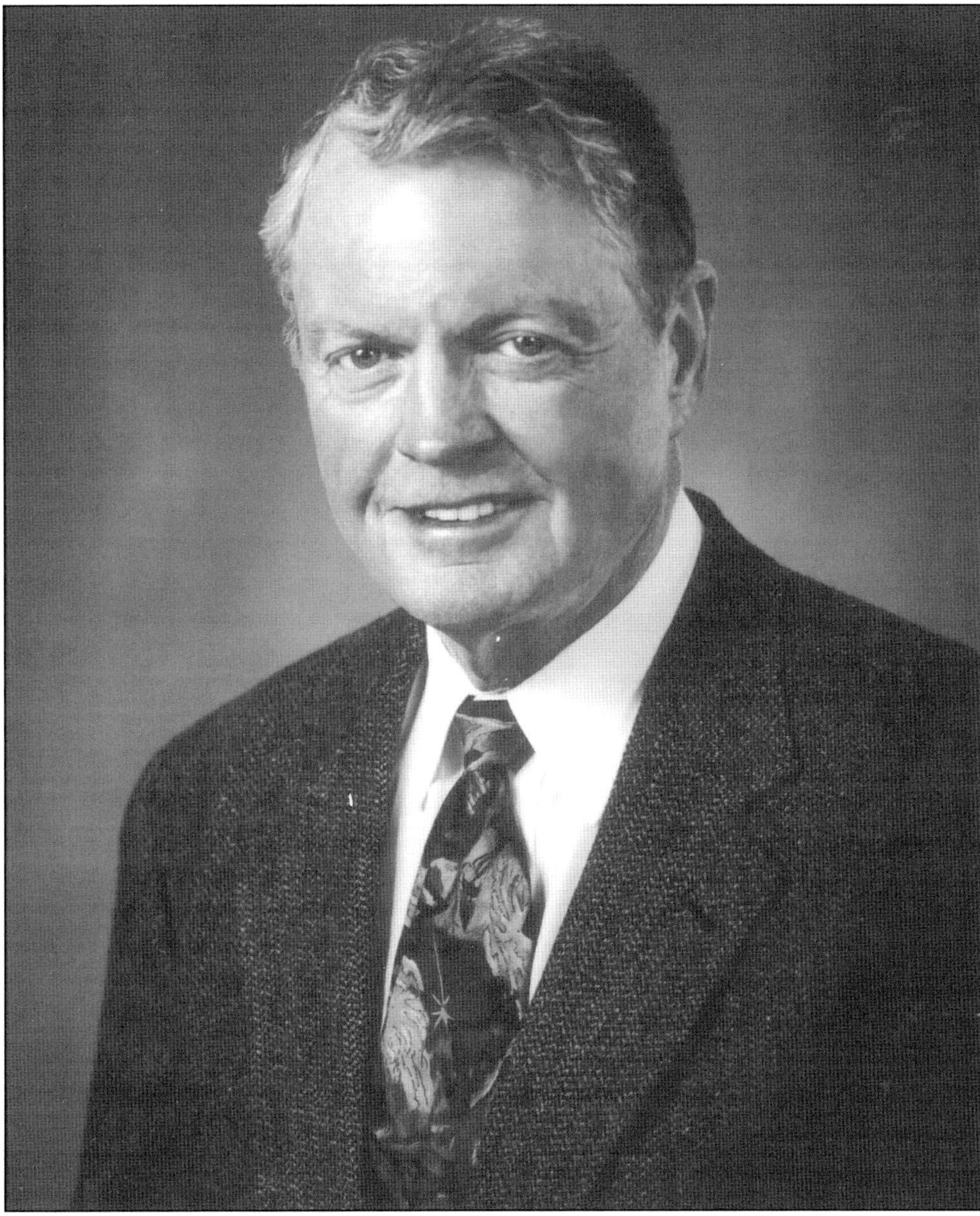

Dr. Tom Osborne is easily Hastings' most celebrated native. While attending Hastings High School and Hastings College, he became a fine athlete. He was drafted by the San Francisco 49ers, and also played for the Washington Redskins. Osborne returned to school and received his Master's and Ph.D. While teaching at the University of Nebraska-Lincoln, he became assistant football coach under Cornhusker head coach, Bob Devaney. He became head coach in 1973, and led the team to three National Championships before retiring in 1998. A divided four-lane highway which links Hastings and Grand Island is named the Tom Osborne Expressway, in his honor. He is the author of three extremely popular books, *Faith in the Game—Lessons on Football, Work, and Life*; *On Solid Ground*; and *More Than Winning*. In November 2000, Osborne was elected to the U.S. House of Representatives for the Third Congressional District of Nebraska.

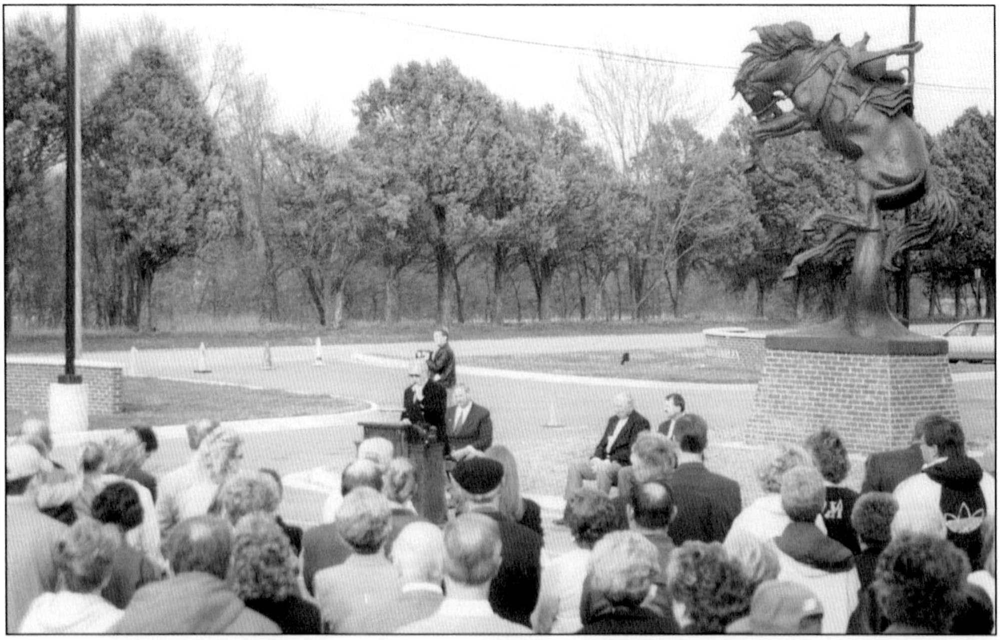

On April 2, 2001, a 21-foot high, 4,000-pound bronze sculpture was dedicated at the entrance to the Osborne Family Sports Complex. Named *The Spirit*, the bucking horse statue represents the Hastings College Broncos mascot. Artist Herb Mignery donated his talents to create the sculpture, which was a gift from local businessman Paul Hohnstein in honor of his family. During the ceremony, Mignery was made an honorary alumnus of Hastings College.

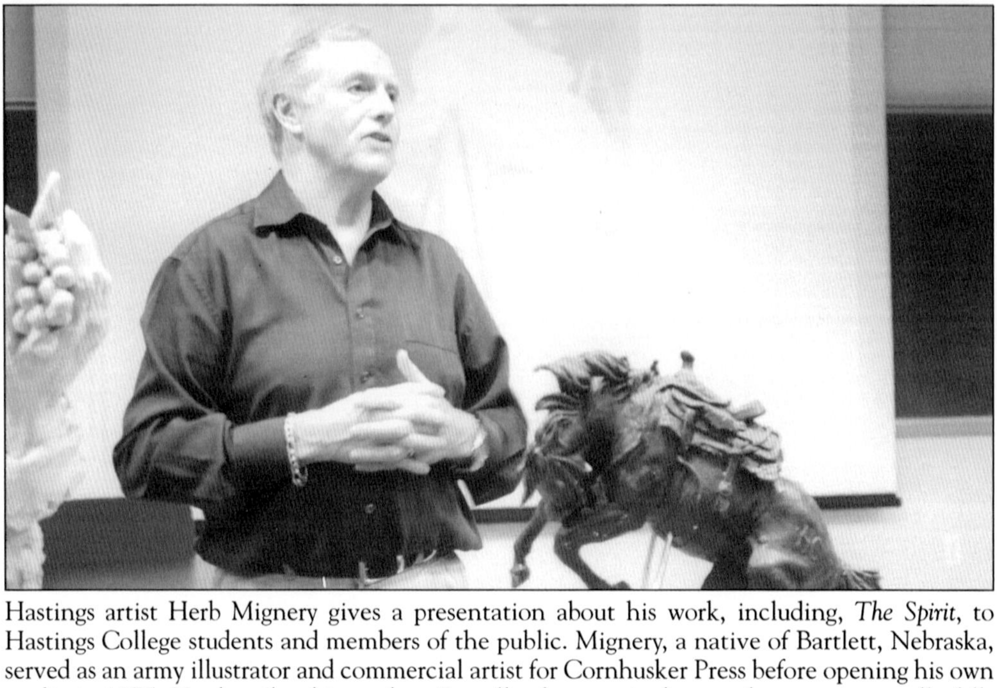

Hastings artist Herb Mignery gives a presentation about his work, including, *The Spirit*, to Hastings College students and members of the public. Mignery, a native of Bartlett, Nebraska, served as an army illustrator and commercial artist for Cornhusker Press before opening his own studio in 1975. He describes his work as "usually characterized as cowboy art, it actually falls under the broad description of Western Americana or even Americana."

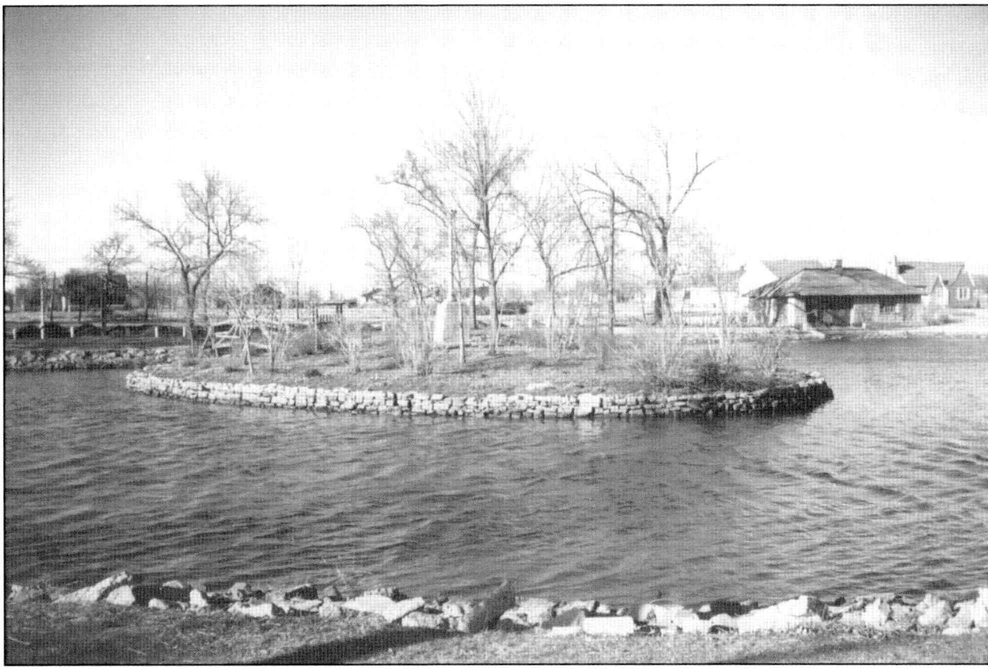

James B. Heartwell developed a 20-acre park for his family and friends at the northeast edge of town. His remaining property that surrounded the park became the region's first planned residential area, which included landscaping in the design. The park was sold to the city in 1899 for $2,000, and is one of the most popular parks. This retrospective look at Heartwell Park around the turn of the century and how it appears today portrays the growth of the surrounding neighborhood. The park is now far from the edge of the city.

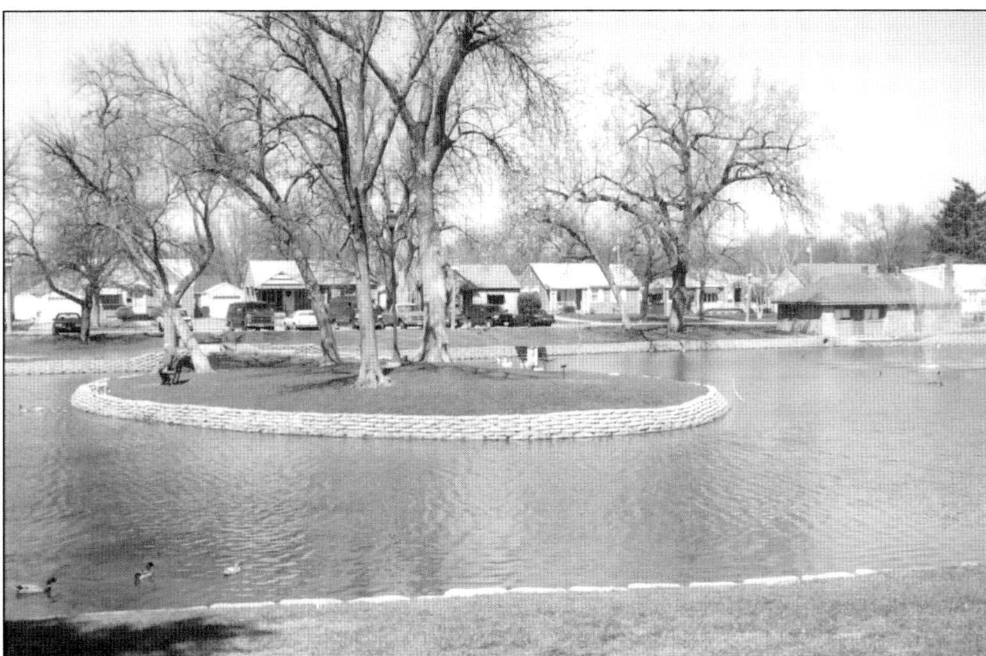

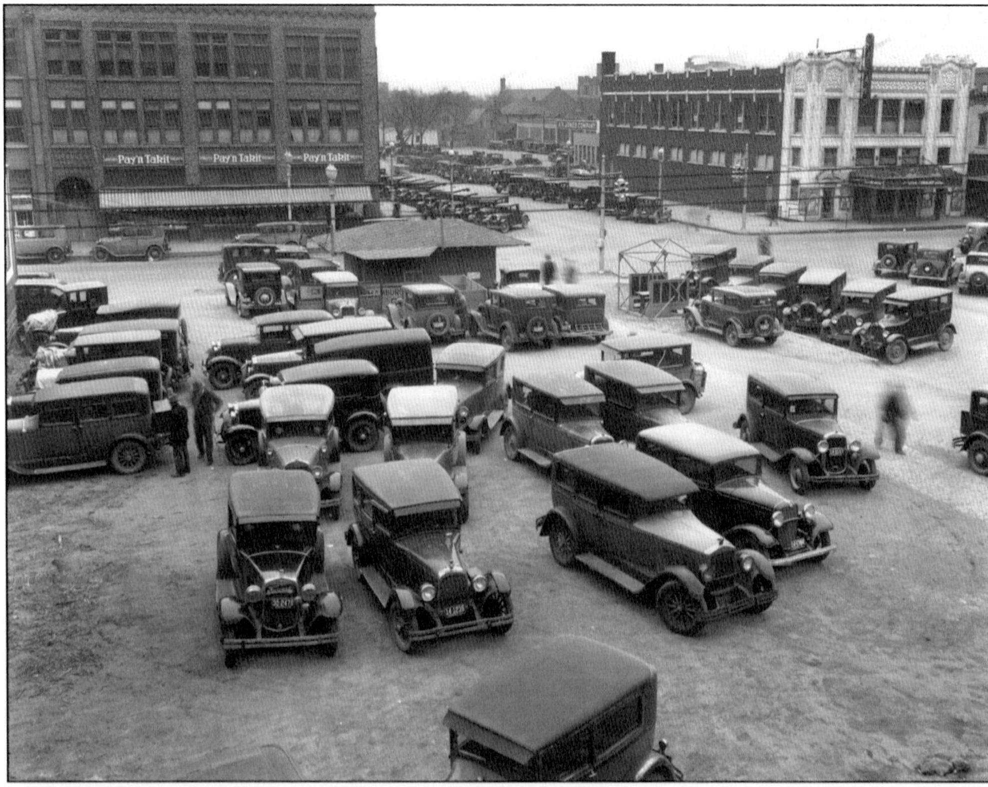


A hamburger stand on the southwest corner of Second Street and Burlington Avenue is dwarfed by Brandes Hall (left) where the Pay'n Takit grocery store was located. The Strand Theatre is the white fronted building to the right. Parking along Burlington was plentiful in 1930. Today, Brandes Hall is the *Tribune* Building, and the Strand is an office building. Burlington Avenue (Highway 281) is a bustling five-lane roadway.

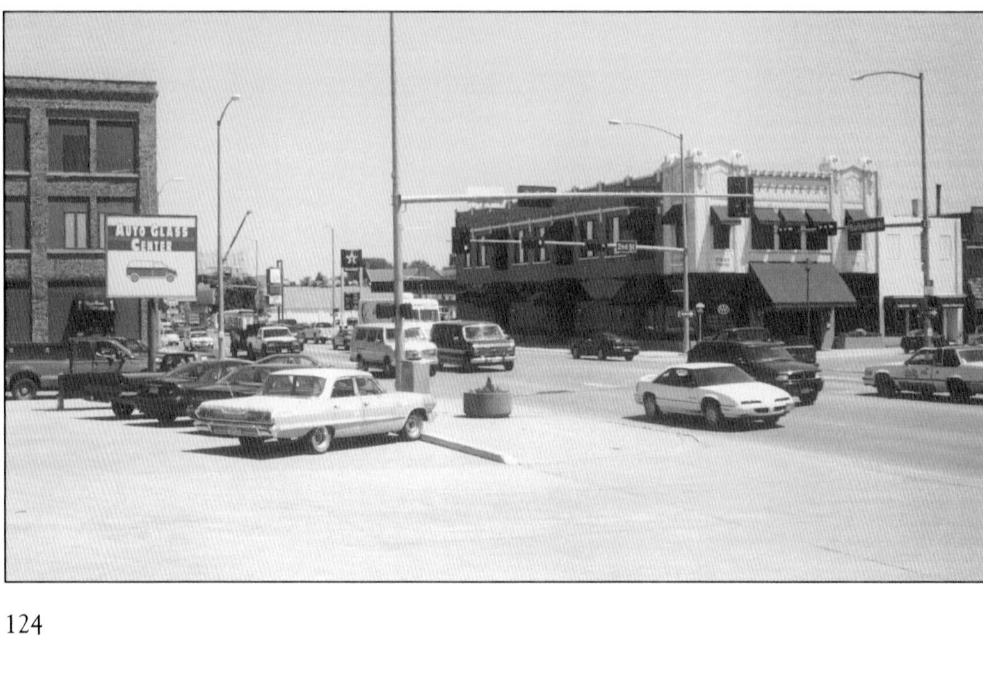

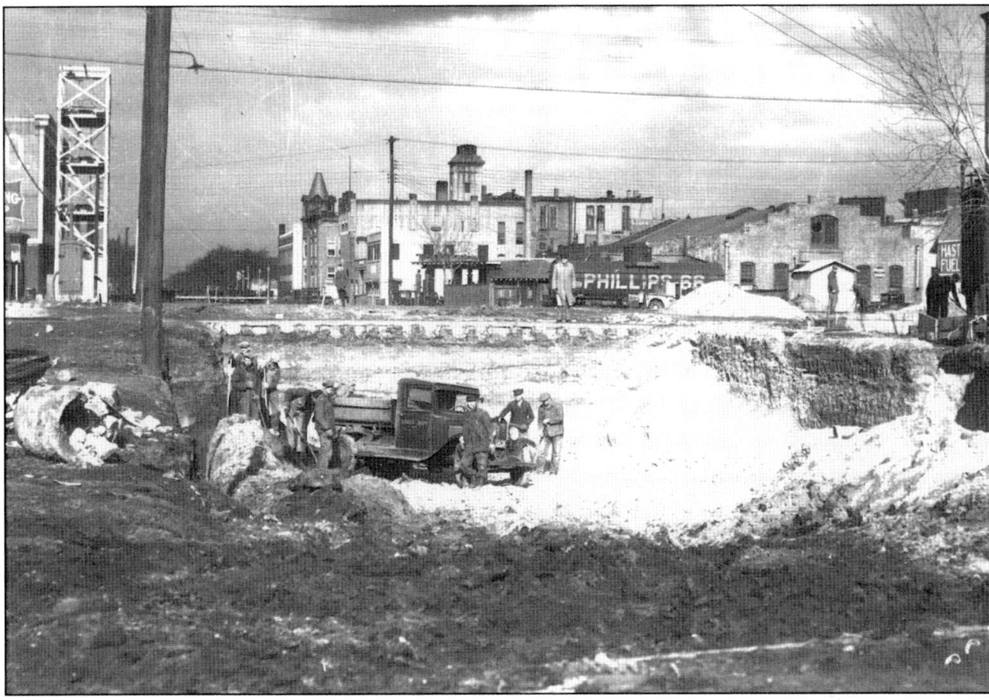


Vehicular and rail traffic increased to point where it became necessary to build an underpass at the Burlington Avenue railroad tracks. The yearlong project was finished in 1934. The old fire station is in upper center of the photo, and the Cushing Grocery Company is at left behind the fire department's training tower. A recent South Burlington Avenue widening project included the underpass.

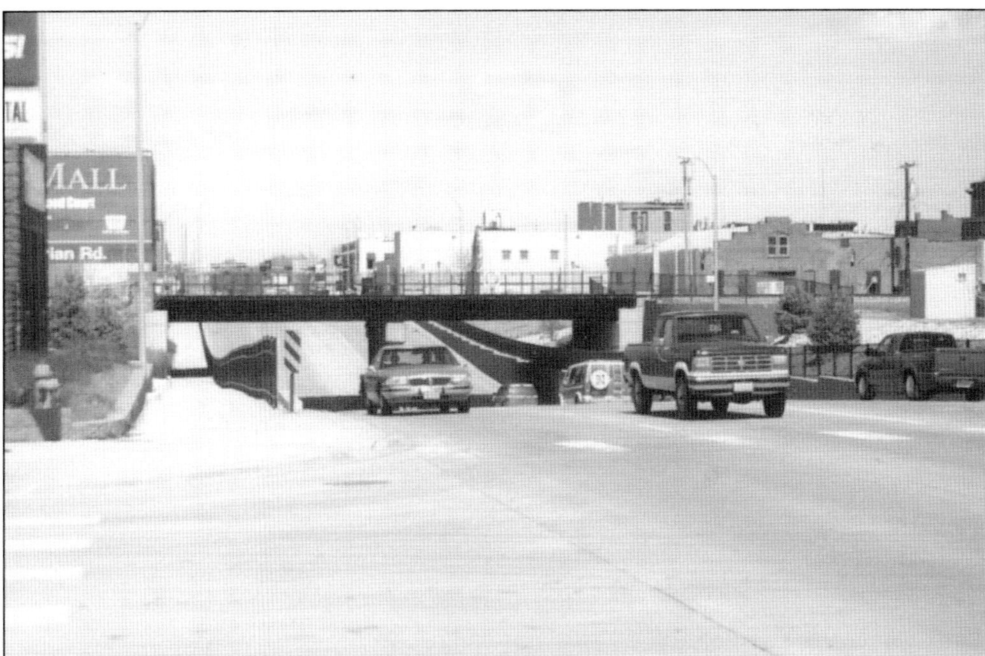

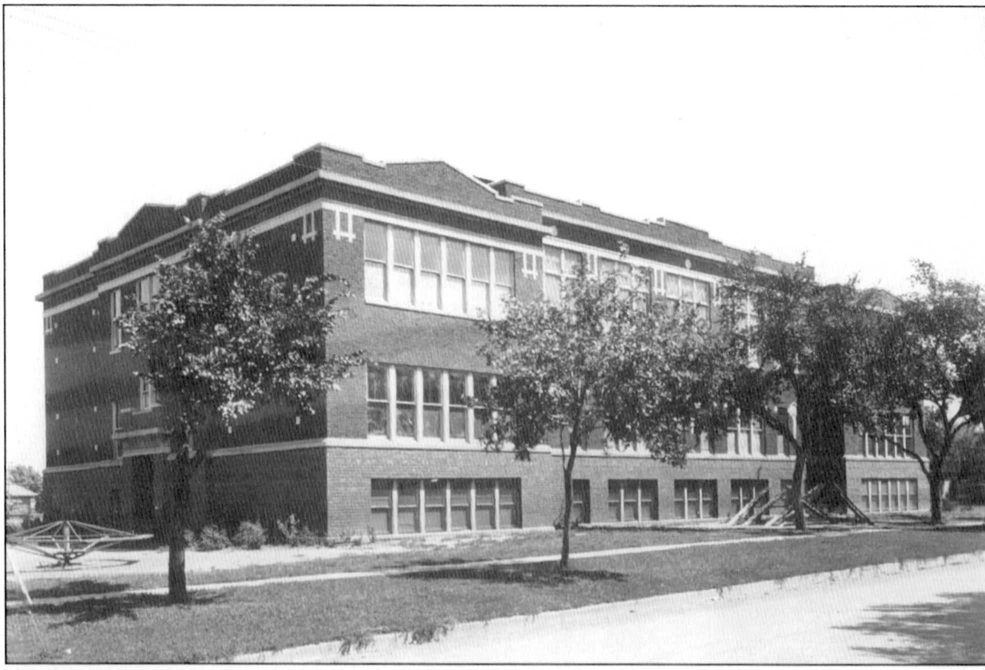

The first elementary school in the city was built in 1880, at B Street and Burlington Avenue. The First Ward School (later called Lincoln School), was replaced in 1912, by a brick, 35,000-square-foot building shown in this 1928 photo. It later served as St. Michael's Catholic School before being sold to the city. An elevator tower was added during the $3 million renovation project and became home to the Hastings Police Department on May 3, 2001.

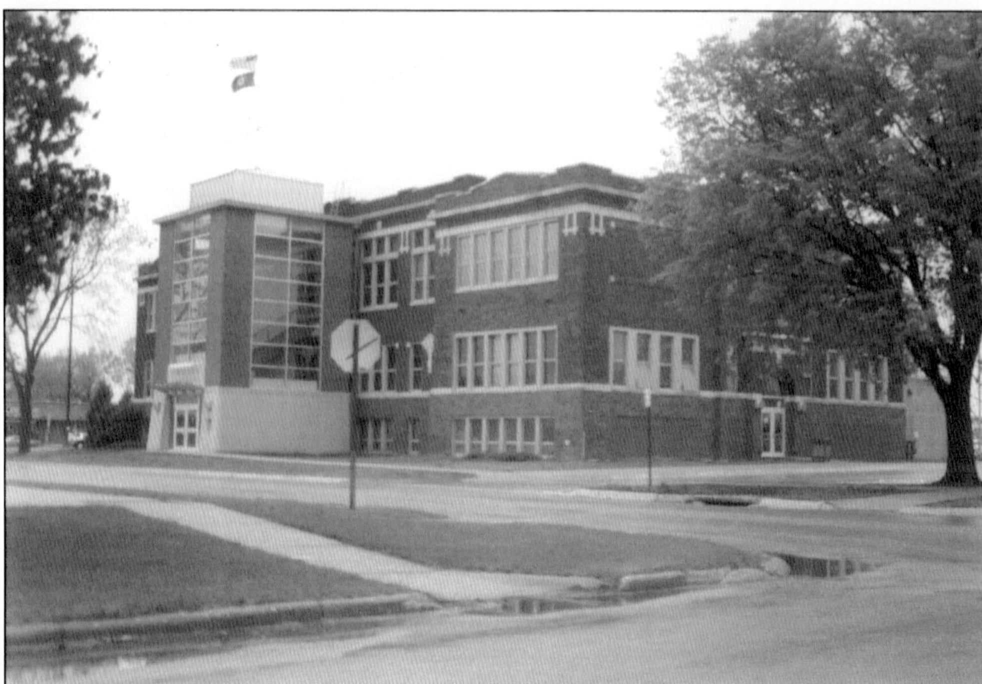

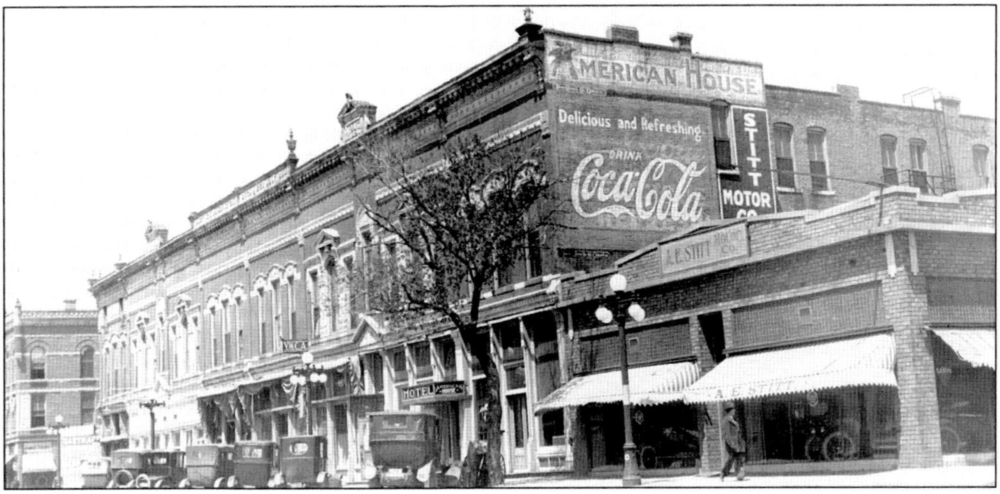


The old Bostwick Hotel was named the American House by 1919, when this photo was taken. The hotel burned during the winter of 1925. The Carter Hotel occupied the site for many years, which was later re-named the Dor-An before being torn down to facilitate the expansion of the Rivoli Theatre. The Stitt Motor Company building later became Rutt's Drug Store and is now The Bike Shop.

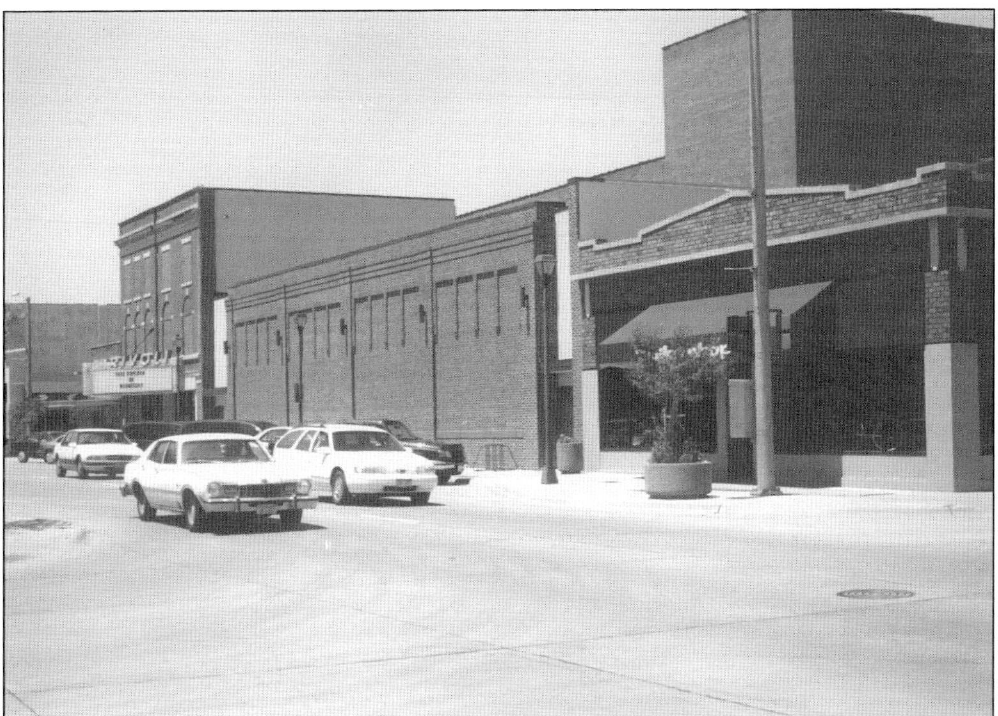

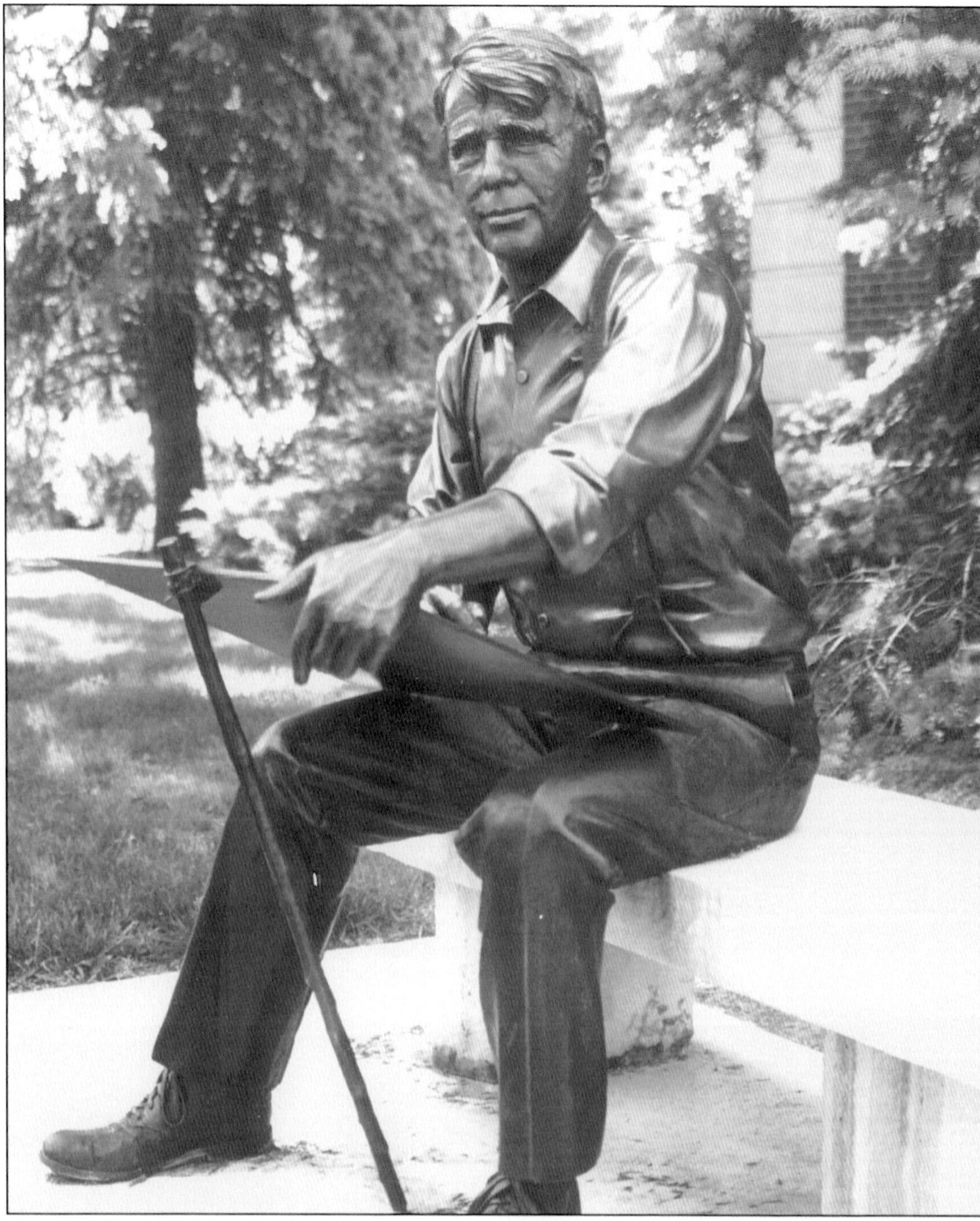

Hastings has become noted for the fine selection of bronze sculptures, which adorn the city. Four bronzes were added to the Hastings College campus within the last year, including this one, *Robert Frost Sitting on a Park Bench*, by George Lundeen. A native of Holdrege, Nebraska, Lundeen received his Bachelor of Arts degree from Hastings College and his M.F.A. from the University of Illinois. He was a Fulbright-Hayes Scholar studying at Academia de Belle Arte in Florence, Italy. He has been recognized by sculpture societies as one of the outstanding sculptors in America today. Perhaps it is fitting to end this book with Frost's words in mind. He recognized that choices are never easy. The progress of a town and its people over nearly 130 years has involved a multitude of decisions, some easy and "safe," and others more difficult and "risky." Earnest progress is often the result of a decision, which was a gamble, "Two roads diverged in a wood, and I—I took the one less traveled by, and that has made all the difference."